Do you know someone who is hurting right n
because you don't know what to say? Do you ¡
their situation?

D1086281

Do these thoughts seem like your thoughts? If
Lauren gives simple, practical suggestions of wl
memorable difference in your friend's life.

Over the years I have observed Lauren's compassionate spirit and willingness to be a light in someone's time of darkness. As a child she stood by me
as I faced the death of two sons, and as an adult she took responsibility for
the family in funeral preparations after the sudden death of my husband,
her father.

Lauren writes from heartfelt experience and has an avid interest in helping
each one of us to help others. We may not know what to do or say, but
Lauren does.

> ~**Florence Littauer,** author of *Personality Plus, Silver Boxes,*
> *Behind the Personality*

When it comes to helping those in need, it's not that we don't want to. It's
rather that we don't know how. *The Art of Helping—What to Say and Do*
When Someone Is Hurting provides us with the practical and realistic information we need to be the arms of Jesus in times of stress and trial. Thank
you, Lauren!

> ~**Gayle Roper,** author of *Autumn Dreams, Summer Shadows,*
> *Spring Rain*

How many times have you wanted to help when you heard about
someone's difficult situation, but you just didn't know what to say or do?
Therefore, you did nothing and felt guilty. *The Art of Helping* is a much
needed guide, filled with proven, practical plans. I use it as a reference in
my responsibilities as Minister of Caring for the Hour of Power Ministry.
Every home and church should have a copy of this book. It will give people
the tools they need to reach out and touch hearts and lives during the
trying times.

> ~**Betty Southard,** author of *The Mentor Quest: Practical Ways*
> *to Find the Guidance You Need,*
> Minister of Caring, Crystal Cathedral, *Hour of Power*

Lauren Briggs has done a terrific job of capturing the essence of helping others in a way that heals rather than hurts. As someone who endured a bone marrow transplant and then the loss of my career and marriage, I can tell you there is truly an "art" to reaching out to those suffering. This book is a MUST read!

~**Georgia Shaffer,** author of *A Gift of Mourning Glories: Restoring Your Life After Loss*

Some people have the touch...the healing touch of sensitivity, availability, and dependability. Lean in and learn from one who does—Lauren Briggs.

~**Patsy Clairmont**
Women of Faith Speaker,
author of *The Shoe Book* and *The Hat Book*

When our seventeen-year-old son Nathan was killed by a drunk driver, we received hundreds of sympathy cards. At first, I saved them all so that I could remember who sent them; however, there were some I could never forget, mainly because of the personal notes included in the cards. I had known Lauren Briggs since she was a young girl, but the day I received her card, I knew this young girl had grown into an extremely caring and sensitive woman. Even twenty years later, I remember she quoted a verse from the Psalms that says our tears are precious to the Lord and He preserves them in His bottle! In that one card, I received permission to cry. I didn't have to apologize for my tears anymore. Lauren's book provides common sense and sensitive ways we can provide meaningful encouragement to those who need our help when we don't know what to do.

~**Marilyn Heavilin,** author of *Roses in December, December's Song, I'm Listening Lord,* and *Grief is a Family Affair*

THE ART *of* HELPING

What to Say and Do When Someone is Hurting

LAUREN LITTAUER BRIGGS

THE ART OF HELPING

Published by Briggs Enterprises
PO Box 8411
Redlands, CA 92375
Laurenbrgs@aol.com

ISBN 978-0-615-47568-4

Cover Design: Koechel Peterson & Associates

Printed in the United States of America
First Edition 2003

5 6 7 8 9 10 11 12 Printing / Year 16 15 14 12 11 10

To my dad,

Frederick Jerome Littauer

February 19, 1929—October 25, 2002,

The man who taught me compassion,

brought me comfort, and gave me confidence.

When I began writing this book,

I never dreamt I would be the one in need of comfort.

To every person whose life has been

touched by tragedy and difficult times,

especially those willing to share their hurts and victories

to teach us how to become effective comforters

CONTENTS

PART *four* CONTINUED SUPPORT

FOREWORD

I met Lauren in her late teeny-bopper years. I loved Lauren immediately because she was fun and full of energy. She loved order and was a doer. She said what she would do and did it.

Her marriage to Randy was precious but not without its heartache. Losing a child during her pregnancy hurt them tremendously, especially since Lauren's passion was to be a mother. She has always been able to do ten things at one time—run a home, care for her elderly Grammy, run a successful business, and minister to hurting hearts.

Lauren taught me much about what helps us during difficult and challenging times. I would have loved for all my friends to have had this book during my five years fighting cancer. Our family has gone through much trauma with our children, and we have lost our parents on both sides.

Lauren is truly a number one mom, wife, and a child of a very strong family who has suffered more than their share. This book is not a negative, but a positive. You will enjoy the gifts shared in *The Art of Helping* and learn how to help others at the same time.

Lauren's mother, Florence Littauer, has been my mentor and friend. It has been a joy to spend time with her and her family.

Lauren's mold was broken at birth. She is talented with many gifts. Her compassionate spirit blesses all who are facing challenges in life.

This is a book that should be on everyone's bookshelves for reference and to be shared with the hurting. May the Lord bless you as you walk through life holding the hand of Christ—the One who went to the cross and suffered the ultimate pain.

Lovingly,
Emilie Barnes

PREFACE

"This is a book you'll want to read before you need it—so that you will have ideas of what you can do and how you can respond—when you first hear the news."

These are the words I wrote on September 10, 2001, while working on this book. Little did I know that less than one day later our nation would face a tragedy of massive proportion.

Little did I know that while writing this book, I would receive the news that my dad had died suddenly, alone, sitting at his desk at home.

We never know what tomorrow brings—in anyone's life.

❖ Are you prepared to help others in their time of need?

❖ Do you know what to say and also what *not* to say?

❖ How can you make a difference in the lives of others in crisis?

❖ Do you know what you can do to help?

There are tangible things we can do when we first hear about a crisis—and as the needs continue. This book provides you with a wide variety of specific things you can say and do to help your family, friends, and neighbors during difficult times.

BOTH SIDES *of the* COMFORT COIN

hen I was thiry-one, former Secretary of the Interior, James Watt, asked me, "What would a young girl like you know about suffering?" He listened as I told him my experiences. After a short time he raised his hand to signal "stop" and said, "That's enough. I believe you know what it is to hurt."

Before I was thirty years old, I had watched my two brothers die of unexplainable brain damage, lost a baby mid-pregnancy, cared for my mother-in-law suffering from multiple sclerosis, moved my grandmother into my home while she battled melanoma, known financial hardship, moved across the continent, and saw my family's beloved dog run over and killed.

During my difficult times, I discovered that most people didn't know what to say or how to help me. As a child, other kids made fun of me, calling my brothers "retards" and "morons." I kept these hurts inside because I didn't want to add to my parents' burden. No one ever knew how much I was hurting.

My experiences caused me to become sensitive to the feelings of friends and family who endure traumatic times in their own lives. I prayerfully send cards of concern, support, and encouragement to people experiencing a crisis. I have walked beside a dear friend and accompanied her to legal proceedings when her husband filed for divorce as she lost her battle to breast cancer. I fund-raised and organized the furnishing of a home for a family returning from the mission field because their son had brain cancer. I felt so helpless. I knew I couldn't cure his cancer, but I could help them set up their home.

My family stood alongside our business partner as he cared for his wife while she was dying of liver cancer. I have helped organize and decorate memory boards to be on display at funerals. I have arranged the front of the church with family portraits and special items for memorial services. We have even purchased a memorial brick to honor our friend's treasured pet that died.

As I look back through my years of raising children, I can see my oldest son on the roof of a cancer patient's house sweeping the leaves off and cleaning her gutters. I remember my middle son assisting a multiple sclerosis patient to participate in the Multiple Sclerosis Walk for Life in his grandmother's memory. I can see my youngest son taking his video games to a hospitalized friend. As a family, we took our instruments and voices on the road numerous times and sang praises with friends in need. My children have known the heartaches of others and have reached out in unusual and caring ways to make a difference in their lives.

ARE YOU PREPARED TO HELP?

In Isaiah 40:1 (KJV) we are commanded, "Comfort ye, comfort ye my people," saith your God. Yet somehow we are fearful and ill equipped to provide comfort. We aren't comfortable with someone else's pain. We're even fearful it might "rub off on us" or that "we might get it" if we are around family and friends who are going through a crisis.

- ❖ Are you prepared to help others in their time of need?
- ❖ Do you know what to say and do to help?
- ❖ What are you doing to reach out and comfort others?
- ❖ How can you be an expression of God's comfort and love?

HOW TO GET THE MOST OUT OF THIS BOOK

The Art of Helping will give you the tools, the words, and the ways you can reach out and comfort your friends and family when they are walking a difficult path. It is filled with personal examples from people who have been there, have lived through the various crises, and have willingly shared what friends said and did that helped. You will have an understanding of what it is like to face a wide variety of difficult times, how to pray with your friends, what to write in a card, and what you can do to make a difference in their lives. This book is divided into four sections:

- ❖ Personal Crisis
- ❖ Health Needs
- ❖ Loss
- ❖ Continued Support

Once you have read the first portion of the book, including the Basic Dos and Dont's sections, feel free to look up the specific topic your friend is facing and read that portion. Each topic stands alone. As you have the opportunity to read other sections, you will find information that may be valuable in other situations as well.

Writing this book was a daunting task. There is no way I could completely and adequately provide all the information you might need. I have, however, provided you a variety of ways to help others. Find suggestions that work in your situation and ideas that you can do. Function within your own gifts. Do what you are good at and what you enjoy doing. Don't use the excuse that you are not comfortable with heartache, sorrow, or pain. Do you think your friend who is walking the difficult path is comfortable? You need to be the expression of God's comfort as you reach out to those who hurt. Use this book as a handbook and reference guide whenever someone you know faces a difficult time.

When I asked my uncle, Col. James Chapman, what he'd learned about comforting in his thirty years as an Air Force chaplain, he thought briefly and shared this experience.

The most valuable lesson I learned happened just a few months after I had been ordained. I was in my twenties and assigned to Amarillo Air Force Base in Texas. Outside the base was a ramshackled community where the residents lived in old World War II temporary housing. A couple worked as caretakers. The husband was a handyman, and his wife looked after the area.

One night another chaplain called me. "Get the police! There's been a murder in Cammes Village." I'd never handled a murder before, and I drove out to the village not knowing what I'd do or say.

When I arrived, I found that the son of this couple had brutally murdered his fiancée. Too stunned to do anything significant or dramatic, I stood by while the police handled details and the body was removed. I moved a few things, made some phone calls, and tried to calm the mother.

When I left at midnight, I didn't think I'd been very helpful or comforting. I felt guilty that I'd not known what to do, so I continued visiting this family as the weeks went on. Whenever I could, I'd drop in and say hello.

As time passed, the son came to trial. It seemed inevitable that he'd be convicted of murder. I planned to sit with the family at the trial. But one day I received a phone call informing me that the son had killed himself. Although I knew I needed to be with the family, once again I felt totally inadequate to meet their needs. What could I say? What could I do?

I spent time with the parents, listened to their thoughts and fears, and offered them my compassion. In the months that followed, I kept going to see the family, just sitting and visiting with them and letting them talk.

One day, the father looked up and told me, "Chaplain, we want to thank you for the time you've spent with us and all that you've done for us. I don't know how we'd have made it through all this if it hadn't been for you."

I didn't know I'd done anything that was either right or helpful. All I knew was that I kept going to see them. I was willing to sit with them and be part of their grief. This taught me very early in my ministerial career that it's not important to have big speeches prepared or to do major things, but rather to be there.

I challenge you to consider people in your community, your neighborhood, your church, or your workplace who are going through a difficult time. Commit to reach out, to show you care, to be on hand to listen, support, and love them. Be an expression of God's comfort and love. You may be the one light they have in the midst of a very dark and stormy sea.

BASIC DOS *and* DON'TS

While there are no pat answers or eloquent words of wisdom that can ever change the circumstances or remove the hurt from your friend's life, there are general concepts we need to understand that will guide us toward being the effective comforters God wants us to be. There are specific things that we can do to make a difference in the lives of those who hurt. They need your compassion, love, and support. The following chart provides specific dos and don'ts of effective comforting.

DO
Respond in a timely manner with a card, a call, or a visit.

DON'T
Don't wait a long time before you make your initial contact.

One of the hardest parts of reaching out is the first contact. We are nervous about what we'll say and how we'll be received. We, ourselves, feel sad, burdened, and scared with the news, so we're not sure that we have anything to offer. Prayerfully ask God's guidance for what you will say or what you will write in a card. Then, step out in faith and write, call, or visit your hurting friend. Once you've made the initial contact, you'll find follow-up calls are much easier.

DO
Offer simple, understanding statements such as
    "I feel for you during this difficult time."
    "This must be very hard for you."
    "I share your feelings of loss."
    "I wish I could take the hurt away."

Comments like these let people know you acknowledge their pain and it's okay for them to feel that way.

DON'T

Don't try to minimize their pain with comments like
 "It's probably for the best."
 "Things could be worse."
 "You're strong. You'll get over it soon."
 "You know God is in control."

Comments like these might be an attempt to offer hope; but to a hurting person, they sound as though you don't comprehend the enormity of what happened.

The first thing we need to do is acknowledge that a crisis/loss has happened. Our comments will then validate their feelings. When we minimize or trivialize their feelings, it indicates we don't understand the depths of their feelings or that we are not interested in how they feel.

DO

Be there.
Be specific with what you want to do to help.

DON'T

Don't say,
 "Is there anything I can do to help?"
 "If there is anything you need, give me a call."

Go to them. Your presence is far more important than your words. Be aggressive with your willingness to help. Ask yourself, "What would I need if I were in a similar situation?" Offer specific things you can do for them like

- "I'm on my way to the store; what can I pick up for you? Do you have any milk?"
- "Would tomorrow be a good day to help you with the laundry?"
- "Would the children like to come over and play this afternoon?"

Don't leave the ball in their court. Most of the time, people in a crisis can't decide or don't know what they do need and would never dream of asking because they do not want to impose.

DO

Expect that they will be different once they have experienced a tragedy.

DON'T

Don't say:,
>   *"When will you be your old self again?"*
>   *"You need to get over this."*
>   *"Just put this behind you."*
>   *"You're not the same."*

Once people's lives have been touched by tragedy, they will never be the same. They will never be their "old self" again. They will find a "new normal" and ultimately discover a way to go on with life, but it will never be the same again. Our lives have continued despite what has happened in their lives, and for that reason we tend to want life to go back to the way it was before their crisis. Remember the faces of the victims' families one year later at the 9/11 memorial services? It was evident they have not "gotten over it." President Bush offered comfort and condolences while the families held up photographs of their loved ones. Tears streamed down their faces, they sobbed at their losses and collapsed into each other's arms for solace and support. Your friends, facing their own crises, tragedy, and loss, feel no less pain than those families.

DO

Agree when the individual expresses his feelings, such as, "That doesn't make sense." "It isn't fair." "I don't understand why this happened."

DON'T

Don't offer spiritual answers or explanations. We don't know why tragedies happen—why certain people go through trauma.

We do our friends a disservice by offering possible explanations. We have no idea why a tragedy happened. Tragedy isn't fair, and it doesn't make any sense. During a time of crisis, people are apt to question their faith. Why has such a thing happened? Where was God when it happened? They don't need to hear horror or success stories of people you know who've been through something similar. Telling someone that everything will be all right when you have never known the depth of his or her hardship is an empty statement.

> ## DO
> *Give spiritual encouragement from your heart, and include Bible verses that have comforted you at a difficult time.*
>
> ## DON'T
> *Don't quote Bible verses as a way to correct or minimize their feelings. Never offer spiritual suggestions from a position of superiority or self-righteousness.*

Put yourself in the other person's place. Empathetic responses are healing to those going through a difficult time. Think very carefully before using any Scripture. Ask yourself if a passage will communicate comfort or condemnation. "All things work together for good" is never a quote for a hurting person. If they claim that verse themselves, then you can affirm that promise, but never offer it as a comfort. At this moment, nothing feels good to them.

> ## DO
> *Encourage them to keep a journal or share their feelings with you.*
>
> ## DON'T
> *Don't say,*
> *"You shouldn't feel that way."*

Often just seeing their thoughts on paper helps them deal with what they are facing. Encouraging a free flow of feelings will help them know you care and are not afraid of their pain. Feelings are not right or wrong. Feelings just are. We need to validate them where they are.

DO

Do say,

> *"I have been praying for you."*
> *"Has this week been any better?"*
> *"Is there something especially difficult you are facing?"*

DON'T

Don't say,

> *"How are you?"*
> *"How are you doing?"*

The real answer to the question "How are you?" is usually something like awful, terrible, or devastated. Your hurting friend won't really want to verbalize that. The best thing to do is to greet your friend with a simple, "Hi, _____," and make a statement of your support or ask a specific question.

DO

Listen to their hearts.

DON'T

Don't say,

> *"I know just how you feel."*
> *"A friend of mine ..."*

Listening is a powerful tool—don't underestimate its value. Listen with attentiveness. Allow the conversation to flow wherever it needs to go. Don't be afraid of silence. Your presence is the important part. Ask how they are feeling: "What are you struggling with right now?"

There is no way you know just how they feel. Even if you have faced a similar experience, share only how you felt; don't presume to know how they feel. Your hurting friends do not want to hear about someone else's similar experience.

DO

Tell them you are praying for them. Ask for specific requests.

DON'T

Don't say,
  "Don't worry, God is with you."
  "Everything will be okay."
  "Just have faith."

Don't say, "I'm praying for you" in a lighthearted attempt to make them feel better. Make sure to spend time before the Lord in prayer, bringing petitions of need. Ask for specific prayer requests, such as getting a good night's sleep, play time for their children, or peace in upcoming decisions.

DO

Say, "I'm so sorry." Then add
  "This must be so difficult."
  "I know how special he was to you."
  "I share your loss."
  "I want to help ..."
  "I've been praying for you."

DON'T

Don't say, "I'm sorry," and end the sentence. Your hurting friend is sorry, too, but can't respond to "I'm sorry." Add a comment or thought that he or she can respond to.

You need to offer something for your hurting friend to respond to. I often ask a question following my statement, "I'm so sorry." Like "Was this sudden?" "Had she been ill?" "Were you able to be there?" Saying "I'm sorry" is one of the most important things we can say; it just doesn't provide a lead-in for a response. Think ahead. What could you say or ask that will allow your hurting friend to respond to your comment?

DO

Allow them all the time they need to deal effectively with the phases of their crisis.

DON'T

Don't put timetables on your hurting friend's recovery.

Your inference that they are not coping well hinders their progress. There are no timelines for recovery, healing, or restoration following a crisis. Don't compare their experience with someone else in a similar situation. Each person handles his or her difficult times differently.

DO

Offer support and encouragement. Respond cautiously and prayerfully with uplifting and edifying ideas when your friends ask for guidance.

DON'T

Don't offer advice. If they weren't solicited, your suggestions may not be appreciated.

Advice is not the same as comfort. Our hurting friends need our nonjudgmental interactions. They need us to offer unconditional love, encouragement, and support. Never give advice unless you have been specifically asked, and even then, be very cautious. We want only to be helpful, but often our advice is not wanted.

When you are asked questions or for advice, share only what you have experienced in your own life. Don't tell stories you have heard about others in a similar situation. Don't say, "I think you should ..." or "I don't think you should ..." Until they are much further down their path of recovery, they really aren't looking for input, answers, or solutions.

> ## DO
> *Remember especially hard times.*
>
> ## DON'T
> *Don't forget anniversaries, birthdays, death dates, and holidays.*

While your life may have returned to normal, your friends live with their crisis on a daily basis. There is nothing normal about their lives. Show your continued support by remembering difficult days. Send a card, make a call, or invite them to spend time with you.

> ## DO
> *Use your gifts and talents to help. Consider what you enjoy doing, what you're good at.*
>
> ## DON'T
> *Don't put yourself under pressure to perform tasks that you really don't want to do.*

Use your skills and talents, and function within your gifts to reach out to others in need. If you are not a good cook, don't feel you must bring a meal. Think of ways you can help that are unique to you.

> ## DO
> *Understand that each person's experience is unique. Needs, hurts, and emotions will vary from person to person, situation to situation.*
>
> ## DON'T
> *Don't say, "I know just how you feel." Or "I understand what it's like."*

Be honest about your experiences. If you haven't endured their particular kind of tragedy, say, "I haven't been through what you're facing, but I want you to know I care about you and will support you through the difficult time ahead." If you have had a similar crisis, tell them about it briefly, adding that you can empathize with their feelings. Of course you can't completely understand what it is like for them because you haven't been through the past experiences that have laid the foundation for their reaction.

DO

Continue to keep in touch, offering support, letting them know you're praying for them. Send thoughtful notes with encouraging words.

DON'T

Don't ignore their needs after the immediate crisis has subsided.

Stay in touch. After a crisis, our lives go back to normal, but the lives of our hurting friends will never be the same.

DO

Realize that their hearts are full of pain and turmoil. Let them know that you will listen to their feelings and that you want to be a part of the process.

DON'T

Don't expect optimism or levity or happiness from your hurting person.

Your hurting friends have such a shroud of heartache around their hearts, it is very difficult for them to feel any joy. They often will feel guilty for laughing or having a good time or will resent other people enjoying themselves.

DO

Indicate your love by saying, "There is nothing that I can say to undo what has happened, but I want you to know that I love you. I'm praying for you, and I want to help."

DON'T

Don't offer clichés or trite statements in an attempt to minimize what they're facing or to cover up your own insecurities.

Try to imagine what your life would be like if you were facing the same difficulty. Pray with them, show your care, and hurt with them.

DO

Allow the individual to make the decisions and take the necessary steps to deal with the trauma. No one can tell another what to feel or not to feel.

DON'T

Don't use "shoulds" or "if onlys" such as
"You should go back to work and get over this."
"You shouldn't feel that way."
"If only you'd spent more time with him."
"If only you'd seen it coming."

We minimize people's feelings when we tell them they should or shouldn't feel that way. Their reality is that they *do* feel that way. They are sharing their concerns, fears, and burdens. Catch yourself anytime you hear the words *should* or *shouldn't* formulate in your mind. Most hurting people have already beaten themselves up over "if onlys" and "should haves", such as "You should have more faith"; "If only you had been there for him"; "If only you hadn't been so strict"; "If only you ate better."

DO

Provide long-term, unconditional support. Let them know that everyone deals with trauma in a different way.

DON'T

Don't be critical or judgmental. Don't say things like
"This wouldn't have happened if ..."
"There must be sin in your life."
"You're not trusting God with this."
"You reap what you sow."

There is no manual or timetable for how to handle a crisis. Let your hurting friends know that you have no expectation of how much time it should take or how they should behave. Assure them that whatever it takes, you will be there with them.

PART

PERSONAL
CRISIS

DIVORCE *and* SINGLE PARENTING

In an ideal world, divorce wouldn't happen. Husbands and wives would live happily ever after. While divorce certainly isn't God's best for our lives, it is a reality for many. We must not look the other way or pretend it doesn't exist. We need to express love and compassion to our hurting friend, not shame and judgment. Divorce is a devastating experience, filled with heartache, loneliness, and sorrow. Divorce produces far-reaching ramifications and long-lasting struggles. Your friend needs your unconditional, nonjudgmental love and support.

WHAT HURTS ME

"I never liked the way he treated you." If the couple ever gets back together you have alienated your friend. That comment is being critical of your friend's choice in a mate.

"There are always two sides to every story."

"You'll just have to let Jesus be your husband."

"Just get on with your life," or "There are other fish in the sea." This doesn't help. LAURA PETHERBRIDGE

Don't judge your friend's heart. My pastor and his wife came to me and said they did not feel I was truly repentant for my mistakes, even though I was devastated by them. I began to sob in front of them, but they insisted God would reveal the real fruit in my heart and that the insincerity would show through soon enough. They remained cold and had no idea of how I was suffering inside. That was almost as devastating as the divorce itself. I was beaten while I was down. JULIE

While separated from my husband by his choice, I heard a radio preacher say, "If your husband is involved with someone else, ask yourself what you've done to push him into her arms." His words devastated me. I had already blamed myself. I didn't need his condemnation. JO FRANZ

I remember being told that God hates divorce. I was a new Christian at the time, and that was especially hurtful to me. KAREN O'CONNOR

When meeting people at a church function, it is not uncommon that my marital status comes up. Upon learning that I am no longer married, their response is often, "Oh—you're divorced," with a sense of disdain or condemnation in their voice. This reaction makes me feel as if I'm less of a person, second rate, and can have no spiritual role in this environment. There is the attitude that I am forever flawed and can never get past it in their eyes. GEORGIA SHAFFER

"There's no excuse for divorce in the church. You should be praying about this!" Did they think I wasn't in prayer for my marriage? I was already wrapped in shame. Their words only added another layer. ADELE

Don't judge or say things like "It takes two to break up a marriage; you must have done something to make him or her leave." That's a lie! I was so hurt by a well-meaning Christian friend who said this to me. It pierced my heart. I was already embarrassed and feeling guilty; this only confirmed my fears. LAURA PETHERBRIDGE

Don't give religious clichés. "It will be all right." "God hates divorce; He will make him come back." "God works all things for good." We are often too angry at everyone, including God, to hear these comments. LAURA PETHERBRIDGE

Those who had never really experienced problems or trials like I was facing were the first to criticize me. ANONYMOUS

General statements like, "Call if you need me," "Let's have lunch sometime," or "You know I'm here if you need something," aren't helpful. Try to identify a specific need and offer specific help. BETH

"You'll find someone else." The implication was that I wasn't a whole person without a mate. It was difficult enough coping with the divorce, without being made to feel as though I was incomplete and unaccepted by others without a mate in my life. Finding someone else was not the point and only attempted to minimize what I was facing. JAN COLEMAN

There were two or three families that made it clear that they were no longer my friends, and I was not welcome to turn to them for even an encouraging word. GEORGE

Don't ask me to share all the details. ANONYMOUS

When spending time with a divorced person, stay away from movies, television shows, or plays that are romantic, deal with divorce, or deal with children hurting from divorce. This emotional trigger is very difficult. LAURA PETHERBRIDGE

Some people told me I wasn't spiritual enough, that if I had had deeper faith, it never would have happened. Don't chastise or shame me. Please, just listen and sympathize. ROSE SWEET

A woman I thought was a close friend was very critical. She didn't inquire about my feelings, how I was doing, or what I might need, but suggested I should talk to the pastor to "prevent" the divorce. BARBARA

Don't fix me up with someone—don't even think about it! LAURA PETHERBRIDGE

I felt hurt, wounded, and criticized when people openly expressed their opinions about my life when they had no idea what I was going through. ANONYMOUS

WHAT HELPS ME

"The future must seem frightening; I'll stay close."

"I'm sure this is a lonely time for you. When can we have lunch?"

"I'm your friend, no matter what. I'm here for you. It's time you focus on yourself and your children." KAREN O'CONNOR

"Tell me what hurts the most, and I will pray for you." "I know God loves you and longs to comfort you during this terrible pain. I'm here for you." LAURA PETHERBRIDGE

A friend in women's ministry helped by assuring me of her continuing love and friendship. She said, "I don't even want to know any of the details. I love you no matter what." She went on to live out her words to this very day, ten years later. BARBARA

Speak truthfully and honestly. For example, say, "Laura, I know this is breaking your heart that Tom is having an affair. I'm so sorry he has chosen to betray you and hurt you so deeply." LAURA PETHERBRIDGE

"I can't take away your hurt, but I can love you unconditionally." This statement was said by my pastor's wife. She then showed her love with her actions. She took care of me, cooked some meals, and was available to listen when I needed to talk. She was a blessing for me and helped me heal. ALICE OLDHAM

The most helpful thing people said was just to affirm that I was in a difficult time. GEORGE

WHAT I WISH PEOPLE UNDERSTOOD

There are some seasons that you can't do anything to change. You can't fix it. I think in our instant society, where any family problem or relationship can be solved during a one-hour television show, we have an unconscious expectation that things will work out to a pleasant solution, and the solution will come along by the end of the week. The depth of the pool of sorrow that I swam through was not so simple. GEORGE

People in crisis need hope. They need hope that this is survivable, that there are second chances, and, mostly, that the God they believe to be sovereign in their lives is good and trustworthy. First Peter 3:15 says, "Always be prepared to give an answer to everyone who asks you to give the reason for the hope that you have. But do this with gentleness and respect." JULIE

Most people around us looked at this situation like leprosy; they just didn't want to get involved. GEORGE

When I was going through my divorce, I felt ostracized by other Christians. I wished people would reach out and include me in things. ANONYMOUS

When the divorce is the result of betrayal, lies, and deceit, grieving over this loss is even more complex than if the spouse had died. You not only face the pain of losing your spouse, but also the deep hurts of rejection. GEORGIA SHAFFER

My sons needed mentors, examples in their lives, because of the absence of their father. ANONYMOUS

I didn't need people taking sides as though this was a war. I felt that I had to step aside from church leadership during my divorce, so I felt I was also losing part of my support system within my church family. BARBARA

I felt like a child. It seemed as if my world had been turned upside down by my husband's public affair and his lack of shame. I felt very alone during that dreadful season in my life. My life had been wrapped up in my husband, and I felt as though I were dying. Part of me left when he left. Some people seemed insensitive to the loss and pain I was going through. KAREN O'CONNOR

I experienced a very traumatic divorce. While there were scriptural grounds for divorce, it was still very difficult to accept that this was, in fact, happening in my marriage. I received a card congratulating me on my divorce. When I opened the card, it sent me into a bout of tears. I hadn't gotten married with the intent of someday having my heart ripped out through a painful divorce. While I may have wanted the divorce due to the repeated unfaithfulness of my spouse, I certainly didn't want to celebrate it! ANONYMOUS

It's very easy to remember someone during the first few days of something tragic, but the real help comes when you remember that person afterward in the weeks and months that follow. That's when they need you the most. KIM JOHNSON

Don't ignore me or look the other way. Even people I counted as friends didn't call, visit, or write. I felt rejected. Even though I was in the midst of a divorce, I still wanted to laugh at jokes, go out for breakfast, enjoy a phone call, or host a tea at my home. I longed for stability during that time. How I wished for friendships and a church relationship while my whole life was blown to pieces around me. ADELE

People going through divorce are in shock, fearful, guilty (even if they didn't leave, they feel like they must have done something), tremendously sad, or even elated if the relationship was abusive. Emotions go from one extreme to another in minutes. This is normal, especially at the beginning. Ride the roller coaster with them. LAURA PETHERBRIDGE

While I was married, many of my friends were couples. Once I became single, I desired to continue my relationship with them, but I was rarely invited to join them. I needed those friends to be part of my life. GEORGIA SHAFFER

Divorces are different. A one-size-fits-all approach to help divorcing friends will not work. There is a time when the hurt outweighs anything else. There is the process of grieving the loss, which is much like grieving any other loss. Because of my divorce, I lost my friend, someone I trusted, my goal of having an intact family, income, stability, respect with my peers, and self-respect. There are days when I feel as if an invisible yet indelible stamp of "FAILURE" is now written across some of the pages of my life. By the grace of God, I know that is not true, but the feelings remain from time to time. GEORGE

I didn't have the strength to reach out on my own. I appreciated it when friends reached out to me without being asked. I especially needed someone to stay in touch on a regular basis, over the long term, without being asked. BETH

People need to understand that the spouse who strayed made a decision to do so—one he or she didn't have to make. The spouse could have chosen to seek help for the marriage with his or her partner. With this realization, those in the body will not be so judgmental of the spouse who was left behind for another. JO FRANZ

The church wasn't very supportive. I never had support from the church family during my struggles. Some churches offer divorce recovery programs but ignore our needs through the difficulties of the process. ANONYMOUS

Death is not the only way to lose a child. When I was divorced, I "lost" my stepson, who'd first leapt into my arms at age two. For ten years I'd been his other mother: I taught him to bake cookies, take his first shower, say his first prayers, and ride his bike without training wheels. I cleaned up after him when he was sick, worked with his teachers, helped him earn pins in Boy Scouts, and lots of other deeply bonding interaction that mothers and sons share. Although my ex-husband walked out on our marriage, he knew that his son's relationship with me was precious and worthy of saving. Many fathers who leave do little to maintain all the loving relationships their children have that might be severed in a divorce. ROSE SWEET

As the child of divorced parents, I realized that children perceive guilt, responsibility, and blame for the divorce. I was told that my parents' divorce and my mother's giving up custody of me was "no problem. You can get a new parent!" I needed people to talk openly with me about the divorce. It hurt me when people treated my dad as if the divorce was his fault. It was Mom who left. Supportive encouragers assured me I was going to make it through this. ROBB

WHAT YOU CAN DO

Friends who just listened and prayed with me were of immeasurable value. They understood without condemnation; they encouraged me without moralizing. The best thing a friend can do is swim alongside and help the divorcing person keep his or her head above water. GEORGE

Buy some good Christian worship music as a gift. I cried so hard I couldn't even pray, but I could sit and listen and pray through the music. LAURA PETHERBRIDGE

During my divorce, people I hardly knew would bring me a small bouquet of cheerful flowers, cards, or baked goodies just to let me know they cared about what I was going through. Good friends listened to me analyze the same things over and over without letting me know how wearisome I was. I had to talk it out and be validated in my feelings. Occasionally, I would have to call a friend late at night because of desperate feelings, and she would come and sit with me and pray until the feelings passed. JULIE

Be available. Many friends dropped out of sight because they didn't know what to say or were afraid to take sides. You can remain friends without saying you are against the other spouse. Make time for your friends. Find out the darkest time for them; mine was Sunday-afternoon family day. Remember, your friend will feel like a third wheel if all are couples and he or she is the only single. A divorced person will be less likely to fall into the trap of getting into a new relationship too soon if he or she has a strong social life with friends. LAURA PETHERBRIDGE

What I needed was the love and encouragement of friends. I needed to spend time in normal settings. With a life upside down in turmoil, normalcy is the best medicine. Phone calls and conversations that didn't dwell on the divorce, yet enabled me to work through some issues, were needed—a listening, non-critical ear. BARBARA

I felt so ugly during my divorce. My cousin bought me a beautiful pair of earrings that I still treasure. They made me feel pretty and really lifted my spirits. LAURA PETHERBRIDGE

My "Christian" husband left me when I was pregnant with our third child. A special couple brought groceries and made sure there was something fun in the bag for my five- and seven-year-olds. When my baby was born, they paid for the diaper service. ANONYMOUS

Buy new bedroom sheets, linens, or a nightgown. The greatest gift I got was a nice nightgown—not romantic, just pretty. It made me feel like I was still a woman even though he rejected me. A friend bought all new sheets, as she couldn't stand sleeping on the same ones he had been in. LAURA PETHERBRIDGE

Strongly encourage your friends to attend a support group, even if they don't want to go or don't think they need it. Offer to go with them. The best healing takes place if they can get around others experiencing the same thing. I recommend http://www.divorcecare.org. It is biblically based. LAURA PETHERBRIDGE

I needed to talk about what I was going through but didn't need advice. I just needed someone to listen, listen, listen. BETH

It was very difficult to be a single mother of three, working two jobs because I received only sporadic child support, and going to school four nights a week. Not once did anyone in my family or church offer to watch my children or help with child-care expenses. I wished someone would offer me a break from the stress of being the provider, nurturer, and caregiver. ANONYMOUS

Accompany your friend to court. This is a terrible experience, even if he or she felt it was necessary to divorce. No one should do it alone. LAURA PETHERBRIDGE

My sister, seeing that I felt unloved and needed affection and affirmation, asked my friends and family to write, draw, or create something special that said how much they loved me and what they particularly appreciated about me. She stuck them all into an album that had those popular, poofy, quilted fabric covers tied with ribbons and lace. When she gave it to me, I bawled my eyes out. It has remained one of my most priceless treasures. I pull it out, dust it off, and sit down to read it whenever I need a "love" fix. ROSE SWEET

Hug us; touch us (same sex only). We now have a loss of personal touch. The bed is empty; the house cold. We need human touch. LAURA PETHERBRIDGE

The day my husband left, my best friend came to my house and stayed with me for a few days. The emotional shock was overwhelming, so having someone with me was a needed comfort. She read to me continually from Scripture and credible Christian books. At the time, my mind was numb, so reading anything on my own was out of the question. Her gift of time and reading helped me immensely. KIM JOHNSON

My wish list: companionship and meals. I longed to just be invited to a friend's home, not to be entertained, and definitely not to be lectured or counseled. I wanted to be around people where the walls weren't falling in. I wanted to feel that I was important to someone. It didn't matter if their hair was done or that the house was picked up. I wanted to know that I was still loved by someone, somewhere. I was happy to be invited over just to watch television! Any meal is wonderful, just knowing that someone knows I am hurting and that I matter. ANONYMOUS

Provide meals, things that can go in the freezer. Concentration levels are at an all-time low. One less thing to think about is an incredible blessing. LAURA PETHERBRIDGE

As a single mother of three children, I had very limited finances. A precious family offered to pay for violin lessons for my youngest daughter. This was a luxury I could not afford, but it was the passion in my daughter's life. What a blessing they are! ANONYMOUS

Help the family get on a budget, find a volunteer in the church who can help, or contact http://www.crown.org to locate a volunteer budget counselor from Crown Financial Ministries. Be careful about lending money. Only lend it viewing it as "if they never pay me back, it's okay." Loaning money breaks up many good friendships. Give them items or pay for tangible things they need instead. LAURA PETHERBRIDGE

What helped were the encouraging notes of love and affirmation from several of the women in our women's ministry at church. There was not one word of condemnation in any of them as they expressed sorrow for the situation and assured me of their prayers and love. BARBARA

Buy books that will give guidance in financial and personal matters. There are great ones out there, but many people can't afford to purchase them. LAURA PETHERBRIDGE

My husband left when my youngest son was an infant. I could hardly get out of bed. The best thing anyone did for me was when a friend came over and sat in the rocking chair and held my baby. I was not emotionally able to do it myself. ANONYMOUS

When my friend was both dying from breast cancer and facing divorce from an unfaithful husband, I was the one who drove her to all of her lawyer's appointments and court appearances. This was one thing I was determined she would not have to do alone. I ached that she needed to spend what little time she had left in a court of law, battling a divorce settlement. LAUREN

Friends offered to watch our children so I could attend a divorce recovery support group or have some time to shop. LAURA PETHERBRIDGE

During the darkest times, people got me out of the house and into the community. They would call and say, "Let's go _____." Fill in the blank with: to a movie, to an antique show, to a concert, on a hike, or on a picnic. ADELE

My son and I were included in a family outing to Hawk Mountain on a beautiful, crisp fall day. My friend packed a picnic lunch for us all, and we hiked up the mountain. Finding just the right spot, we sat on boulders and watched an amazing variety of birds migrate. I still cherish that memory, as it was something I could not have done on my own at that time. GEORGIA SHAFFER

Help with attorney fees, counseling, childcare, day-to-day living expenses like groceries and utilities if the ex isn't paying. Help find a place to live or help in selling the house. LAURA PETHERBRIDGE

I had neighbors who knew I lived alone and have multiple sclerosis. They made sure the snow was cleaned off my car each morning, brought the paper to my front door, and watched out for me. One neighbor was a nurse and checked in on me regularly, bringing meals at times and keeping me company. JO

Buying school supplies is stressful, especially when funds are tight. A co-worker took my three children to K-Mart to buy their school supplies. It was such a blessing that someone offered to meet this need. Another friend sent me gift certificates inside encouraging greeting cards. Others anonymously sent money, store gift cards, and gift certificates.

Make sure your friends have somewhere to go on holidays, anniversaries, and birthdays. Many times a single parent is left home alone on these dates while kids are with the other parent. This is an extremely lonely time for them. The first Christmas is absolutely the worst. Help them put up decorations for the holidays. LAURA PETHERBRIDGE

Having been a single mom, I know that there is a need to have some quiet time to think and work through the many difficult issues that we face as a single parent. I ask single parents if I may have the pleasure of watching their children for a couple of hours or even a full day. My youngest son is now five and needs playmates. It is a perfect excuse to have other children in our home and provide the needed break for the single parent. Single parents tend to carry a lot of guilt already. If they felt as though they or their children were a burden, they would never accept my offer. By presenting the offer as beneficial to myself and my son, who can refuse? LECIA SEGAARD

A wonderful gift was that people were not afraid to invite me to their homes for dinner or parties even though I wasn't a "couple" anymore. It was very strange for me to attend as a single person, but they made me feel completely welcome. KIM JOHNSON

A very dear couple, who lived far away, called every few weeks or so to see how I was getting along and often just to let me cry on their shoulders. What I remember the most about these friends was that they offered to send me a round-trip airline ticket. They told me I could come out and stay with them for as long as I needed, in a safe, beautiful, and peaceful place, so I could take a break from the pressures of my current situation. ANONYMOUS

For most single mothers, finances are tight. Every penny counts. One friend tucked a phone card in with a note of encouragement. I was so grateful for her thoughtful gift. GEORGIA SHAFFER

The junior pastor at my church was willing to meet with me at any time, for any length of time, just to let me talk, vent, and pray. Many times we met at a local coffee shop or college campus to walk, talk, and pray. He didn't judge me or try to feed me comfortable platitudes. He was just there and allowed me to bleed and encouraged me to keep my eyes on the Lord. GEORGE

Two couples made themselves available to me at any time of the day or night. I remember calling them up in the middle of the night in tears. As I poured out my hurt over the phone, they seemed to scrape me off the floor and lift me up into a chair. Their prayers with me gave me comfort and hope that God still loved me and cared for me. JO

My husband and I pray together each night. Our prayer list includes single parents and their children. We must never forget the importance of prayer. We practice "purposeful listening" when talking with single parents. In a casual conversation, they may mention a need in their lives that they would never have the courage to bring before their peers. Most often our help is in the form of anonymous gifts, but occasionally, they will mention something very specific, such as a favorite brand of hand lotion that they can no longer afford. In such a case, we purchase the item and present it with a card signed by our entire family and let them know that we appreciate them as an individual and for their ministry within our church. If the gift is for a male, my husband presents the gift. If it is for a female, then I present the gift. LECIA SEGAARD

I was told that my ministry was over. I would never again teach a Bible study. I would never again play the piano or organ for church. I would never again sing before a congregation because I was a divorced woman. Shame hung over my head like a nuclear fallout cloud. I attended a church meeting in another town. A woman there asked me to accompany her. The song I played was "If the Lord Says." The first phrase was, "If the Lord says I'm a blessing, then I am. If the Lord says I am healed, then I am." As I played the piano and listened to the words of this simple song, a transformation went on in my heart. After the service, the singer tore the song out of her songbook and handed it to me. She said, "I think the Lord wants you to have this." From that day, I began to recover. If I begin to feel worthless, I remember the words to the song, and those negative feelings vanish. ADELE

My idea for helping single parents is what I call "adopt a family." This is when a two-parent family takes a single-parent family "under their wing." This might mean including them for Sunday dinner, picnics, church events, camping, boat rides, amusement parks, etc.—whatever that family typically does together. This gives the children a wonderful Christian example of what a two-parent family looks like and feels like. I am convinced that the "big brother" type program would work with families as well as it has with individuals.

The best thing you can do for someone in this situation is give your time, encouraging and supporting without judging or pushing personal opinions on him or her. Be quick to pray with the person about everything and slow with expectations. Allow people the freedom to heal at their pace, not yours. Understanding and grace are invaluable. This is an extremely emotional and painful experience that takes extra time to overcome. KIM JOHNSON

When my husband left, I couldn't talk about it at all. I told no one what had happened. Several months into this silence, someone asked, and I dumped on her. Instead of telling me to shut up, one friend gave me an empty journal book. She said, "What you're saying is so valuable, would you please write what you just told me? You never know when one of my children might need it." That was honestly the first time I realized that anyone else could ever hurt as I did. I went home that night and penned the words that became *Surviving Separation and Divorce.* SHARON MARSHALL

Our church has a special parking area for single parents with young children. This not only helps the rushed parent but gives them a little place of consideration. It also serves as a safety net in a very busy parking lot. JANET LYNN MITCHELL

SPECIAL HELP WITH CHILDREN

Men, take boys under your wing and become the dad they are now missing. Even if the dad is in their life, he typically will remarry quickly, leaving the child feeling abandoned. It is critical that they have a role model who will spend time with them.

Listen! Let the child know you hear them. Many times a kid will open up to someone other than family. Children are fearful of siding with one parent, so you could be a safe person with whom they can share their feelings—especially teens. Speak kindly and calmly to them. Their world is spinning.

Carpool or help with the transportation. Now, with only one parent, there is less chance of the parent being available to meet all of the transportation needs.

Help the family find a counselor who specializes in meeting children's needs.

Make homemade treats, like cookies, etc. Mom's too busy for that now.

Help the children make Christmas and birthday gifts for both parents.

Speak kindly of the other parent. Be honest if they are making poor choices. Don't hide the truth, but address the behavior, not the person.

Don't be afraid to discipline when you are watching them. Many single parents are very loose on discipline because they feel guilty for the child's pain. These children are often begging for boundaries; this shows love.

ALL SUGGESTIONS IN THIS SECTION ARE FROM LAURA PETHERBRIDGE

WHAT TO WRITE IN A CARD

You are in my thoughts, in my heart, and in my prayers.

I know you are going through a difficult time. I care about you and will be here for you. You are precious to me.

I can't begin to know what you are experiencing, but please know that I'm praying for you and your children each day.

There are no words that can change what you are facing, but please know that I love you and that I care.

As you walk this lonely road, be assured of my friendship and my support.

PRAYER

Dear heavenly Father, You know how (<u>name of hurting friend</u>)'s heart is broken and hurting. I ask that You would come beside him/her and make Your presence known. I know it is never Your desire for Your children to suffer. I come to You now asking for protection and comfort. Fill those lonely moments with Your love. I ask for Your guidance in the many decisions that lie ahead. Please go ahead of him/her and prepare the path that he/she must walk. Help me to be the friend (<u>name of hurting friend</u>) needs at this most difficult time. I ask Your special blessing on his/her life. Amen.

AN ESTRANGED *or* REBELLIOUS CHILD

There is no friendship, no love, like that of the parent for the child.

HENRY WARD BEECHER, AMERICAN CLERGYMAN

There was a period of two years when my oldest son, in his late teens, wanted nothing to do with us. He chose to be on his own. He lived in the neighboring town, but wouldn't even come for Thanksgiving dinner. We missed him terribly. There were times when I would walk by his now tidy room and wish for just one sign of life—maybe a dirty sock on the floor or an unmade bed. Even our dog missed him. She would lie in the hallway outside his room with her nose stuck under the door just to catch his scent.

I tried to stay in touch, to keep the lines of communication open without being overbearing or pushy. We attended every concert his band performed in the Southern California area and waited to greet him afterwards. We complimented the show and his performance, but he had little to say to us.

I had never known such heartache. While I had experienced losses and difficult times, I had never experienced total rejection from my own child. He was apart from us for two years. The road to restoration was long and slow, but today he joins us for every holiday and works alongside his father in our family business.

All contributions have been made anonymously out of respect for the contributors' children.

WHAT HURTS ME

My extended family members are the most difficult for me. I come from a long tradition of Christianity for which I am very grateful.

43

Unfortunately, it is laced with legalism. The questions about our daughter's welfare seem more like judgmental inquisitions than concerned inquiries.

Parents who have not experienced a prodigal find it very easy to wonder why this problem exists. It hurt when people approached us to tell us they couldn't understand why kids would go astray if the parents raised them right. Those kinds of comments poured salt on the wound. They put the burden of guilt on us, pulling us further down.

Someone prayed over me and stated that he didn't know what I had done that God would do this to me. I felt the man thought God was punishing me! I don't believe God is punishing me. He is teaching me His ways. I have learned about a broken heart, and I hope I can help others.

There is still a lot of shame and feelings of denial within the Christian community about drug and alcohol abuse. It flies in the face of "If you were a good Christian family and raised your children according to biblical principles, this wouldn't happen to you."

One Sunday after church, an elder's wife came up to me, and as I shared about my daughter, she responded by saying, "I guess I don't know what that is like. I know my daughter would never do something like that." Her arrow penetrated deeply. I will never forget her hurtful words. I pray she never finds out what this pain is like!

The things that were said that really bothered me were simplistic advice like, "Just kick her out," given by people who had never had to face that decision, friends who had never been there themselves.

Don't compare my experience with stories of other rebellious children.

Don't give me advice, asking, "Have you tried … ?"

Don't breech the family's confidentiality. Some friends took the liberty to share with others in our adult fellowship about my wayward daughter. Often prayer requests can be a spiritualized form of gossip. Confidentiality is very important, because when the child does return to the family, he or she does not need to be forever living down poor choices.

WHAT HELPS ME

"How's (child's name) doing?" or "Have you heard anything from (child's name)?" Just because a child is estranged or rebellious, he or she still exists, and we appreciate your interest and concern.

"I know how much you love your child. I will be praying with you for his/her protection."

"I'm sure this is a very difficult time for you."

"I know the desire of your heart is to have reconciliation with your child. I support you in the decisions you are making."

"I know you must be hurting. It's difficult when our children turn from us. I would like to pray for you and your family daily. I am committed to our friendship."

WHAT I WISH PEOPLE UNDERSTOOD

A wayward child is not the direct result of bad parenting. The parents already feel guilt and have a sense that they did something horribly wrong to result in their child's rebellion. The emphasis needs to be on God redeeming all things—mistakes included—as we trust Him and take responsibility when appropriate.

I wish people understood that this estrangement is not because we did not love our child enough, or that we didn't discipline him or her enough. I wish they would not see the actions of the child and point the finger at the parents. I wish they would not judge us.

There is always a painful, empty spot in your heart, especially when you see complete families.

The toughest part of our son's rebellion is that he rejected us. He cannot stand to be around us and avoids us as much as he can. I can't even describe what this rejection is like, but it wounds to the bone.

Parents need encouragement and praise. Remember, parenting is a job that comes without a manual.

I was the first and only one of my friends who was experiencing a child with an addiction problem. Therefore, no one could relate to what I was going through. The thing I missed most was the chance to pray with people who had experienced the same fears and frustrations I had. There were Christian-based groups for people with addictions, but nothing for the families. It made me feel that Christian families don't have these problems. The help I got did not come from a Christian environment, but rather from counselors and family groups at the rehabilitation center.

Satan's biggest target is our children. He doesn't stop there. He wants our marriages too. Through all of this turmoil, my husband and I almost separated. One day as we were taking out our pain on each other, I looked at him and said, "You are not the enemy, and neither am I." He agreed. We started praying together, and for the first time we put total trust in the Lord, knowing that He loved our daughter far more than we did.

During our prodigal season, many people tried to help us, but when you are going through this, you never think your child is going to come back. You see the hardness in their hearts, and you know it will only get worse—and yes, it feels like your child died.

There were many times when the only thing I had to hold on to was God's promise that my child would overcome her illness. My daughter's addiction was totally bewildering to us since no one in our family had experienced this. We had no idea where to turn or who to talk to.

Once an adult child has chosen a wayward path, he or she needs to be unconditionally loved back to the right path. It is sometimes a very slow process. Resolve to let him or her see the nonjudgmental love of Christ in you.

Our crisis is past, yet we are living in a paradox. We feel very vulnerable and have tender, wounded places in our hearts. We personally feel our daughter's failure to live as a committed Christian, but we are loving her unconditionally. To do so does not mean we condone all her behavior or agree with all her choices. On the other hand we are not embarrassed or ashamed of her. We are grateful for our current relationship, though it has changed, as do all relationships with adult children.

WHAT YOU CAN DO

When my older, wiser best friend heard that my daughter had moved out, she simply said, "Do you want me to come over?" I replied that it would be really nice to see her, though there was really nothing she could do and I had no tangible need at that moment. I didn't realize how much it would mean to see her van pull in the driveway some time later. She simply came in and sat with my husband and me. She let us debrief while she listened. Hearing our own voices tell the story helped us gain perspective. She then offered this most helpful and profound insight: "Your daughter didn't want to leave; she just knew she couldn't stay." Immediately, instead of feeling angry at the pain she had caused, my focus shifted. I became aware of *her* needs. I had never experienced the "just being there" that is often talked about, but this lady demonstrated in a moment of crisis what that looks like. She truly was "Jesus with skin on" to us that afternoon.

Mother's Day is a rough day for a mom of an estranged child. We were on a trip on Mother's Day, and as we boarded the bus, one young girl turned to me and said, "I know you are hurting, and if it helps, I'll be a daughter to you, and you can be the mother to me that I do not have." She encouraged me throughout the trip that my daughter would come home, because she did after her rebellious years. God sent an ex-prodigal to minister to my broken heart and give me hope.

A friend encouraged me to claim a verse for my child. The verse that I claimed for my daughter was Romans 11:29 (NRSV), which says that the gifts and calling of God are irrevocable. I know that my child has gifts God entrusted her with and a calling on her life—this keeps me going even when I see nothing in her life that indicates she's interested in God. God says His call and gifting is irrevocable—nobody can revoke what He has established.

My friends encouraged me to keep the lines of communication open even though the child's choices were not in alignment with my values.

What was most helpful were my listening friends, who let me share my heart without being judgmental. Friends who made a genuine commitment to pray for our family and our daughter were especially needed. I was reminded that "good seeds" were sown in my daughter's life, and they will bear fruit in time. God has told me time and time again not to evaluate the crop prematurely. He is in charge of the harvest.

One evening I was crying and asking God "Why?" when our Sunday school teacher's wife called and asked if I had a prayer need. We were new to the class, so she didn't know us well. I briefly explained that our daughter had left us and that she was my prayer need. She said, "I have a Scripture for you." It was 2 Chronicles 15:7 (TLB): "Keep up the good work, and don't be discouraged, for you will be rewarded." It was God's answer to the question I had just been asking! The next morning I asked if she had called the whole class. She explained that I was the only one she had called, and she had felt led to call me at that very moment. I'm so grateful that she was obedient to God's call!

Encourage your friend with a prodigal child to keep a journal with letters written to their child, Scriptures that offer encouragement during that time, and written prayers. When the child does return and is reconciled, the journal can be given to him or her as a gift—a tangible evidence of faith at work! For the prodigal to see how much intercession and love was happening while he or she was gone can be humbling and moving. [1]

Create a prayer support for the parents. Ask the parents to write down their concerns for their child such as fears, hurts, resentments. Write these concerns down on individual cards. Each person in the prayer support group can take one card and pray about that concern for one week. Check in with the parents, maybe share a meal together, and discuss what is happening in the family's life. [2]

Remind the parents of a prodigal that it is okay to laugh and to enjoy other aspects of their lives. Just because one family relationship is strained doesn't have to block what is good in the rest of the family. Take hurting parents to a funny movie or play. Tell them that you know life has been stressful and that laughter is good for the spirit. [3]

Help your friends make a list of obstacles that are in the way of reconciliation with their child. Seeing the obstacles on paper helps clarify their thoughts and needs. Simplify each obstacle to a one- or two-word label that you can use as a focus. Pray consistently for God to remove the obstacles. [4]

WHAT TO WRITE IN A CARD

There is no greater love than the love of a parent for a child. Please know that we are praying with you for his/her safety and decisions.

I know your heart is breaking, and if there were some way I could change things, I would. Until this situation improves, I will be praying for you and _____ (child).

This is a difficult time for any parent. I know how much you love _____ and only want the best for him/her. I will reach out to _____ any chance I get. You have been strong in your faith and great parents. I admire you and love you.

If you have experienced a similar situation with your child, share how you felt during that time and then offer encouragement. I might say, "I can remember how much it hurt just to walk by my son's bedroom. I had such an ache in my heart as I felt his rejection. Slowly, one step at a time, the path toward healing began. Please know that I share your hurt and am praying for your son's/daughter's return."

PRAYER

When praying for someone, we want to validate where they are at the present and offer hope for the future. Even if the parents can't believe for themselves, we want to activate their faith by believing for them and using God's Word. I feel it is important to help the parent realize God's heart in all of this. I like to use God's Word and His promises and pray them back to Him.

Lord, You know the pain that (<u>name of hurting friend</u>) is in over this situation. I ask You to meet her/him right now and minister Your comfort and hope. Lord, I am thankful that You are bigger than (<u>name of hurting friend's child</u>)'s rebellion, and You promise to complete the good work You've begun in (<u>name of hurting friend</u>)'s life. I entrust him/her to You right now, knowing that You love (<u>name of</u>

hurting friend) and are working in ways I can't see.
JAN FRANK

Lord, I come to You with my friend (<u>name of hurting
friend</u>). You know how his/her heart is aching right now
over the situation with his/her child, (<u>name of hurting
friend</u>). Father, You understand what it is to have wayward
children. How Your heart aches over those You love who've
gone astray. You love (<u>name of son/daughter</u>) even more
than (<u>name of hurting friend</u>) does, and You desire
him/her to return to a life that honors You and to a relationship with You. I ask You right now, in the name of
Jesus, that You call the child back to Your fold. I thank You
that You say in Your Word that You seek the lost little
lambs. I ask You to speak to this child in the deepest parts
of his/her heart and woo him/her back by Your love.
Thank You that Your Word says that it is Your kindness
that leads us to repentance. Please, dear Father, show kindness and mercy to (<u>son/daughter</u>) and bring him/her home
to Your heart of love. In the meantime, strengthen and
encourage (<u>name of hurting friend</u>) and give him/her Your
Father's heart of love, patience, and compassion. Teach
him/her to love as You love and to wait with expectation
for all that You will do. I will give You all the praise.
JAN FRANK

RESOLUTIONS

My daughter is a delightful young woman, and God is obviously
working in her life—slowly, but working.

My daughter finally stopped running and faced her pain. She is a
committed Christian now who looks back and sees God never left
her.

Our son has rejoined our family, but he does not have an active faith.

We are rejoicing today, watching how He brought her back. SLOWLY, but nevertheless she is back. She still has her strong will, but her heart is supple.

Forgiveness is immediate; reconciliation is a process. I can forgive my daughter, but the celebration and reconciliation will come later.

EMOTIONAL NEEDS— DEPRESSION

Our friends and family dealing with depression or other emotional needs are not in that place by choice. If they could snap their fingers or say a prayer to change their condition, they would. We need to validate and affirm the reality of their pain. Because their condition isn't a visible injury or illness, we often underestimate its role in their lives and deem it unrealistic or insignificant. As a support system for them, we need to be understanding, patient, and helpful, not judgmental or critical.

WHAT HURTS ME

"You shouldn't feel this way." I had a minister say to me, "I'll pray for you" in a condescending way. Talk about kicking someone when they're down! You'd think a minister would be more compassionate and understanding. I'm sure many are, but if they've never experienced depression, they can be too harsh or critical. When you're depressed, you don't need a pep talk; you need help. DENA DYER

People gossiped about me. They said, "Shirley's crazy. She is a mental case." Others would not listen to me and pretended or acted as if everything was normal. People would come to see me, skirt the issue of my pain and problem, and ignore my complaints. Some tried to make jokes to make me laugh when laughter was impossible for me. SHIRLEY LINDSAY

What really put acid on the open sore was when friends would say, "If you were truly a Christian, you would not be depressed. You would have the joy of the Lord." That only added guilt! GLORIA

"Depression is just selfish. Confess to God. Pray more."

"You've got to pull yourself up by your bootstraps and get on with life."

"Cheer up!"

"Just count your blessings," or "Be thankful for what you have."

"It must be PMS or your time of the month."

"Look how bad other people have it."

"What do you have to be depressed about?"

WHAT HELPS ME

"I love you no matter how you feel."

"I am here for you; I'm not going anywhere."

"Do you want to talk?"

"I came by to give you a hug. Do you have time to talk for a few minutes?"

"I know this is a struggle for you. I support you and care about you."

WHAT I WISH PEOPLE UNDERSTOOD

Depression wrapped itself around me so tightly I never thought it would end. I developed panic attacks and lived in a state of introspection. Logic took flight! People wanted me to explain what I was feeling. A thousand questions came at me, but I couldn't answer because I was in a dark pit of fog. GLORIA

I just wished people "understood." Try to put yourself in my place; empathize with me; show you care and hurt with me. Don't treat me according to what feels good for you or what meets your needs. Find out what my needs are. SHIRLEY LINDSAY

Many depressed people are ill; they have a chemical imbalance in the brain. Whether or not it started from emotional and/or spiritual issues is of no consequence. We need time, love, patience, medical attention, and encouragement to take our medication without being made to feel weak. Don't try to talk us out of depression. Do encourage us to get help, to exercise, and to get out of the house. It's a delicate balance between being pushy and being sensitive; but with God's help, you can minister hope and healing to someone who's struggling with depression. DENA DYER

Depression is often not a choice. I do believe there are some people who do choose to be grumpy and complaining and sour about the whole world. But the real phenomenon of clinical depression is not a choice. I want to be happy, but sometimes my physical body won't allow that because of biochemical and physiological stuff happening inside my brain. I cannot control this, but I do want things to be better. Sometimes I need more help and encouragement than others. Most of the time, I just need people to act normal and not make a big deal of this depression thing so I can work through it more calmly and without feelings of guilt or fear of rejection. I sometimes attempt to hide because I don't want people to know I'm depressed, and I'm afraid they'll be irritated, frustrated, or disgusted. LUCY AKARD SEAY

Generally I'm a cheerful, upbeat person, and when I became depressed, my friends didn't know how to take me. They ignored me and even shunned me instead of asking what was wrong or just showing they cared. The message I received was that they loved me only when I was happy. They literally wouldn't have anything to do with me since I wasn't making them laugh anymore. We all deal with problems differently. I needed friends to talk it out. LAURIE

Depression creeps up on me like an early-morning fog. One day I feel competent, resilient, and ready for whatever life slings at me. Then, without warning, I have lost my bearings; I can't find me. I sink, and my body feels the heaviness. My body carries the weight of disconnection from myself, and I hate being me. BRENDAN O'ROURKE

Before I was diagnosed, I felt totally exhausted and empty for months on end. I couldn't remember details or think more than an hour ahead. Nothing amused me because I didn't have the strength to laugh. Daily stresses were magnified. My body became a stranger to me. The effort it took to do necessary things drained me. I hibernated as much as possible to protect my miniscule energy level. All these months I had no clue that I was experiencing depression. BRENDA NIXON

WHAT YOU CAN DO

My best friends and spouse help me by listening when I need to talk and encouraging me to seek godly counseling. They invite me out for lunch, to a movie, or shopping. They volunteer to watch my son so I can get extra rest and help me to laugh and not take myself, or my problems, so seriously all the time. DENA DYER

I understand that mental illness is one of those things that people don't understand, and they tend to shy away. It was the visits of friends that were invaluable to me. It meant so much to know that other people cared. The phone calls and notes were very supportive. ANONYMOUS

During a tearful episode at church, my sensitive yet confused husband took me away and sat with me as I cried uncontrollably. He didn't say anything—no questions, lectures, ridicule, or advice. His peaceful presence was helpful. That's what I suggest you give your hurting person. BRENDA NIXON

My friends accept the reality of my struggle and do not try to change me, avoid me, or make me see the reasons I shouldn't be depressed. They regularly reaffirm their love for me and their unconditional acceptance. They often say that they are sorry that I struggle with this. They treat me separately from the depression. I am not defined by depression; it is just something that I struggle with. They label me as a friend who struggles with depression, not their depressed friend. LUCY AKARD SEAY

A good friend told me it was okay to be mad at God. He already knew how I felt and was big enough for me to talk to Him about how I was really feeling. ANONYMOUS

One friend visited with me and shared Psalm 40:1–2: "I waited patiently for God to help me; then he listened and heard my cry. He lifted me out of the pit of despair, out from the bog and the mire, and set my feet on a hard, firm path and steadied me as I walked along." She said for me to write, "Help me," beside the Scripture. She said that one day I would be able to write, "He did it." It was a promise she shared with me, and ultimately I was able to say, "He did!" She didn't try to give me a quick fix, but she gave me God's promise that He would steady me as I walked along. ANONYMOUS

My neighbor came to visit me in the psychiatric ward. She told me God wanted to give me a brand-new life. I scoffed at that and told her about my flamboyant alcoholic past. "See, God wouldn't be interested in me," I finished. She smiled and said, "My dear, you are exactly what He is looking for." I gave my life to Jesus that day.

Virginia Johnston has continued to encourage and pray for me through all these years. ELLEN BERGH

During my season of despair, I wanted so much for someone to sit with me, let me cry, talk, and put my head on their shoulder and expect nothing from me. I didn't want answers. I just wanted a person to come alongside and walk with me where I was—in the valley, not on a mountaintop. I got to know a friend in the latter part of my illness who loved me for what she knew I was under-neath all that agony. She reassured me she would never cease being my friend no matter how strange I acted. God sent friends to spoon-feed me His Word, because prayer and Bible study were dif-ficult for me at that time. He ministered to me through the lips of my friends. GLORIA

Friends would allow me to pop into their homes to share coffee and pray with me for different needs. They would watch my children when I needed a break or had some errands to do. I appreciated their sacrifices. Hearing from friends that they wanted to help me showed me I was not alone. LYNN JONES

Friends from college showed up and claimed the Scripture promise found in Jeremiah 29:11: "'For I know the plans I have for you,' declares the LORD, 'plans to prosper you and not to harm you, plans to give you hope and a future.'" That gave me great hope that maybe I wasn't doomed to always live in a mental hospital. It meant so much when friends visited me in the hospital, even though I know it must have been tough for them to know what to say. Knowing that others were praying for me and had faith that I would recover gave me great hope. I saw hope in the faces of my friends. ANONYMOUS

Having worked with many depressed clients in my psychology prac-tice, I am convinced that we seldom address the need for reassurance via holding. What a depressed, sad, hurt, scared person needs is to be held in a safe, non-sexual manner and to hear the words of attune-ment from someone who cares. We can visualize Christ doing this for us, but there are times when we need to feel the actual, physical con-firmation of another human being responding to our cries.
BRENDAN O'ROURKE

If your hurting person faces therapy because of childhood issues, he or she needs your support. It is helpful to give the person permission to take time to heal and understand the gravity of the pain as much as is possible. Take time to listen.

Don't judge or offer simplistic answers or overspiritualized solutions.

WHAT HURTS ME

"Just forget all that and move on."

"That happened a long time ago; you should be over that by now."

"Just give all that to God, and He will take care of it."

As the support system, we need to understand that these issues are deep. Childhood issues affect a person on a spiritual and emotional level. It takes time to heal and life often gets worse before it gets better. The process of working through emotions often takes longer than we want, but with loving support and God's help, a person can be restored to wholeness. JAN FRANK

WHAT TO WRITE IN A CARD

I know you're going through a difficult time. I'll stay close.

I'd like to wrap you up in love and take the hurt away. May you know God's presence in the midst of your struggles. Rest in the knowledge of my friendship, love, and support.

I am praying that you will feel God's gentle hand touching your heart and guiding you through each day.

In the midst of your darkness, may God's light shine through. Please know that I love you and that I care about you.

May you feel surrounded by love during this difficult time.

Continue to send notes of encouragement, love, and support. Emotional needs are not resolved quickly. Your friend will need continual reassurance of your unfaltering support.

PRAYER

Lord, You know the feelings that (<u>name of hurting person</u>) is struggling with right now. His/Her feelings don't surprise You or cause You to feel any differently about him/her. You love and accept (<u>name of hurting person</u>) right where he/she is. You know he/she desires to feel Your joy, yet there is heaviness in his/her heart. He/She is wrestling through legitimate feelings of anger, sadness, and abandonment. Even David, who wrote the psalms, often found himself in despair, but You were there to help him and You even call him a man after Your own heart. Help (<u>name of hurting person</u>) to know You see his/her pain, and You are here to offer comfort, reassurance, and hope. Amen.

JOB CHANGE
or LOSS

Much of our self-worth is defined by our careers. When we experience a change in our jobs, it creates a significant impact on our lives. As a support system, it is important to understand the implications of this kind of loss in a person's life. It may be easy for those of us who are secure in our careers to glibly quote Scriptures about faith, trust, and God supplying all your needs. It is a very different situation when you are the one without a paycheck, with no options, facing financial ruin.

WHAT HURTS ME

"Are you sure you're trying hard enough to find a job?" ANONYMOUS

Most friends offered Scriptures to encourage me to have faith that God was in control and that all things work together for good—eventually. There was nothing to halt my tears or relieve my anger and sense of utter frustration. SUSAN GAINES

Don't assume that someone is in this crisis because of his or her own shortcomings. Love expects the best of someone. ANONYMOUS

"It's time for you to move on." This kind of a loss is similar to losing several family members at once. To tell us it's time to move on is akin to telling a woman whose mom has died that she has no right to continue grieving. SHARON GRESHAM

I had two separate women approach me and ask me what we needed materially during our time of unemployment. I hesitated, but they really pushed me to give them specific answers. I finally responded that we needed groceries and gas. It was humbling and somewhat humiliating to admit that we were really struggling just to have food to eat and gas for my husband to drive to interviews. After that, one of the women never followed up with me at all. The other woman called me back several days later to say that she had decided she really couldn't do anything to help us. I felt so raw and vulnerable. It was as if I had bared my soul and someone had poured salt in the open wounds. ANONYMOUS

WHAT HELPS ME

"I'm praying for you. Is there something specific I can pray about for you?"

Encourage your friend with the positive qualities you see in his or her life, such as skills, gifts, attitudes, and the fruit of the Spirit: "The peace of God is so strong in you"; "You are an encouragement to me."

We were blessed to have special people in our lives to support us during my husband's unemployment—people who reaffirmed their love for us, people who said they believed in my husband and knew that he was a good worker and a wonderful employee. These friends said they admired us and were challenged and inspired because we turned to God with our struggles. They said they would pray for us and were faithful to call for updates and continue to tell us they were praying for us. ANONYMOUS

During the peak of my struggle, I shared my concerns with a friend. Thankfully, she didn't quote the usual Scriptures or encourage me to have more faith. Instead, she read to me Hebrews 5:7: "During the days of Jesus' life on earth, he offered up prayers and petitions with loud cries and tears to the one who could [but didn't] save him from death, and he was heard because of his reverent submission." If loud crying was appropriate for Jesus when He felt overwhelmed by what was being asked of Him, and it wasn't a sign of declining faith on His part, then perhaps it was okay for me to cry. I didn't need to feel bad grieving over something that was painful and out of my control. It was sweet to discover how Hebrews 5:7 is a balm when there are no ready answers or relief. SUSAN GAINES

WHAT I WISH PEOPLE UNDERSTOOD

It has been hard to see people drop us like a hot potato when they found out my husband was unemployed. I can't figure it out, and it hurts me deeply. It feels as if people think unemployment is contagious, and if they associate with us, they'll lose their jobs, too.
ANONYMOUS

I wished people would realize that when we lose a job, we lose a part of our identity, our daily association with friends, our security, our feeling of value or worth, as well as our income. It is a truly disrupting event. GEORGIA SHAFFER

Having arrived home from the mission field to learn that we could not return, we grieved the loss of a job, the loss of our mission status, the loss of a dream, and the loss of our friends. SHARON GRESHAM

Understand that the job of the unemployed is to find work or develop a business. I actually have less free time when unemployed because of my job search. People seem to think the unemployed should be available to do them favors and run errands during business hours. That is when I am out making contacts. ANONYMOUS

We didn't want to rack up credit card debts by eating out, going to movies, and other unnecessary expenditures when we had no income. Don't ask your unemployed friends to spend money when they have no money to spend. ANONYMOUS

Grieving takes time. Regardless of how strong we are with the Lord, we need to take time to grieve. People weave in and out of the stages of grief. We need permission to let the tears come and go.
SHARON GRESHAM

WHAT YOU CAN DO

A friend gave a couple a Precious Moments figurine because the husband was out of a job. She said, "My husband was out of a job and got one. Your husband will too." She went on, "Give this figurine away when he gets a job." This figurine is being passed around to others who are going through trials. It is a symbol that God has been faithful to this couple and to many others. He will be faithful to you. That figurine has many stories to tell. Who knows where it is.
BETH HEDIN

I am so thankful for those who not only let us grieve, but held us to their hearts. SHARON GRESHAM

My pastor gave me his listening ear and understanding support. He was there for me. ANONYMOUS

Don't give unsolicited advice. If you have something to share that is so valuable and unique that you must share it, ask permission first. Speak humbly. "I know I can't know your situation fully, but I would really like to help if I can. Would you mind if I ask you some questions and see if I have any ideas? Have you looked into …? Have you considered … ? What do you know about …?" ANONYMOUS

Men took my husband out to lunch and just encouraged him, man to man. ANONYMOUS

When you offer financial help or pay for a meal or for attending an event, do so privately and maybe even anonymously. It is difficult for people in need to be recipients of "public assistance." When you give, don't make it a public thing. ANONYMOUS

One friend brought us a large box of meat from Sam's Club including chicken, ground beef, pork steaks, and beef steaks. This meat lasted us for weeks. Another friend brought us two big grocery bags of fresh vegetables from his garden. A couple at church asked if they could treat us to lunch one Sunday after church. Our church offered to help us with bills through the church's benevolent fund. Our Sunday school class took up a special collection for us and gave us a large sum of money as their love offering. That money helped carry us through weeks with no income. One lady pampered me with a basket of goodies from a specialty bath store. ANONYMOUS

I really appreciated it when friends invited me to their homes for dinner or a visit. I really needed friends and support during that difficult time and could not afford activities that cost money. ANONYMOUS

WHAT TO WRITE IN A CARD

I can't believe this has happened. I want to help. [Then offer specific things you can do.]

I know you are going through a difficult time. I love you and am praying for you.

I am available to help you prepare your résumé, get it printed, and then send it out. When would be a good time to get together?

This change must be hard to understand. I don't understand, either, but I love you and care about you.

I have several friends in your industry. I'd like your résumé so I can pass it on.

These are such uncertain days. I want you to be certain of my support, love, and prayers.

You have been a faithful friend. Now it is my turn to be there for you.

PRAYER

Lord, You understand the uncertainty that (<u>name of hurting person</u>) and his/her family are facing right now. You know their concerns for the future and the trials they face daily. Please open for them the doors of opportunity and close the doors that are not part of Your perfect plan for their lives. Wrap them in Your peace as they struggle with the difficulties before them. Help them to claim the promise that You will supply all their needs according to Your riches, despite how they feel. I praise You in advance for what You are going to do in and through their lives. Amen.

DIFFICULT CHANGES

Difficult changes can include anything that causes pressure—a physical change, a change in places of worship, an empty nest, a broken engagement, or a compilation of many experiences all at once. Often, the most difficult changes are the unexpected ones. We are not prepared and are taken by surprise. A hurting person needs our understanding, our companionship, and our support.

WHAT HURTS ME

"I just don't know what I would do without the Lord!" That only added to my guilt that I might not have been trusting God enough. I don't know how I could have trusted Him more during that time. SHARON GRESHAM

"Just give it time. Get more involved. Make new friends." These comments belittled me and invalidated my feelings. CARRIE P.

"If you'd been a better parent, maybe they would not have left so soon." My ex-husband said this to me at a time when I was hurting. I had dedicated my life to my children while raising them basically alone. I tried to ensure that my children had everything they needed. I prayed over every decision, yet I felt helpless against those words. SHERRY CUMMINS

"Everybody experiences crises. Suck it up!" SHARON GRESHAM

Don't give spiritual answers like "You need to submit; give it up to the Lord and have more faith." We need comfort and acknowledgment that we are going through a tough time.

There were times when I'd arrive at work, set my purse on my desk, and begin weeping simply because I could not understand why or accept that God was allowing this to happen. I was completely overwhelmed. What I needed to realize was that there are occasions where the appropriate thing to do is grieve without shame or fear of being perceived as less than faithful. SUSAN GAINES

"It's your turn to enjoy yourself." While this is true and may provide some relief and comfort to the parent whose children have left home,

it is also painful. What the parent really wants is to go back to the job she has known for most of her adult life—being needed.
SHERRY CUMMINS

"You have to be patient. God is going to do something great in this."
SHARON GRESHAM

"You know, when we don't trust the Lord during times of crises, we can't expect Him to meet our needs. It's a sin not to trust Him." I was trusting the Lord, but that didn't change the pain of my circumstances. SHARON GRESHAM

Many people gave me platitudes, pat answers, and patronizing remarks. They ignored my hurt. They were not there for me. They expected me to "just get over it." SHARON GRESHAM

"Good riddance." My youngest child left home one year before high school graduation. She was having difficulty working through her feelings. I had agonized over how to deal with it, and she left before I could help her work through issues that she needed a mother for.
SHERRY CUMMINS

One man told me, "You make things all about you," and "You're not as smart as you think you are." ANONYMOUS

WHAT HELPS ME

"I'll come with you and support you." CARRIE P.

"I'm sorry you are going through this time."

"I love you. May I give you a hug?"

"May I pray for you?"

"How are the kids doing?" An empty nester often has just come out of a very busy period of life with plenty to talk about with friends whose children are in the same activities. Empty nesting does not provide the same opportunity to share. Show an interest in his or her children and what they are doing as they enter adulthood. SHERRY CUMMINS

I went to be with our daughter at the end of the semester. Her landlady possessed a sensitive heart for the hurting. She sensed my need, invited me in, made tea, and encouraged me to sit with her and share my heart. She listened and said, "I'm sorry for all you are experiencing. I am here anytime you need to talk." SHARON GRESHAM

WHAT I WISH PEOPLE UNDERSTOOD

I needed someone to acknowledge that I was not crazy, and I was facing real problems with real issues. CARRIE P.

I gave everything to the Lord, but the burden did not go away. I soaked in His Word daily; still I needed the burdens lifted. I felt as though six huge boulders had fallen on me, flattening me. I received one crushing blow after another. I sobbed for another person to share the load. I knew the Lord was with me, but I sensed I needed a person to be "Jesus with skin on." Most people's responses actually added more boulders, more weight of guilt. SHARON GRESHAM

What is interesting about an empty nest is that while the parents know it is coming, the day seems far into the future. The empty nest may not happen when or as expected. Even when it is anticipated, an empty nest is still a shock to the system. SHERRY CUMMINS

Our twenty-year-old son, James, left home to join the Air Force. My grief over his departure caught me by surprise. I cried for five days, slept with his teddy bear, and stopped eating, as nothing tasted good anymore. I felt foolish and horribly embarrassed. How could I let myself get so emotionally out of control? For some reason, I was having the hardest time of my life. I was crazy with worry and just couldn't move forward. KIM SADLER

WHAT YOU CAN DO

No one tried to give me advice. My friends simply listened and sympathized. I tried so hard not to be thought of as a gossip, but I needed a place where I could share my struggles and just be me. CARRIE P.

All they needed to do was hug me and tell me they were sorry for my hurt. I could have used a phone call where they said, "I'm praying for you today." I would have enjoyed an invitation to share a meal with some friends. Please listen without trying to solve my problems. SHARON GRESHAM

My mother-in-law became my angel. She was able to support me through my experience with stories about her own struggles in life. A phone call or a cup of coffee with her would brighten my day and my outlook on life. She had a gift for encouragement. ERIN K.

Invite your friend whose children have recently left home to join in new and different activities. The empty nester is entering a change of lifestyle and may need a little guidance on which way to go. This can be a lonely time, especially for a single parent. Ask him or her out for coffee or dinner. SHERRY CUMMINS

The people at my bank gave me tremendous support when I needed to sell my house and move into a condominium. They went above and beyond the call of duty. To celebrate my new lifestyle and to thank all my friends who had walked with me through my difficult time of over five years, we had a party at my new home. We laughed together and rejoiced in how far I had come. I will always be eternally grateful. GLADYS

My friend Dee found me sobbing on her doorstep. Her children are grown and gone, but her heart understands the trials of motherhood, including the pain of separation. She opened not only her front door, but also her arms. I collapsed into welcoming arms and wept. She rocked me back and forth, just like I used to rock James when he was small enough to hold. She gave me permission to cry. She sat me down to a fresh spinach salad, homemade desserts, and coffee. At her kitchen table, she shared stories of her own grief when her son and daughter moved out. She identified with how hard it is to let them go. She shared Psalm 25:8–10 with me. It was God's promise that she clung to as her children left home. She lovingly challenged me to shift the focus of my thoughts from my interpretation of the circumstances to God's. It was time for James to go, and it was time for me to trust God to take care of him. KIM SADLER

A tiny seed of hope began to grow in my heart. A day with my optimistic friend, Mary, included lively conversation that always lifted my spirits. Discussions often centered on our faith in Christ, as she encouraged me to seek Him for the strength to overcome my trials. "In seasons of joy or pain, always remember—God's love for you is greater than you can ever imagine." She said, "We're all special in His eyes." The truth of her simple words of encouragement shot straight into my heart, compelling me to keep trusting the Lord. CINDY HEFLIN

WHAT TO WRITE IN A CARD

I know you're going through a rough time. I am praying for you and care about you. [Suggest a time when you can get together.]

I want you to know how very much you are loved. During this time of transition, I stand with you and support you.

While we look forward to new seasons in our lives, the change is often difficult. Please know that my love for you has not changed.

God comes to us where we live and loves us as we are. No matter what lies ahead, He is with you—and so am I.

This change must be hard to understand. I don't understand, either, but I love you and care about you.

One friend sent a card in which she wrote, *"You have been there for me so many times, how could I not be there for you? Consider yourself bear-hugged."* SHARON GRESHAM

PRAYER

Lord, I come before You with this difficult season in (<u>name of hurting friend</u>)'s life. You know these changes have caught (<u>name of hurting friend</u>) by surprise in some ways. Even though he/she is trusting You, walking through this is hard. He's/She's never traveled this road before. Lord, I thank You that Your Word says that You will direct (<u>name of hurting friend</u>)'s path and will walk beside him/her throughout the journey. Bring him/her blessings along the way, Lord, and help him/her to know Your faithfulness at a deeper level. Amen.

A move can be compared to a loss. When people move to a different city, they experience the loss of their home, comfort, community status, identity, and many friends they may never see again. It is important to understand the magnitude of the loss they are experiencing. Losing their support system and saying good-bye to their position and involvement in community activities are intangible losses that are difficult to explain. There is a grieving process that goes on that most outsiders do not understand. Your friend will need your support before the move as well as after the relocation takes place. Your relationship will not be the same, but it does not need to end. Find creative ways to stay in touch and continue your friendship.

WHAT HURTS ME

"Well, you can always write."

"Let me know if I can help." That is a vague offer and is neither specific nor meaningful. After nearly twenty years in one city, my husband, children, and I moved across the country. The sorting, packing, cleaning, and collecting of boxes compounded other details like utility bills, change of address forms, gathering medical records, and saying our good-byes. When people said, "Let me know if I can help," I rarely thought of how they could help. Besides, even if I did think of something, I couldn't find the telephone to call them.
BRENDA NIXON

Don't plant doubts about your friends' future or suggest that their lives are unstable. VAN WALTON

Don't break off the relationship because "It's too difficult or painful to have a long-distance friendship." With the use of e-mail and great phone rates, distance should never be a reason to end a relationship.
VAN WALTON

WHAT HELPS ME

"I've seen what special friends you are. I know we'll miss each other."

"I will call you every Thursday night at 9:30 so we can catch up and stay in touch."

"I will be praying specifically that you get connected to other friends who love and support you as much as we do."

"I know this is what you need to do, but know that we will miss you. Your friendship, your laughter, and your support mean the world to me."

People praised us for our adventurous spirits and positive attitudes during difficult times of picking up roots and moving. VAN WALTON

A friend reminded me that my husband's job and the resultant transfer was actually God's provision for our family. VAN WALTON

WHAT I WISH PEOPLE UNDERSTOOD

Being separated geographically from a precious friend is not death, of course, but it is the death of an intimacy that will never be replaced. Being Christians gives us the assurance that our home is in heaven and we're "just a passin' through." However, like many transitions, there is pain. CLAUDIA

For the first two years, I battled loneliness and depression that comes from having no family or familiar friends with whom I could recount funny stories or share personal history. No one came to "just drop in." ANONYMOUS

WHAT YOU CAN DO

When we packed to move across the country, we had thousands of details to remember. Sometimes our brains' circuits were overloaded. Our friends brought us dinner so we could relax for a moment and eat. That was a detail we didn't have to think about. Taking the brief break energized us to continue our work. BRENDA NIXON

People watched my children while the movers packed and moved us. Friends offered to clean my house after the movers had emptied it. VAN WALTON

When a friend learned that we were packing to move, she offered to defrost the refrigerator in the apartment we were leaving. Of all the things going through my mind, that one hadn't even entered my brain. She arrived with her own bucket, sponge, and cleaning supplies. She was a genuine friend. MARY HUNT WEBB

Friends and families from my son's high school showed up to move us. They helped us pack, move, unpack, and put things away after I was forced to sell our house and move into a rented condominium. ANONYMOUS

Host a good-bye party honoring the family moving. Give them a scrapbook with pictures, programs, and events you've shared. Prepare a gift basket and ask the attendees to write special memories or blessings for the family. Send them off with a piece of local memorabilia from the community they are leaving. VAN WALTON

When we were being transferred, a neighbor volunteered to clean the bathrooms. "I'm really good at cleaning bathrooms!" she said. The way she said it made me laugh, as if she didn't have another talent in the world. She didn't stop with the bathrooms. She went home for her vacuum cleaner when she saw the movers ready to pack my vacuum. She vacuumed the whole house after the movers left. We had not been close friends, but she was a neighbor who saw a need and filled it. MARY HUNT WEBB

We were moving from a cold climate in Canada to the warmth of Florida. Our church held a going-away party for us. I knew it would be a sad occasion for us, as I couldn't imagine there would be much to celebrate. As we walked in the door, we were greeted by groups of laughing, giggling church members dressed in wild, flowered shirts, shorts, and sandals! These were our conservative Canadians? It was less than sixty degrees outside, but you would have thought it was ninety degrees inside. Beach music blared through the speakers, rafts, floats, and umbrellas outlined the stage, and for the entire evening we laughed through our tears at how far we'd all come and the changes God had made in our lives. They showered us with gifts of suntan lotion, sunglasses, beach towels, and sand pails for our kids. They wrote hilarious skits and songs about our going down south. Through it all, there was not a poor sport or a pouting face. Our final and most treasured gift was a massive king-size quilt. Each square was an original creation, and on it were the precious names of each family or individual who had been a part of our lives. CARON LOVELESS

This was to be the last Bible study my precious friend Cherie would attend. She thought it would be a regular Bible study. I taught for ten minutes and then announced, "Today we are going to give a tribute to our beloved Cherie." I started by telling two stories about her faith, then the other twelve ladies shared what Cherie had done for them and how she had ministered to them through the years. We cried, laughed, took pictures, and even planned a trip to Idaho for all twelve of us the next year. Instead of a memorial service for the dying, this was for the living, and none of us will ever forget it. This was a wonderful closure for such an important time in someone's life. CLAUDIA

When we arrived in our new community, neighbors brought over picnic lunches on moving day. I was given a personal invitation to join others on a social outing. A lady from the church we began attending offered to pick me up and take me to a church function. VAN WALTON

WHAT TO WRITE IN A CARD

Fortunately, there are excellent cards available on friendship and for when someone is moving. Find a card that expresses the reality of your friendship. Be sure to include a handwritten note specific to your experiences—things you've shared together, the laughter, and the hard times. Commit to stay in touch and support your friend with prayer.

I wish I could be with you and hold your hand. I'm praying that you will find a great support system where you are.

Because we have celebrated each other's joys, we have the strength to share each other's burdens.

All that we love deeply becomes a part of us. You will always be a part of me.

May you know God's presence in all that lies ahead.

Whenever you need someone to talk to, know that I am here and my heart will listen.

Continue sending little notes or cards to brighten your friends' day. Let them know how often you are thinking of them—and what you are asking God to do for them.

PRAYER

Lord, thank You for new seasons of life. You know, Father, the feelings of anticipation for what is ahead but also the sorrow of letting go of what has been. Help (<u>name of hurting friend</u>) to see Your hand in this move and to trust You for good things in it—even through the lonely times and the adjustment of finding a new doctor, hairstylist, and dry cleaner, guide (<u>name of hurting friend</u>)'s steps. Help (<u>name of hurting friend</u>) to get connected to other friends who love and support him/her as much as those he's/she's leaving. I thank You in advance for this new chapter in (<u>name of hurting friend</u>)'s life and trust that You will bring forth good fruit in and through him/her as a result of this move. Amen.

ELDERLY PARENTS

As children, our parents took care of us. Often there comes a time when the roles reverse and we take care of our parents. This can be complicated and emotionally demanding. Your friends and family in this situation need reassurance, understanding, and compassion. They need to know that you see the additional strain in their lives. There are times when a parent's immediate needs take precedence over the family's needs. Your friends or family members will be blessed when you enthusiastically step in and help fill the gap.

My mother is by no means elderly, but following my dad's death there were many things she needed us children to handle. We all willingly jumped in—each handling areas we were good at—and saw that her needs were met. This came at a cost to our own families and our own work schedules. Anytime you can help your friends in that situation, it is a welcomed relief.

WHAT HURTS ME

"How could you put your own mother in such a place?"

It didn't help when people told us that Dad's illness was the worst illness in the world! We needed to find some ray of hope, have some good times with Dad, despite his illness. BETTY CORBIN

Friends kept saying, "Call us if there is anything we can do." One evening, when we did have a need, I called a member of our Sunday school class. She was very short with me and told me to call our minister. I felt like she had slapped me in the face. BETTY CORBIN

WHAT HELPS ME

"I know how much you love her. I'm sure you're making the best decisions for her."

"I know this is hard on you. You are doing a great job caring for your dad."

"I don't know what your mom would do without you. You are the light in her otherwise bleak day."

Our minister asked for a favorite Bible verse to use at Bill's memorial service. I suggested, "Nothing can separate us from the love of God." The minister reminded us that this is true, even when someone has Alzheimer's disease and no longer has his or her mental capacities. The disease doesn't separate them from the love of God. BETTY CORBIN

"May I pray with you? Would you like me to add you and your parents to our prayer chain?" KAREN JENSEN

A nurse that worked at the daycare center where Bill went told me, "You have to laugh, or you'll go crazy." You don't laugh in front of the person, but it's okay to talk about a funny situation later and laugh about it. BETTY CORBIN

WHAT I WISH PEOPLE UNDERSTOOD

I went through the difficult decision of having to place my mother in a nursing home. It was all the more difficult because I had said on numerous occasions, "Don't worry, Mother, you will never have to live in a nursing home." I was a nurse and was confident I could care for her, yet her needs were twenty-four hours a day, seven days a week. Once in a nursing home, she failed quickly and was only there for three months. I kept thinking, *I could have cared for her another three months.* But at the time, we never know what or for how long the needs will be. PENELOPE CARLEVATO

We were very tired and stressed. We didn't need a lot of demands made on us. We were unable to do some of the things we would have done before. BETTY CORBIN

My mother moved across the country to be near me because of her poor health. She moved into an apartment in the same town in which I lived. Suddenly I was again a full-time daughter, despite the fact that I was an adult and had lived on my own for over fifteen years. ANNA

"Alzheimer's is the long good-bye" (Nancy Reagan). Truer words could not have been spoken. You lose your loved one, and the roles are reversed. You become the parent. Because my mom's short-term memory is gone, I prompt her to reminisce. This makes both of us feel better, and I learn more about her past, even when she can't

remember what she had for lunch. As a family member of someone
with Alzheimer's, you begin to grieve while your parent is still alive
and needing care. This is a very difficult emotional balance to
manage. KAREN JENSEN

We need to talk about our ailing parents. It was very apparent that
Mother was not going to get better. We all knew it, but it was hard
for many to discuss. I had spent most of the summer flying back and
forth to care for Mother. I was exhausted, both physically and emotionally. PENELOPE CARLEVATO

WHAT YOU CAN DO

"You are so involved in meeting your mom's needs, let me bring you
dinner tomorrow night." Or, "I'd like to take your children to a
movie."

Don't avoid spending time with your friend and his or her parent.
Your presence can bring a breath of fresh air to an otherwise dry and
difficult day. I have visited the parents of my friends in the hospital,
the nursing home, and at their home. If a grandparent attends a
school function where my child is, I make a point of going over and
visiting with them.

Encourage your friend to get some respite. Volunteer to stay with the
parent so your friend can have a break and do something fun or some
needed shopping.

As I bathed my mother, I thanked the Lord for all the physical parts
of her earthly tent. As I washed her face I thanked the Lord for her
eyes that watched me grow, the lips that kissed me good night and
cheered me when I graduated from nursing school, the arms that
rocked me through the night, the hands that taught me to play the
piano and tie my shoes, the legs and feet that ran after me when I was
a toddler, and the knees she knelt on for countless hours, praying for
me and our family. This was an act of healing and thanksgiving for
me. PENELOPE CARLEVATO

We were overwhelmed with the difficulties of caring for my husband's
father, finding him a suitable place to live, and meeting his medical
needs. A couple from our Sunday school class, who had a parent
with the same diagnosis as Dad, invited us to lunch. They shared
their experiences and their knowledge of assisted-living facilities and

listened to our challenges with an understanding and compassionate ear. Because they had experienced many of the problems we were going through, it was helpful to talk with them that day and many other times during that complicated time. BETTY CORBIN

When my mother relocated to live near me, my friends were very helpful. My friends included her in activities to which I was invited, welcomed her to our church community, visited with her, acknowledged the new demands she made on my time, and hosted a very special birthday celebration for her. ANNA

My brother and I would have loved to have had food brought to us in the room. We knew Mother's time was short, and we didn't want to leave her room. PENELOPE CARLEVATO

When caring for elderly parents and having your home as well as theirs to keep up with, it is a blessing when someone makes a weekly or monthly commitment to mow the lawn, wash the car, pick up groceries, or run errands. It is so helpful when someone makes a commitment that can be depended on without having to be asked or reminded. PAULINE

My Grammy Chapman was at a retirement home for the last three months of her life. My children enjoyed going to visit her, and to this day, they still go to the same home and sing or play for the residents. If you are a part of a performance group, offer to take the group to the facility where your friend's parent is.

Our minister, Rev. Lewis, visited Bill's nursing home regularly. He would tell us about his visits with Bill. We knew that Bill enjoyed having company, and we really appreciated the fact that Rev. Lewis visited. BETTY CORBIN

Mother's pastor was such a special help. When he came to visit, he was full of joy and included me in the conversation, even when Mother was no longer responding. He shared with me how special her ministry had been to him, the church, and the community. PENELOPE CARLEVATO

It was helpful when someone wrote to us, or told us, how faithfully we cared for my father. Most of our friends didn't know him, but they knew us. We often wonder if we've done the best for our parent. It was helpful to us when someone indicated that we did well in caring for him. BETTY CORBIN

WHAT TO WRITE IN A CARD

All that we love deeply becomes a part of us. I see how much you love your mom. She will always be a part of you.

I admire the way you care for your dad and the patience you have shown. I'm sure you have enriched his life.

Your dad has a quiet strength that I admire. I see the same quality in you. You are a blessing to him.

The journey through life has many passages. Caring for our parents is a particularly difficult passage. The time spent caring for our parents, although difficult, can have the rewards of memories being filled in, the "I love you's" filled up, and the peace of knowing you were there for them. KAREN JENSEN

PRAYER

Dear heavenly Father, You know the special bond between a parent and a child. You know the love (<u>name of hurting friend</u>) has for his/her mom/dad. Yet, You also know the difficulties of his/her care and the heartache of watching him/her decline. I ask that You provide (<u>name of hurting friend</u>) with a special peace and wisdom as he/she cares for (<u>name of hurting friend's parent</u>). Help him/her know that You are always there, even in the most trying of moments. I ask that a special measure of understanding be given to his/her family, as he/she is torn between the needs of his/her mom/dad and those of his/her family. Amen.

A prayer that was especially meaningful for us during this time was a benediction used by our retired minister, Rev. Harry Rankin:

Gracious heavenly Father, help us to be patient with every person. Help us to live victoriously in spite of every circumstance. Give us an inner joy that no individual and no situation can take away from us. Go with us, abide with us, lead us this day and always. Amen.

We prayed this over and over as we took care of Bill. I still have this prayer posted on my refrigerator. I first put it there in 1994.

BETTY CORBIN

ABUSE *or* VIOLENCE

A buse can happen to anyone, and it does—young children, battered women, men, and the elderly. Abuse happens to those with the best jobs, in the best schools, with incomes high or low. You may be the person who is needed to provide support to the one victimized, or you may be called upon to bring healing to the abuser. Either way, you need to be knowledgeable, available, and loving. You may be the one person who can bring hope to a devastating situation.

WHAT HURTS ME

To the victim:

"You will be fine. Just get this behind you and forget it."

"If you had just been a better wife or mother, this wouldn't have happened."

"If you'd had a wedding ring on, this wouldn't have happened."

"If you had only left sooner, this wouldn't have happened."

"Just hit this head-on, and you can go on living again."

To the abuser:

Don't react with shock when someone confides in you. A friend reacted with shock and condemnation when I shared my abusive actions with her. I vowed I'd never tell anyone else. KATHY COLLARD MILLER

WHAT HELPS ME

To the victim:

"This is not your fault. You did not cause him to do this to you."

"What do you need?"

"How can I protect you?"

"This is not something you have caused."

"Can I get you to a safe place?"

"Do whatever you need to do. I'm here to help you."

To the abuser:

"I understand how hard raising children is."

"I have never known such extremes in my emotions as I have with my own children. I have never felt this depth of love before, but I also have never known such extreme frustration before."

"Relationships can be very difficult. I know this is not how you want to act. Let's get you some help."

WHAT I WISH PEOPLE UNDERSTOOD

The victim:

There are all kinds of abusers from all kinds of lifestyles. You just never know. But I wish people would not look down their noses and say, "It would never happen to me," because it can. I used to think the same thing, until it did happen to me. ANONYMOUS

Someone had to take care of me, get me states away from my abuser, and help me see clearly. I couldn't even think for myself at the time. I was in such shock.

I always thought it was my fault, that I caused him to do this to me.

One does not need to be married to be abused. People feel trapped in relationships even before they are married.

I wish people understood how painful it is to admit what is going on and tell someone you are being abused. We feel shame. We believe what we are being told by our abuser, who claims to love us. It is also not easy to leave, pull up stakes, and run from danger. It is hard to leave the known for the unknown.

The abuser:

I was being abusive to my two-year-old daughter and was terrified to tell anyone. I figured I was the only one who did such a horrible thing. My behavior worsened as I feared being found out.
KATHY COLLARD MILLER

WHAT YOU CAN DO

The victim:

I needed to talk and reach solutions to the things that were tearing me up. The chaplain listened to me.

Do your research. Become familiar with local resources for victims of abuse and violence. Believe what your friend is telling you about the abuse she is receiving. Encourage her that she does have options, that help is available. Attend support group or counseling sessions with her.

The abuser:

Offer to go with them for counseling or to a support group. Assure them that you know this is not the way they desire to behave.

Provide baby-sitting, so the parent can have a break from the demands of parenting.

Be available to talk on the phone, or go over and be a sounding board so they can share their feelings.

Let the parent know that you will come to rescue his or her child anytime he or she needs help.

When I briefly and fearfully shared a little bit about my anger with a neighbor, she didn't react with condemnation. She identified a time that she had gotten disproportionately angry with her children. That gave me hope and was the turning point for me toward healing.
KATHY COLLARD MILLER

When I finally had the courage to share with my Bible study group, they committed to pray for me. At my request, they also held me accountable for my future behavior. That was very significant in my healing. KATHY COLLARD MILLER

WHAT TO WRITE IN A CARD

To the victim:

I know this is a difficult time for you. May you be wrapped in a cloak of protection and peace as you seek shelter and safety. I'm here for you and will do all that I can to help you.

You have taken the first step. Let me walk alongside you as you continue on your path to a safe and healthy life.

I can't believe this has happened to you. I'll stay close.

You are precious in God's sight. It is never His desire for you to experience such pain and abuse.

I want to provide a safe and sacred place where you can begin your healing and find strength for your future.

May God give you still waters to calm the storm in your life. I am supporting you with love and prayers.

I'd like to wrap you up in love and take the hurt away.

To the abuser:

I know you desire what is honorable and what is right. I support you in your effort to change your reactions and develop temperance. Please come to me when you need reassurance that you are heading in the right direction and are making wise decisions. The road ahead is not an easy one, but I will be with you. I am encouraged by your commitment to a healthy future.

As you look to God to guide you, may you find the strength to make the changes you desire.

You've taken the first step toward healing. May God's love surround you, strengthen you, and give you hope.

PRAYER

For the victim:

Lord, You know the depth of what (<u>name of hurting friend</u>) is experiencing and feeling. Help him/her to know that there is nothing beyond Your ability to redeem. Please comfort (<u>name of hurting friend</u>) and show him/her Your abundant mercy. Heal the wounds, both physical and emotional, and restore his/her health. In Jesus' name, Amen.

Dear Jesus, You are our refuge and comfort in times of trouble. Protect and keep (<u>name of hurting friend</u>) safe. I ask that he/she feel Your loving arms around him/her as he/she seeks protection and guidance. Amen.

For the abuser:

Dear Father, You know the heart of my friend (<u>name of hurting friend</u>). It is not his/her desire to perpetrate such pain on those he/she loves. Yet, at this moment, he/she doesn't have the skills and the coping mechanisms to overcome those urges and frustrations. Give him/her the strength to follow through with wise counsel. Help (<u>name of hurting friend</u>) to trust You and release his/her anger and rage to You. I pray that he/she will remain accountable to You and his/her support team for the growth that is to come. I thank You for the work You have begun in him/her and ask for continued strength. Amen.

LEGAL ISSUES *and*
FINANCIAL PROBLEMS

As I wheeled my friend into the courthouse for yet another court hearing, I was struck by the overwhelming cloud of negativity that hung in the air. I realized that, with rare exception, every person in the building was there because of a lawsuit, a crime, or a tragedy. We were there because my friend, while battling terminal breast cancer, was being sued for divorce by her unfaithful husband. I could not fathom that in her few remaining months, her husband would force her to appear in court over divorce and financial issues. I was her companion at every legal meeting and court appearance. Not only was the experience emotionally draining, but the atmosphere in the courthouse itself was depressing. We were in the presence of angry, broken, violent, and hurting people.

WHAT HURTS ME

"If you had been wiser (smarter, more careful, more faithful), this wouldn't have happened."

"Will you lose everything?"

"You shouldn't have done that."

"Why didn't you see this was happening?"

"You should have known better."

"I can't imagine how you allowed this to happen."

There was a small group of friends who did not believe that a Christian should sue anyone. Instead of support, or even prayers, we were looked upon as the rebellious Christians. JANET LYNN MITCHELL

Many "friends" have talked behind my back and have ridiculed me to others while putting on a supportive face in my presence.

WHAT HELPS ME

"I want to be here for you so you never lose sight of our friendship and my support of you."

"I am so proud of you. Your peace and your faith are a blessing to me."

"The details aren't important. I just want you to know that I care."

"I can only imagine how hard this is on you. I want to help."

"No one knows the depth of what you are facing. I care, and I love you."

"I don't need to know the details. I just want to support you."

Offer your encouragement and support.

One of the most healing words that anyone has ever said to me was, "Janet, what happened to you was wrong!" These people validated my pain and my experience. They knew that God would bring good out of this painful experience. JANET LYNN MITCHELL

WHAT I WISH PEOPLE UNDERSTOOD

Often, legal problems and financial concerns are coupled with another crisis in a person's life. There may be legal proceedings following an accident that caused a permanent disability. Financial problems may be the result of the loss of a job or the inability to work due to chronic illness. It may be necessary to attend court hearings and trials because a family member was killed by a drunk driver. These complications make the situation all the more difficult and tragic to handle. Your friend is juggling not only the grief and reality of his or her crisis, but the additional burden of financial or legal problems in its wake.

Surprisingly, numerous Christian friends and home church connections vaporized when we were no longer the financially successful people we had once been. People turned away from us. They treated us as if we were an embarrassment to them.

This is one of the most difficult, draining experiences of my life. Please don't judge me, abandon me, or gossip about me. This is when I need your unconditional love and support the most.

I wish that people trusted my relationship with God. I knew that God had asked me to take a stand for godly principles. I did not know how my trial would turn out. I did not know how God would use my obedience. This was up to Him. People who have watched this situation unfold have seen God work in marvelous ways. After winning in state, appellate, and federal courts, I was blessed more than I could imagine. In 2000, a bill was signed into law protecting future victims in the state of California—born out of my medical disaster.
JANET LYNN MITCHELL

WHAT YOU CAN DO

Before my trial, close family and friends gathered at my home, and we prayed together, dedicating my trial to God for His purpose and glory. JANET LYNN MITCHELL

Include your hurting friend in your social circle and invite him or her out to dinner—your treat.

Offer to watch their children on court dates, or just to give them some time alone.

I have a business partner, a true Christian brother, who has prayed for us and stood in the gap created by friends abandoning us.

Provide support and understanding. Don't ask for more details. Wait for your friend to tell you what he or she is comfortable sharing.

I had friends who were willing to help me meet my family's needs during the trial. An elder in my church heard about my situation and chose to come out of retirement as a lawyer and try my case. She was seventy-six years old at the time. JANET LYNN MITCHELL

WHAT TO WRITE IN A CARD

This must seem unbelievable. I cannot imagine what this is like for you. I love you and am here for you.

I know you're going through a difficult time. I am praying for you. I would like to take you to lunch next week. I'll phone to set up a date.

How I wish I could wrap you up in love and take your hurt away. May the knowledge that you are loved and supported be a comfort to you.

Amidst this terrible storm, may you see calm waters ahead.

I needed you, and you were there. Now, I want to be there for you.

This must be hard to understand. I don't understand, either, but together, we'll take it one day at a time.

PRAYER

Lord, I pray for (name of hurting friend) during this most stressful time. You know the anxiety and insecurity that (name of hurting friend) feels. Thank You that (name of hurting friend) can be assured of Your provision and love, no matter what happens. Make Your presence known as (name of hurting friend) walks this difficult path. Father, I ask that I will be a friend who (name of hurting friend) can count on for support and understanding. Amen.

Lord, I pray that You would go with (name of hurting friend) into this proceeding. Help him/her to entrust the outcome to You and to speak truth when called upon to do so. Lord, I pray for just decisions and that righteousness would prevail. But most of all, I pray that (name of hurting friend) would have deep assurance of Your steadfast love no matter what the future holds. Thank You, that no matter what happens, (name of hurting friend) can know that one day, all things will be accounted for in Your kingdom. Amen.

PART
two

HEALTH
NEEDS

INFERTILITY *or* FAILED ADOPTION

A couple struggling with infertility experiences the loss of their dream every month when the wife finds out she is not pregnant. The pain of infertility isn't at all what most people think it is. It isn't like looking at someone's house, car, clothing, or other possessions and wishing you could have them. It isn't covetousness. Rather, it is the pain of loss—like grieving a death. Disappointment is a constant companion as month after month no child is conceived. This is a very mercurial existence.

WHAT HURTS ME

"You've been married so long and no kids. Don't you want children?"

"Why don't you have children?"

Try not to complain about your children to someone struggling with infertility. Most parents probably do not realize how hurtful it can be to hear facetious, disparaging, and negative remarks about their children. Most women who want a child would be grateful for any child, and do not want to hear you complain or take yours for granted.
MELODY ROSSI

"If you had children, you would understand." We don't seem to be able to have children. We'd love nothing better. I've wept, prayed, schemed, and researched, to no avail. Adoption is even out of reach.
ANONYMOUS

Don't put spiritual guilt on me by saying, "You're not spiritual enough. If you had deeper faith, it would happen." ROSE SWEET

Don't say that you understand, because you don't, unless you have gone through the same type of problem. If you have, you still don't know what I'm going through. It's best if you share what you experienced without suggesting that you know what I'm feeling.
JULI HUDSON

Don't offer input regarding fertility treatments you've just heard about. Little do you know, I've tried all of those, and then some. It seemed particularly inappropriate and bothersome when men discussed this issue with me, as though my reproductive issues were small talk. MELODY ROSSI

Don't say the classic lines, "If you relax and stop wanting it so badly, it will happen." "God will send you kids. Just be patient; it will happen." Well, it didn't. "If you pray harder God will listen." ROSE SWEET

Don't tell me how easy it was for you to get pregnant. It makes me feel like a complete failure. JULI HUDSON

Don't give me solutions; just listen and empathize. ROSE SWEET

It is very hard for people struggling with infertility to hear people talk about abused kids. Most of us find that a difficult issue, as no one wants to hear about innocent children suffering. However, for a couple who cannot have a child and who may be struggling with issues of fairness, it is extremely difficult to hear about those who have had children and then abused them. Be sensitive to this issue. MELODY ROSSI

WHAT HELPS ME

This is the one topic in the book where it is better to say very little. When your friend chooses to initiate a conversation about her infertility, you need to be a ready and willing listener. Agree with her feelings and affirm her frustrations. We mustn't give false hope, because we have no way of knowing if she will ever have a child. We run the risk of adding to her emotional roller coaster if we are continually asking if there was success this month. I have a friend who has wished for children for years. Every few months I will ask a casual question like, "Has there been any change?" or "Did the doctor have any new input?" I usually mention that I want her to know that I am continually praying for them but don't want to make her uncomfortable by asking her or bringing it up all the time.

"I know that having a baby is the desire of your heart."

"You mean so much to me. I want you to know that I hurt with you."

"Have you had any different information or a new diagnosis?"

"I care about you and am wishing with you."

Reassure your friend that God isn't punishing her. JULI HUDSON

WHAT I WISH PEOPLE UNDERSTOOD

My infertility was a crushing, knock-out blow. Every month, twelve months a year for eight years, I endured shattering disappointment. It undermined my sense of being. Like an acid, it ate away at my sense of being a complete woman—trying, hoping, praying, believing, and not being able to accomplish deliberately what millions of women do casually, even accidentally. NATALIE [1]

I do not feel complete as a woman while I am struggling with infertility. Instead I feel damaged and inferior. In fact, I think women who have children also feel that way about me. Everywhere I look, I see things that exclude me from society and make me feel like an outsider. I am in constant pain. My very womanhood is threatened. Therefore, I may be much more sensitive to small, seemingly insignificant things, which doesn't make any sense to others. I may not want to be at gatherings that are geared for "families," because I don't feel that I am a part of one. MELODY ROSSI

Once I allow myself to imagine having a child, I begin to wonder what the child would be like—just as expectant parents do. The infertile couple has experienced many deaths of their would-be children. Once infertility is deemed final and permanent, the couple not only experiences the loss of all the children who might have been, but also the death of their dream of becoming parents. The scope of the loss is enormous. MELODY ROSSI

I need room to be upset at times. I will probably get upset when yet another couple is pregnant. It makes my own inability to conceive more painful. JULI HUDSON

After multiple miscarriages, I learned not to put due dates on the calendar to protect myself from the pain. I also wondered, *When is it enough? When do I stop trying?* I don't have the answers to that one. It is haunting and discouraging. Verses and stories of hope are always wonderful to hear. I would love to have a prayer partner and someone with whom I can search the Scriptures. ANNA HEBB

When a couple is infertile, others sometimes wrongly assume that they want to be around babies or children, so as to vicariously experience parenthood. For most of us, nothing could be further from the truth. In fact, the sight of a baby can bring an infertile woman to tears. Our arms ache to hold our own child, not someone else's. Do not ask an infertile woman to baby-sit unless she offers. Be sensitive about baby showers and having her spend time around your children unless she has indicated she wants to be there. Being around babies, small children, or pregnant women can be torture for a woman who is struggling with her inability to have a child. MELODY ROSSI

After years of trying to have a child, an infection left me without any hope of ever conceiving. As my health improved, the reality set in that I would never bear a child. It was heart-rending. Be aware that I am lugging around a terrible weight that no one seems to notice in me. I am desperate to have someone understand how heavy that weight is. Validate me, enter into my pain, and cry with me. Imagine what it would feel like to lose your child, and understand I have lost my dream of a child every month for years. MELODY ROSSI

There may be no deeper, more painful struggle for a woman than dealing with infertility. It rips at the very core of who I am as a woman. I feel like an outsider in society, and if you have children, I may not feel like I can relate to you. I think those who have children see me as inferior, and I may feel inferior myself. If I am in the midst of this struggle, I may be very emotional at times and may not even know why. When I see a baby, my arms ache, and something catches in my throat. I feel like a failure, like damaged goods, and as though my life will never amount to anything. I am searching for meaning and may think that no one with children has the same struggle—so if you are, please let me know! If I am in the midst of fertility treatments or trying to adopt, I am enduring a lot of unknowns and a great deal of discomfort and disappointment. My doctor visits are not routine. Each time I go, waves of anxiety may sweep over me as I am poked, prodded, and subjected to hormones and chemicals that are designed to assist me in what everyone else has done naturally. Your compassion and understanding can be a lifeline to me when I am drowning! MELODY ROSSI

WHAT YOU CAN DO

Someone who had gone through infertility treatments herself and had adopted two children encouraged me deeply by telling me it would be all right to quit trying to have a child. She understood the pressure I felt and was the first person who "gave me permission" to quit without feeling like a failure. MELODY ROSSI

If you are close to your friend and sense the time is right, you may be able to lead her into areas where she can utilize her mothering instincts without feeling broken, damaged, or empty. Be willing to go with her to the nursery at a shelter or some other place where she could minister to children. Although she may not be ready or willing to exchange her dream of a baby for short-term interactions with other children, eventually, exchanges with little ones who are hurting may bring a great deal of healing to her soul. MELODY ROSSI

My friend Amy was with me at a luncheon when we found out another girl we taught with was pregnant. I was upset but tried not to let it show, and Amy saw that. She talked to me about other things, and then, when we had both left, she called me on my cell phone to see how I was. I really appreciated her concern and appreciated how she waited to talk about it until we were away from everyone else. JULI HUDSON

Please be aware that Mother's Day, as well as many other holidays and social settings, can be very painful for someone struggling with infertility. Help your hurting friend realize this, too! Suggest that she not feel compelled to attend church on Mother's Day—and certainly don't ask her to do anything to participate in this celebration for other women. Ask her how she feels about attending baby showers. If someone invites her to a baby shower, help her evaluate whether it is emotionally safe for her to attend. Give her permission to "sit this one out." MELODY ROSSI

My sister and my girlfriend, both on separate occasions and unbeknownst to each other, sent me Mother's Day cards and said that there is no one else in the world they would rather have raise their children if something happened to them, other than me. They let me know that I had been a true mother in every sense of the word to their children. That felt good and was reassuring. ROSE SWEET

Only a few close friends were able to come alongside me for my infertility heartache. None had experienced infertility themselves. They were just wise and compassionate women of God. Perhaps the biggest thing they did was to encourage me to talk—mostly by showing me that they understood the immensity of the issue. So few people understand the depth of pain involved in not being able to have a child, but these two women were able, by recognizing how empty their own lives would be without children, to see how hollow mine must have been at that time. They just stood with me in the pain.
MELODY ROSSI

FAILED ADOPTION

Kathy Henkel has experienced the heart wrenching sorrow of a failed adoption. She offers her insight into how we can best offer comfort to those who have lost a child in this way.

WHAT HURTS ME

Someone said, "Look on the bright side! Isn't it good she died before you got there to adopt her?" I wanted to respond, "Yes, but it would have been even better if she had lived, and if our hearts hadn't been ripped out!"

Don't gossip! People who were not my friends, but mere acquaintances, were anxious to be the first to spread the news that I did not get my baby. It did not matter to them how much pain I was in. They just wanted to be the star of the moment to share the details of our loss.

WHAT HELPS ME

"This is such a long process. I hurt for you that you have had this tragic loss."

Our social worker advised us to allow ourselves time to grieve. This advice validated our feelings that we indeed had a loss and that we needed to go through the stages of grief.

WHAT I WISH

The moment a couple is told of a baby available for adoption, they begin bonding and falling in love with that child. When the baby dies or the adoption falls through, it doesn't matter that they never saw her or held her. I guess the emotional response is a lot like a miscarriage. It is possible that another child will be placed with the couple for adoption, but they still experience the death of a child and the death of a dream.

HOW YOU CAN HELP

After the baby we were to adopt died, I needed to return the airline tickets, but doing so emphasized the finality of our dream. My sister took the day off work to go with me to return the tickets. Then she took me to the mall. She walked me into the baby department and bought a baby dress for an eighteen-month-old baby girl. With that dress, she gave me what I needed most. She gave me the gift of hope, encouraging me to look forward. This was not the end, just a very painful delay.

WHAT TO WRITE IN A CARD

I want you to know that I am praying for you today—and tomorrow, too.

You are in my thoughts and in my heart.

I know you are going through a difficult time. May you find comfort in the knowledge that I care and am praying for you.

I am hurting with you, waiting with you, and sending you my love.

We have shared many joys. I desire to share this struggle as well.

I am here to walk beside you as you face whatever lies ahead.

Together, we'll take this one day at a time.

PRAYER

Dear Lord, please come alongside (<u>name of hurting friends</u>) as they suffer through this heartache. If You have a child for them, please open the doors that will lead them to that special one You have chosen to be in their family. In the meantime, Lord, please help them to feel whole and complete. Help them to see the plans and purposes You have for them that no one else can fulfill. Please cause their marriage to be strong during this time of strain and adjustment of dreams. Lord, build a hedge around them, and don't let insensitive people foolishly say things that cause them to ache. Do not allow their pain and disappointment overtake them. Lord, give me words that will soothe the places in their hearts that are broken and empty. Amen.

MELODY ROSSI

Your prayer before you spend time with your hurting friend:

Dear Lord, help me to understand (<u>name of hurting friend</u>)'s sorrow. Help me to say the words that will comfort her, that will encourage her, and that will protect her from those who do not understand her heart. Help me to see her as You see her, and give me words that will soothe all the places in her heart that are broken and empty. Amen.

MELODY ROSSI

SURGERY—HOSPITAL STAY

I hate hospitals" or "I don't like being where people are sick" is often a comment offered as an excuse for not visiting a friend. However much you may not like hospitals, nursing homes, or sickrooms, you can't possibly dislike it as much as the person staying there. You may not wish to be there, but you can go home—back to your normal, healthy life. If your friend is seriously ill, facing surgery, or recovering from an injury, you need to visit. You need to be there for him or her. It is important that your friend feels supported, protected, and prayed for while enduring a physical crisis.

WHAT HURTS ME

Avoid telling another person in recovery how they should feel. Each person's pain tolerance is different and should be respected. People are not "troopers" or "wimps" depending on their response to pain. BRENDA NIXON

When we were first told that surgery would be necessary, it seemed that people came out of the woodwork to tell us about every unsuccessful surgery they had ever heard of! MARILYN HOGAN

Don't say, "This is God's will," or "I'm sure you'll be fine." Don't talk about yourself or give advice. Ask how they are feeling, what has been done today. Focus on them, their experience, and their feelings.

Don't make comparative statements like, "My surgery was a piece of cake, so you shouldn't have any trouble." BRENDA NIXON

Don't make trite comments like, "Oh, you'll be fine." Only God knows the outcome of a surgery. BRENDA NIXON

WHAT HELPS ME

"The future may seem frightening. I'll stay close."

"I am here to help you through this."

"Your body will let you know when you are ready to get back to your routine."

"We will take care of it for you—don't worry."

"This is a major event with significant physical and emotional consequences. I will be here with you all the way."

"What has this been like for you?"

"You need your rest. Don't feel bad about being tired."

WHAT I WISH PEOPLE UNDERSTOOD

When I am sick, I struggle with my own inability to do anything. Please don't have expectations of me. Love me for who I am in my present condition. See me as the same person, even though my physical body is in crisis. Help me feel that I matter as a person in spite of my inability to do the same things I used to do. I might be too sick to do the adjusting, so it helps me if my friends can find new ways to relate to me. MELODY ROSSI

People in a hospital are there because they need extra care and rest that is designed to help them recover. Soon after my surgery, a friend came to visit and stayed four hours. It was exhausting for me to attempt to carry on a conversation. MARILYN HOGAN

My anxiety is not a gauge of how much or little faith I have; rather it is a human response to the anticipation of an uncertain event. I feel emotionally vulnerable. I need sensitive, kind, and tolerant people around me, not those who casually preach, "God will take care of you; don't worry!" BRENDA NIXON

My accident resulted in a permanent disability. I wasn't looking for friends to fix the situation. I knew they couldn't. I just wanted support. I needed someone who would be a good listener, someone who could empathize, spend time with me, or cry with me. Some friends were so uncomfortable with my situation, they dropped out of my life. I've never seen them since. VICKIE BAKER

One friend understood that with two young teenage daughters, there might be some shopping that Dad couldn't take care of. She worked around the girls' schedules, took them to the mall, took them home, and kept the purchases within the budget. Practical acts of kindness may not look like big deals, but to the family, they are a huge lift. MARILYN HOGAN

For those who don't have the "gift of gab," bring a small gift or flowers, offer your greetings, make inquiries about the person's health, and then leave. Some people came by to see me and stood at the end of the bed and didn't say anything. They expected my husband to entertain them. AMANDA RANKIN

When you visit your friend in the hospital, take your knitting, needlework, or book, and tell your friend you will be there if he or she needs to sleep. It can be very comforting just to have someone stay by one's side. MELODY ROSSI

During our crisis, our priorities changed and things went undone. RUTH HAUGER

Recovery can be prolonged after surgery or an accident. It's easy for friends and the church staff to slack off on contacting someone in recovery. This is the opposite of what is needed. Recovery can be a very lonely process of hard work to regain strength or mobility. Continued encouragement through calls, prayers, and visits goes a long way in uplifting the physically challenged. JO FRANZ

WHAT YOU CAN DO

When my husband was in ICU after his stroke, someone gave me a gift bag filled with peanut butter crackers, granola bars, cookies, candy bars, fruit, magazines, silly simple games, and note cards. It was wonderful. For a few days, I lived out of that bag! AMANDA RANKIN

I was hospitalized during Christmas, which is a very lonely time in a hospital. My husband stayed by my side and didn't have a chance to eat. Friends from church showed up that night with a full Christmas dinner for him. MELODY ROSSI

A young mother of two preschool children called my husband and said that for the time I was recuperating, which turned out to be three months, she wanted him to deliver all our laundry to her on Monday morning on his way to work. She then washed and folded the clothes and had them ready for him on Tuesday. MARILYN HOGAN

A friend of ours returned home following surgery just before Christmas. Our family packed up our instruments and electric keyboard and went to visit him. We set up our portable orchestra in his living room. We sang Christmas carols and played holiday tunes.

Years later, I received a thank-you note saying that we'll never know how much that meant to him.

Two gentlemen from our church drove the sixty-five miles from our hometown to the hospital to sit with my husband throughout the hours of my surgery. Their support was also an encouragement to me, because I knew my husband would not be alone with his imagination and fears. BARBARA ANSON

Bring a small cassette or CD player with earphones and some praise tapes and books on tape. The patient can use the player during times alone or to pass sleepless nights. The caregiver can listen while the patient is napping. LINDA GILDEN

Friends brought baskets of fresh fruit, knowing hospital fruit would probably be canned. Another friend asked what I needed. I told her I missed my journal, so she put together a lightweight notebook and brought a pen for me. Fresh roses, just cut from her garden, were brought by another friend. JO FRANZ

I was in ICU on my birthday. My uncle brought in a long banner written on continuous-feed computer paper. It read, "Happy Birthday, Vickie! We love you!" It was taped up on the ceiling directly over my head. It was a terrific encouragement. VICKIE BAKER

When we came home after my husband's open-heart surgery, I had been up with him for forty-eight hours straight. A friend arrived and said, "This isn't working; you're coming home with me!" She packed us up and took us home with her for ten days. She let me sleep during the day while she took care of Tony. Then I could be up and down all night and not fall apart from lack of sleep. AMANDA RANKIN

A friend sent out the message that while people were visiting me in the bedroom, they would find the ironing board up and ready. While they talked to me, they could iron, too. MARILYN HOGAN

Several friends offered to bring me a hamburger or taco when hospital food got to me. VICKIE BAKER

One of my daughters brought freshly baked chocolate-chip cookies, her favorite praise tape, and a cassette deck for me to listen to. The music put me in the right frame of mind for the rehabilitation needed each day. My husband brought me cappuccino on his way to work, spent his lunch hours with me, and every evening, he would lie on

the bed with me for an hour to assure me of his love and devotion.
JO FRANZ

My hospital stay was long and very discouraging. When I finally got well enough to walk a bit, I had to take my IV poles with me. It was quite a struggle to shuffle around on that cold hospital floor in my slippers and robe, leaning on that contraption, and trying to keep all my tubes untangled. Some friends came to visit and said they would help me walk around the ward. Once I got out of bed, I realized they were wearing slippers, too! As silly as it sounds, it was a huge gesture and communicated a kind of solidarity that touched me deeply.
MELODY ROSSI

When my husband was in the rehabilitation hospital, a friend took all of his cards and stuck them up on two walls of his room. There were tons of them! It was a reminder that everyone loved him and hadn't forgotten him during this very scary time of our lives.
AMANDA RANKIN

I felt I needed visual motivation for my rehabilitation, which would involve learning to stand and walk again. I asked my husband and daughters to pick out pictures of things I looked forward to doing again. They brought photos of me skiing, riding the tandem bicycle with Ray, and of course, spending time with the family. JO FRANZ

When you take meals to someone, take them in disposable containers. This saves the recipient the trouble of returning dishes. It is a huge help. RHONDA WEBB

A group of friends cleaned my house, did the laundry, mowed the lawn, and cared for my pets. One friend, who had helped me with bookkeeping before, opened and sorted my mail. She wrote out the checks for my bills and left them for me to sign and put in the already stamped and addressed envelopes. AMANDA RANKIN

One lady came every Tuesday and Friday and cleaned the bathrooms. Then she would visit with me for a while. I looked forward to getting to know her, as she was not a close friend when she first came.
MARILYN HOGAN

It was delightful when friends brought videos to the hospital or my home. It was important that they not be rented, as it would have been difficult to return them. When I was confined to a bed, the hours passed so slowly, and this really helped. One person loaned me a

number of wonderful books—entertaining novels and books that corresponded to my interests. These distractions were so welcome.
MELODY ROSSI

After my surgery, I had very little appetite. A special friend brought some strawberries, got vanilla ice cream from the cafeteria, and made me a little sundae. It tasted so good after the food in the hospital that it really got me started eating again. MARILYN HOGAN

When I returned home from the hospital, many people brought us meals, which was great. One friend was so smart, she brought over a basket with two loaves of bread, a variety of sandwich meats and cheese, mustard, mayonnaise, and some chips. RHONDA WEBB

One friend with a limited budget called long distance each evening to see how I was doing and visit a while. Her easy manner and gentle encouragement caused me to feel loved. She timed her calls to fall during the lonely time between the end of visiting hours and when I would go to sleep. BARBARA ANSON

I was in the hospital for our daughter's thirteenth birthday. I had planned the party, a friend made the cake, and my husband hosted the party. Later that evening, he brought my daughter, her gifts, some birthday cake, and Polaroid pictures of the party to let me be a part of her becoming a teenager. MARILYN HOGAN

I was nineteen years old, in my hospital room three thousand miles away from any family member or friend, preparing for my tenth surgery. A nurse I didn't recognize stuck her head in the door and said, "Janet, what is your favorite candy?" I told her that I loved milk chocolate with chewy caramel in the middle. That evening an older couple knocked on the door.

"Are you Janet from California?" the gentleman asked. As I answered that I was she, he reached toward me, taking my hand. He embraced it, holding it, offering me the touch of another human being. How did he know that I longed for my father's touch? Sitting next to me, he offered me a box of milk chocolate caramels.

His wife began to explain the facts surrounding their surprise visit. "The nurse told our church about you. She's been with you in your last few surgeries and knows you are here alone. She asked us to pray for you. We have been praying for you, but tonight we thought we'd come find out just who we'd been praying for." That night was the beginning of a wonderful friendship.

They phoned daily and returned every few days. With each visit, they would take my laundry, wash it, and return it neatly folded in a bag. Often, I'd find a piece or two of my favorite chocolates sitting on the nightstand by my bed. I was amazed! A surgical nurse cared enough to tell her church about me, and the church put their faith into action. They were my heaven-sent encouragers!

Dare to reach beyond your comfort zone, extending your hand to a stranger. Strangers are just friends waiting to happen. In the body of Christ, no one is a total stranger.

JANET LYNN MITCHELL

A dear Christian friend, Florence, came to my room and sat on the edge of my bed. She took my hand and quietly said, "My dear, what is going on?" I had been hemorrhaging and was scared. Very softly and calmly, she held my hand and prayed. I had prayed, but not like she did! After her prayer, I had a warm sense of peace fall over me. Florence's gentle prayer calmed my deepest fears. I ended up in the hospital having surgery. When I came to, my husband told me that Florence's husband, Charlie, had been with him in the waiting room, praying with him. Charlie clasped our hands together as he prayed to the Lord. What a blessing to have mature godly prayer warriors as our friends. LYNNE REITZ

WHAT TO WRITE IN A CARD

To let you know that I am praying for you today—and tomorrow, too.

You have a long road ahead. I'll stay close.

May the love of family and friends carry you through your recovery.

Know that you have a friend to stand beside you. I'm here for you.

You've been there for me; now it's my turn to be there for you.

May the knowledge that you have friends who care surround you and strengthen you in the days that lie ahead.

I was lying flat in bed unable to move, speak, or even breathe on my own. The best thing friends did for me was to send cards and letters. The cards went right up on the wall as a cheery reminder that someone outside of those four walls cared. Personal letters and notes meant even more to me. They usually weren't elaborate—just a "Hi, I'm thinking about you, praying for you, my heart aches with you." They were written from the heart. VICKIE BAKER

The week after my surgery, hurricane Hugo ravaged our city. I felt there were so many ways I could have helped had I not been recovering from surgery. A get-well card arrived from an elderly church member. In it she wrote, "Take the time you need to get well, and don't feel guilty." That simple phrase changed my attitude. I realized that I had been so concerned about the hurricane victims and so frustrated by limitations in the ways I could help them, I was not giving my body time to heal. JOY BROWN

PRAYER

Father, (name of hurting friend) and I come to You with concern in our hearts and pain in his/her body. I ask that You fill him/her with a spirit of peace and trust, while You build a special fence of protection around him/her. You know the difficulties of this condition and the depths of (name of hurting friend)'s needs. We ask Your special comfort to allow for a good night's rest and renewed strength to meet the demands of a new day. Lord, please bless and watch over all of the caregivers; may they have a spirit of tenderness and understanding. Be with the family as they stand alongside (name of hurting friend) during this difficult time. Amen.

CRITICAL *or* TERMINAL ILLNESS

I have been signing my e-mails with the phrase, "Every day is a gift" for the last year. How thankful I was, when Dad died suddenly, that I knew we both viewed each day as a gift. None of us knows what tomorrow may bring, but a person facing a critical or terminal illness often has a realistic picture of his or her possibilities. We don't know if this loved one will experience remission, have total healing, or face an untimely death. Our job is not to give false hope, but to love, care for, and walk alongside him or her during this most difficult time. Someone with a terminal illness has learned very quickly to make each day count. It is important to be a part of making each day a special one, one he or she is thankful to have had.

However uncomfortable the situation is to you, your discomfort is a drop in the bucket compared to what your loved one faces. You will find that once you make the initial contact, follow-up visits become much easier and more natural.

WHAT HURTS ME

"I know how you feel."

"I've been through the same thing."

"Won't you be glad to be with the Lord?"

"Let me know what I can do to help."

"I know a lady who had just the same thing you have."

Don't quote Romans 8:28 or other Bible verses to minimize what the person is experiencing. Don't ask if he or she has been praying about this; it presumes that the condition is something he or she could change. Don't ask for details about the illness; let your friend share what and as much as he or she wants to share. ALIDA SHARP

"It's okay if you die, because all your children are baptized. You have done your job." It's not okay with people who love me if I die right now! I have seven beautiful grandchildren to enjoy. I am confident of my salvation, but this remark is inappropriate. MARLEEN

I know people meant well, but it was difficult to hear them say, "She's in God's hands." I know this to be true, but it made me feel helpless, and as a parent, it's only natural to want to help your child, to make him or her better. JEAN DOBOS

Many people compared their illnesses to Dad's brain tumors. When they would talk about their long battle with an ulcer, I wanted to say, "Are you going to die of an ulcer?" Please don't compare your experiences with my loved one's. RAELENE PHILLIPS

I needed to talk about all these shocking changes in my life, yet everywhere I turned friends and relatives would cut me off by saying, "God will heal you," or "You are just that much closer to heaven." BONITA KILGORE

Don't offer simplistic answers, spiritual or otherwise. That kind of comment can cause your friend to feel unnecessary guilt or anxiety. JUDITH HAYES

Some visitors bad-mouthed the medical profession. They suggested diets, supplements, and alternative treatments in Mexico. I happen to feel I have been led to excellent doctors who have helped me live well, long beyond what statistics would suggest. When I am sick, I don't want to argue or have people be critical of my medical choices. I want to feel loved. Don't share medical alternatives, unless you have been specifically asked to research other possibilities by the patient. MARLEEN

My son was on large doses of narcotics because of his extreme pain. Emergency-room visits were brought on by spikes in his pain. Each time he would ask for more medication. A physician accused our very sick son of being a substance abuser and chastised us for supporting his habit. It was probably the most difficult day of my life. During an illness, moralizing has no constructive part in the healing process. VAN WALTON

"If you die, we'll see you in heaven." MARLEEN

WHAT HELPS ME

"I can understand you need your rest."

"How can I pray for you?"

"How are you feeling about what you are facing?"

"I'd like to take you to your next treatment."

If you have been in a similar place, share with me how it affected you, how you coped, and what you needed. Be careful not to suggest that you know what I'm going through or how I should feel.

"I would like to drop dinner by tomorrow night. Is there anything you or your family especially like or have been wishing for?" Ask if there are any special dietary needs or restrictions. MARTHA POPE GORRIS

"We love you. We're praying for you. You are precious to us." CHARLES FLOWERS

A friend with a similar diagnosis told us that though she would never have wished for this to happen, she knew she had been blessed in ways she would not have been without that diagnosis. It was an encouragement to my aching heart. DONNA WATTS

"I'm here for you. Whatever you need, you've got it." Follow up with specific things you are willing and able to do. Most people will not ask for help and often don't even know what needs there may be.

WHAT I WISH PEOPLE UNDERSTOOD

Words are cheap; hugs are huge! ROBB DENNIS

If you know someone who has been given a difficult diagnosis, don't let your doubts about the diagnosis stop you from helping and encouraging that person. Even if the diagnosis might be wrong, that person still has to deal with the news. The tests, doctor appointments, and not knowing for certain what's wrong can be very stressful. MICHELLE MCPHERSON

As a mother with young children and a rare virus that attacked my central nervous system, I needed more than words, cards, or calls. I needed real help. LYNNE REITZ

The most important thing is for people to listen to the person who has a terminal diagnosis. He or she is probably already struggling with faith issues. Everyone wants to be healed, but then realize that this may not be reality. Many times I tried to share my despair with church members over my poor prognosis. I felt out of control of my life. In our culture, we start moving away from a person as soon as we hear that he or she has a terminal illness, leaving that person without someone close to share his or her feelings. Remember, when a friend dies, you lose only one person. When a friend is dying, he or she is grieving over giving up everybody he or she knows. BONITA KILGORE

Understand that chemotherapy can mean anything from taking a pill as you go on with life to three- or four-hour infusions that leave you limp, aching, and retching for days. I don't want to hear about people who never missed a day of work when they had chemotherapy. When I asked my doctor, she said they weren't getting the "industrial strength chemo" like I was. My side effects were not a matter of character. MARLEEN

When I was ill with cancer, so many people were sending meals, cleaning my house, and taking care of the children. I felt guilty. How was I ever going to repay all of these people? I didn't even have the energy to write a thank-you note. It was overwhelming. Then my mom opened my eyes. "Who are you to deny them the joy of ministering to you? These people are the Lord's hands showing His love for you." I could then see Jesus meeting my needs. BETH HEDIN

People react differently to crisis. Some people need to be around others to help comfort them in stressful times. I preferred solitude. I found comfort in knowing how many people were concerned and were praying. JEAN DOBOS

I am usually an outgoing, happy person, but I was very distracted and extremely scared when my son was ill. Friends wanted to divert me, but I could not concentrate on anything but my son's illness. I felt so single focused. Some of my friends eventually gave up on me.
VAN WALTON

Because of the constant pain, it was difficult for me to look or feel like socializing. Many times I could not visit with people.
MARTHA POPE GORRIS

Children put a whole different dimension on the serious illness of a family member. You have to balance the children's need for normalcy and a routine, hope, simple pleasures, and outright joy against their equally important need to understand and accept what is happening and may happen in the future. MARGARET WINTER

Honesty is always the best policy. I let helpers know I'm trusting them to be honest with me if I ask them to do something they cannot, if they are unavailable, or if their schedule changes. CINDY HEFLIN

After I was completely recovered, there were still those who viewed me as "the sick one." I felt like I was wearing a sign on my chest that said, "Cancer Woman." One friend in particular would approach me at get-togethers with a pained look on his face and say, "How are you feeling?" KATHY THOMAS

As a friend, I was afraid of being close to cancer, so at first I stayed away. I was afraid to touch and care for someone whose body was filled with tumors and cancerous fluids that made her belly bulge. I didn't know if I could handle seeing my friend in severe physical pain. I was fearful that her pain would become my own and then I would feel too overwhelmed to help her. I was also guarding my heart from becoming too emotionally attached to her in the face of the reality that her condition was terminal. I am so glad I overcame my fears and found the joy of giving in true friendship. Although these past months of caring for my friend have been tiring and emotional, I do not regret it for a moment. I have not only had the privilege of getting to know her more intimately, but I have also been a witness to the bravery and elegance of one facing adversity and ultimate death. I am also grateful for the opportunity to serve another human being and give of my resources, strength, and faith. JUDITH HAYES

CHILDREN OF CRITICALLY OR TERMINALLY ILL PARENTS

If an illness is prolonged, a child's ability to process it changes over time because he or she is growing and maturing at the same time. Children need explanations in terms they can understand, and they need you to give them words for emotions that are brand new to them.

Children need to have some input and need to be involved, but they do not need to be responsible to make adult decisions or shoulder adult burdens. It is important that they not become substitute adults in a kind of partnership with their healthy parent.

Don't underestimate what children can understand. However, don't expect them to see things the way you do, even when you've been given all the same information.

Seeing the situation through children's eyes, asking what they understand and expect, enables us to involve them in a way that they can process what the illness means. MARGARET WINTER

WHAT YOU CAN DO

My cousin advised me to spend as much time enjoying Mom as possible. I did my best to arrange time off, and friends took care of our daughter so I could be with Mom. When I would visit, I took CDs of music and groups that I knew she liked. I played them for her, and despite her intense suffering, we were able to connect through music. ROBB DENNIS

The news was stunning, and we were at a loss as to what would happen. I remember a woman I worked with offered to take notes when I met with the neurosurgeon, since my husband was out of town. This was so helpful, because when a person is in a state of shock, he or she tends not to hear or understand everything. It is so overwhelming. JEAN DOBOS

One of the benefits of modern technology is communication through e-mail and Web sites. When a family is facing a critical illness, they don't have time to tell everyone who might be concerned the details, needs, and condition of their loved one. Many people are sending out e-mail updates and prayer requests to their e-mail list of family and friends. You can help by managing the information and sending out the e-mail. It is also possible to post updates on a Web site, which enables the support community to stay in touch without bothering the family.

My mother celebrated her seventieth birthday while my father was in a coma. That afternoon, all the nurses on the floor brought Mom a cake. That gentle message reminded us that life will go on and we can celebrate happy times in spite of sad times. RAELENE PHILLIPS

When you go to visit, ask the person or the family to tell you if he or she thinks it is a bad time, when it is time for you to leave, or if it would be better if you came less often or stayed a shorter time. Believe and abide by the answers. Don't take it personally if he or she prefers a shorter visit. Similarly, believe it if you are told that it is wonderful to see you and he or she would love you to visit more often. Everybody is different, and the preference of one sick person may not be the same for the next friend, even with the same illness. Offer multiple choices: Would you like to chat? Would you like me to bring movies or music? Would you like me to read to you? Should I bring a deck of cards? Don't be surprised if the person does not react the way he or she used to or with the enthusiasm you had hoped for. He or she may indeed be responding with as much pleasure as he or she is capable of feeling. MARGARET WINTER

When my husband was diagnosed with cancer, the elders of our church came to our home to pray over my husband. They made a personal effort to come together as a group. Their prayers, presence, and concern meant the world to us. KAREN O'CONNOR

A friend suggested that we put a sign on the front door—red for "This isn't a good time to visit" and green for "We welcome your visit." It worked well. Even the delivery men respected the sign. BETH BLANCHARD

Friends took the time to call after each test to check in with me. Many people cooked for my family. One friend, who was herself experiencing stage-four cancer, was my e-mail buddy and regularly encouraged me with personal prayers and stories that uplifted me through my darkest days—especially when I was losing my hair! Even though Janet has since passed away, I still find myself reading over her old e-mails. ALIDA SHARP

The consistent calls, cards, and e-mails assuring us that we are loved and being prayed for were a blessing. KAREN O'CONNOR AND CHARLES FLOWERS

Provide opportunities for children to visit, make cards, draw pictures, or write letters to a terminally ill patient. It is important for them to feel that they did something personal for someone who needed them. It helps them feel as if they did everything they could. MARGARET WINTER

My Bible study group committed to pray for me during my cancer surgery. These ladies prepared the evening meal for me in their homes and delivered it. One in particular remains vivid in my memory, as she put a flower in a little vase on my tray. I shall never forget this kindness. JANE SMITH

My husband's job took him away at odd hours. My dear friend, Carol, came over to my house one day and said, "Okay, you're coming home with me!" I was shocked. I protested that it was too much for her, and she couldn't do that. She said she'd talked it over with her husband, and that's what they wanted to do. She packed some clothes for me and my children, helped me put on a robe, and took me to her house. I was confined to bed, so taking care of me was a huge undertaking. She put me in her main floor bedroom and nursed me back to health. She took care of my kids, too! She took me to the doctor three times a week for blood tests and doctor visits to monitor my condition. When my husband was available, she would have him over for dinner as well. Even when I was strong enough to return home, Carol still helped with the children, laundry, and dishes. LYNNE REITZ

During a critical illness, my friend, Debbie, stopped by to comfort me. She came into my room with a large wicker basket. Inside it were seven gifts, all wrapped in white tissue paper with ribbons tied around each one. She also included a special verse and a thought for the day with each gift. She told me to open one gift per day. So, for seven days, it felt like Christmas. What a special blessing that was. As I recuperated, I looked forward with intrigue and anticipation toward waking up the next day to open my surprise. I praise the Lord for her act of kindness. It truly helped my healing process. JACQUELINE CROSS

My surgery took a huge toll on my body, and recovery was very slow. I was unable to find numbers, pick up the phone, or dial. I needed people to be perceptive. I needed them to call and see if I felt like a chat or a visit. It was helpful when they asked if I needed another meal, if I had any dietary restrictions, or if I needed a ride to the doctor's office. ALIDA SHARP

When you make an offer to help, make sure it is something you are able and willing to do. A friend who had offered to help with child-care made a face when my husband asked her for the second time to watch our daughters. We never asked her again. MARTHA POPE GORRIS

A dear friend was dying from cancer. We decided we should shower her with love for forty days. We picked out the forty days on the calendar and asked her family and friends to do something nice for Val during that time frame. Each person picked a day or two when he or she would "shower Val with love." The personal gifts included videos, books, dinner, homemade baked goods, flowers, cleaning her house, and going to the pharmacy and paying for her medication in advance. Some things were simple; some were lavish. It blessed the givers so much, they waited a few weeks and did it again. My sister traced Val's hand and distributed copies to remind us to pray for her. I've helped get the forty-day Feast of Love started several times. Sometimes, I fill a basket with flavored tea bags, sugar lumps, two cups and saucers, and something sweet to eat. MARCIA VAN'T LAND

Listen, listen, listen. Listen not only with your ears, but also with your heart. Allow your friend to openly express his or her pain, both physical and emotional. Be as nonjudgmental as possible. Provide respect and dignity. Honor your friend and his or her family's feelings. Find ways of bringing joy into the home. Bring colorful flowers, a shiny balloon, favorite foods, or even a funny video. JUDITH HAYES

My Aunt Katie had chemotherapy every Tuesday morning. The "Crafty Ladies" at her church also met each Tuesday morning. They spent time in prayer for her and made a special angel. Each time she returned home from therapy, there was always a different handmade angel at her front door as an indication that she had been prayed for that morning.

When my husband was hospitalized for months, my friends mobilized. They mowed the grass, kept food in the refrigerator, did my laundry, and cleaned my house. One friend slipped in while I was at the hospital and changed my sheets. Another friend opened and read my mail. When I came home from the hospital at midnight, my mail would all be sorted, and I'd find a pile of bills that were made out, the checkbooks balanced, and a Post-it note that said, "Sign these checks." I did, and she mailed them. AMANDA RANKIN

I was encouraged to seek another medical opinion at a cancer center several hours away. A friend, who lived where the center is, took the day off from work and went with me to the doctor appointments and tests. It turned out to be an all-day ordeal. My friend's mere presence and positive attitude gave me strength. I'll always be grateful.
MICHELLE MCPHERSON

Friends came and cleaned my house without my knowing and did it anonymously. They did everything from picking up the clutter of two preschoolers to cleaning the bathrooms. DONNA WATTS

The friends who "stayed" with us throughout the long and frightening journey is what stood out most for my family. These were the people who vowed to pray for us and stay in contact. Weeks would pass, and their companionship remained. If they were far away, their caring and brief phone calls or e-mails were certainly strength builders. One group showered us with "Prayer Grams." The cards came regularly for six months. VAN WALTON

My son was grown and didn't live with us, so I was alone in the house while my husband was hospitalized. Every evening when I got home from the hospital, I would find a dinner plate of food placed on my front porch. A precious woman in my neighborhood served up one plate of her family's dinner for me every evening.

I needed someone I could talk to, but no one wanted to listen to my feelings. I thought of a friend I knew who volunteers with the local hospice program. When I told her of my diagnosis, she said, "I will be right over." I was able to unburden myself to a compassionate friend, who not only understood, but listened. Allow your friend to talk it out with you; be a good listener. BONITA KILGORE

A friend came every few days and watered my plants. Another friend organized dinners. I received gift certificates for coffee at Starbucks and other specialty stores. One special friend sent us a card of encouragement every few days. ANNIE VANCE

The Navy chaplain's wife showed up one afternoon after school and vacuumed my house. That blessed my socks off! MARTHA POPE GORRIS

My mom and friends accompanied me to my doctor's appointments. They were essentially my ears. Many times, I found myself fading to this place in my head where I would think, *Is this really happening? I can hardly believe this is me going through this.* Then I would snap back to reality and find that I had missed the last minute of conversation. It was helpful to have someone there who was truly listening and helping ask questions. After each appointment, on the ride home, we would go over what was discussed. KATHY THOMAS

While I was recovering from major surgery, a co-worker brought me the video series, *All Creatures Great and Small.* She would bring one set, and when I was finished, she would stop by, visit, and leave me the next set. I realized these were valuable to her, and it was such a nice escape to watch this series. ELLEN SCHOUEST

After the week of meals ended from my church, one friend continued to bring dinners for several weeks, always bringing enough for at least three nights. ALIDA SHARP

While we were states away from home with our son in the hospital, friends provided unique gifts. We received comfort gifts such as hand cream, body lotion, Chapstick, coffee mugs, and tea bags. Others sent us individually wrapped cookies, fudge, and little hand creams or soaps for us to give to the staff to show our appreciation. One friend sent us a package of stamped thank-you notes. We had newspaper delivery arranged for while we were there. We were given a gift certificate to the hospital's coffee shop, a long distance phone card, a CD of soothing music, a book on tape, a devotional book, and a typed sheet of favorite quotes and uplifting Bible promises. A friend sent a fluffy comforter and "real" pillows from her home. VAN WALTON

I need lifelong weekly infusions, and the nurses were having difficulty administering them. At our Bible study, 3x5 cards were handed out for everyone to record his or her prayer requests. I shared my fears, frustrations, and frailty. We each picked a card, promising to pray for that person's need for the week. While I was out, I received a call from my unknown prayer partner. She recorded the message that she was praying for me and listed my specific concerns. I played it over and over again. I cried. What was significant to me was to know she cared and prayed for me and my particular needs. JUDI REID

The most meaningful moments were those when two or three elders from our church gathered around my son's bedside and prayed for him. We were a broken and needy family. We were very scared. VAN WALTON

A friend gave me a gospel-music tape to listen to while driving to my doctor appointments. My nephew and sister brought a stuffed animal to me. Friends and relatives sent cards of encouragement and left messages on my answering machine. MICHELLE MCPHERSON

Illness at Christmas is simply overwhelming. My husband had surgery in November, and it looked like we wouldn't have our Christmas tree up that year. Our neighbor came over and saw that our tree wasn't up. He hauled out the box and started putting up our aging, temperamental tree. He made repairs in our electrical outlet and took it all in stride. He was a true blessing. One year I had pneumonia over

Christmas. Our pastor's wife came to visit and asked what my concerns were. I said what worried me most was getting the Christmas tree ornaments taken off the tree and packed away. She asked where the boxes were, and with that she got them and took all the ornaments off the tree and wrapped them while we chatted. These were acts of kindness I will never forget. MARY HUNT WEBB

My pastor took me out just a week before my mom died and suggested I make some pre-arrangements with the funeral home. He said, "It is so difficult when you do it afterwards, and you don't always make the best decisions as you are in shock." This might not be the right thing for everyone, but it would be nice to offer this suggestion and volunteer to accompany your friend to the funeral home. EVELYNE TIMBERLAKE

Someone brought a decorated Christmas tree, complete with lights. Our daughter couldn't see well at the end, but she could see the lights. BETH BLANCHARD

We had to travel one thousand miles away to be at our son's bedside. My younger son was taken in by parents of his friends, his teachers, and his youth pastor. His teachers gave him grace to miss assignments and respected his reflective days. They removed pressure and just loved him. They e-mailed me frequently to assure me he was in good hands. Friends took him home from school, fed him, carpooled him, and let him sleep in their homes while my husband and I were away. VAN WALTON

When my husband was dying of cancer, I had friends who would drop in with groceries: juices, brownies, cereal, yogurt, cookies, tea, etc. It was so nice not to have to be running and spending time at the store for things like that. One friend called every morning to ask what she could pick up for me. Some days it was nothing, but it was so helpful to be asked. ANNIE VANCE

We found out on Mom's seventy-fifth birthday that she had a brain tumor. Four weeks and one day later, she was gone. During that last month, we moved Mom to my sister's, and I moved in to help. The support team at my sister's church was overwhelming. Every night there was a hot meal brought to the house. People phoned and visited, not only with us, but also with Mama. They didn't shy away from talking to her even though she was extremely disoriented and confused. Those who had loved and known her throughout her life wrote notes and cards, and many drove long distances to see her. Just the fact that people took care of our needs without being asked and took the time to write the card or make the phone call was tremendously strengthening for us. I still glean comfort from those times. JUDY WALLACE

A charming friend with a merry heart sets up a day every couple of months to come see me. She checks at the last minute to be sure it is still a good day, but I have the pleasure of looking forward to her visit. She brings a picnic with colorful paper goods and a big thermos of tea so she doesn't have to ask for anything when she sets up, and there is no cleanup. Sometimes she brings picture albums of family trips or a funny picture book to share. Once she gave me a manicure and a pedicure to celebrate the return of healthy fingernails. Another time she gave me a drawing lesson. She always has several great ideas, but she checks to be sure I feel up to it. Sometimes we just talk, laugh, cry, and hug. She tries to keep it upbeat but is a good listener who also shares her ups and downs. MARLEEN

People let us know they were praying for us. We got a big United States map and put a little sticker everyplace we knew someone was praying. There were so many! People came from down the hall in the hospital to see Jackie's map. The doctors were very interested in it as well. It gave us a chance to tell them we believe in prayer. BETH BLANCHARD

One neighbor family came every night, and we would all pray together as I tucked my husband in for the night. ANNIE VANCE

I began losing my eyesight to retinitis pigmentosa and was no longer able to drive, even though I had young children. My friend Mary offered, "You know, I'm always out with my two children. I'd really love the company if you ever need a ride." Mary arrived promptly the next afternoon. Her cheerful nature was as sunny as the sunshine I was missing. Each Tuesday afternoon, with the children buckled securely and plenty of books and snacks, we set out for an afternoon on the road! Soon, I realized traveling with Mary was more than just a trip to the bank, library, or drugstore. It was fun! With games and songs, she entertained the children as we made our rounds "all through the town." Her joy and laughter were good medicine to my weary soul. CINDY HEFLIN

Try to avoid bringing us things that must be returned. If you bring it, please come and retrieve it in a short while. Someone brought bags of books to the hospital, and we had to take them all home with us.

Don't bring food in dishes that must be returned. We can't keep track of who brought what, let alone return them. BETH BLANCHARD

One of the most touching aspects of being part of a team is witnessing how each person has his or her own special gifts to offer. When a friend was seriously ill, one person came once a week and cleaned the entire house. Another changed the bed linens and washed them for the entire family. Yet another owned a submarine sandwich shop and would bring a variety of sandwiches for our friend to eat. A sweet couple volunteered to take our friend to pick out her own coffin and make her funeral arrangements while she was still able to walk and make rational decisions. We were a team, and we conducted ourselves in that spirit. We all knew why we were there. Our primary focus was the care and comfort of our friend and our communal love for her. Find your own special place of service to your friend. Seek direction in how to fill the unique vacuum in his or her life, and then offer to help. JUDITH HAYES

Note cards are so helpful because I can read and reread them when I feel up to it. I save cards in baskets and reread them when I feel down. MARLEEN

THOUGHTS FROM BOB BARNES REGARDING THE LAST FIVE YEARS OF EMILIE'S ILLNESS

People truly don't know how to respond in difficult times. I even find this difficult for me, even though I have gone through the "valley of the shadow of death" with Emilie. We all need help when these occurrences come our way. I can honestly say that we never had any unusual remarks said to us. We have had nothing but great expressions of love and thoughtfulness during these last five years. Some things that have happened on the positive side of the ledger have been

- ❖ More than 4,000 cards and letters of encouragement.
- ❖ More than 8,000 e-mails sent from all over the world;
- ❖ Telephone calls of inquiry, concern, and love;
- ❖ Food brought by countless friends;
- ❖ Prayer partners supporting our situation;
- ❖ Friends helping sit with Emilie while I had a break;

- ❖ Volunteers to drive Emilie to a doctor's appointment while she had chemotherapy or radiation;

- ❖ Churches who have requested prayer in their Sunday bulletins or newsletters;

- ❖ Posting our "handprint" newsletter on our Web site where prayer partners were updated on Emilie's condition;

- ❖ Volunteers helping us move so we could be near her oncologist;

- ❖ Friends and family who traveled to Seattle while we were there for her bone-marrow transplant;

- ❖ Cheerful visits in the hospital;

- ❖ Continuous bouquets of flowers to brighten our room.

WHAT YOU CAN DO (FROM BOB BARNES)

JUST DO IT! Often one says, "Call me if you would like a meal, a pot of soup, an errand run." Just do it for the person. Don't wait to be called.

BE SENSITIVE TO TIME. Don't overstay your welcome. Make your visit sweet and brief. Be very sensitive to the energy level of the one you are visiting. It's better to be too brief than too long. Leave before the person wants you to leave. Remember, you may not be the only telephone call or the only visit for the day.

DON'T ASK FOR TOO MANY DETAILS. Don't make the caregiver have to tell the same story over and over again. You are not the only person he/she has had to tell. Just be satisfied with a speedy report. You don't need to know everything.

GUARD THE ARTICLES, VIDEOS, AND CASSETTE TAPES YOU SEND. We know you are well-meaning when you send all these miracle products, but in most instances they bring confusion and doubt to the patient. One of the important parts of recovery is that the patient has utmost confidence in her medical provider. Yes, it is true that we need the latest information in order to make wise decisions, but the patient doesn't have the time or energy to research all the crazy marketing products on the subject. All these product suggestions are overwhelming to the patient and causes the person to doubt their doctors. The patient needs encouragement, not more alternatives.

WHAT TO WRITE IN A CARD

We send you greetings of love and wishes of comfort. May you find comfort in each other's arms as you wage this most valiant battle. You are in our thoughts and in our prayers, this day and always.

The future must seem frightening, I'll stay close.

How I wish I could make this cup pass from you. I'd like to take a magic wand and make it all go away. Since I can't do that, please know that I love you and will be with you as you travel this road through uncharted territory.

I pray for you every morning when I take my walk [or any other specific time you pray for your friend]. I have been praying specifically for _____ [and state what you have been praying for].

May you feel supported and loved by the knowledge that we care and are praying for you.

I have no idea what the future holds for any of us, but I know who holds the future. May you experience a gentle calmness during this storm in your life.

In whatever lies ahead, may you feel God's gentle touch and know He is with you.

Take time to write how special this person is in your life, the impact he or she has had. Make sure you say all you need to say. Don't leave anything unsaid.

PRAYER

Lord, I come before You with (<u>name of hurting friend</u>). I thank You that You are the great physician. You made our bodies and know precisely how they function. Lord, it is my desire that You totally and completely heal (<u>name of hurting friend</u>)'s body of this illness. Thank You, Lord, that You love (<u>name of hurting friend</u>) and have a future and a hope for him/her that cannot fade away. You promise to carry (<u>name of hurting friend</u>) through, no matter what is ahead and that You will never leave him/her. Give him/her the peace and assurance of Your constant presence. I ask all these things according to Your will, knowing that Your ways are high above our ways and that Your grace is sufficient. Amen.

W hen I first put out a request for people to share what has been helpful and hurtful as they faced a difficult situation, I was stunned by the flood of responses I received for chronic illness. I have come to believe that this is one of the more difficult areas of need. With virtually every other situation, we live with the hope that things will get better. But when someone is living with a chronic illness or chronic pain, we must face the reality that, short of divine intervention, it won't get better. In fact, it will only get worse.

Friends dealing with a chronic illness need long-term, continual support and assistance. We seem to be willing to rally around someone facing an immediate crisis, but we are less eager to enter into a situation where there is little hope that the condition will ever improve. Yet, these friends may be the ones who need us the most.

WHAT HURTS ME

"At least you still have your mind."

"Be glad it isn't worse."

"God heals everyone. By comforting people in their pain, you are preventing them from knowing God. Your work is not of the Lord."
LISA COPEN

"You look great!" This is nice to hear, but it also makes it more difficult for people to understand the beneath-the-surface issues we face. The silent message in that statement is, "You don't look sick. Are you sure there is something wrong?" JUDI REID

I had friends who insinuated that my condition was merely "normal aches and pains." Others told me to "get a grip!" KATHY KORHONEN

Don't say "I understand" if you haven't been there yourself. And even then, be careful not to suggest that you know how the person feels. You don't. Just share what it felt like for you when you were experiencing something similar. LISA COPEN

"Maybe if you got some exercise, you would be in better shape."
When informed of the boomerang of post-polio muscle atrophy thirty
years after my recovery from polio, my mother told me if I had exer-
cised after a hospital stay, this never would have happened. Most
people have no idea what is best for my condition. ELLEN BERGH

"Well, you don't look disabled." I was asked, "You can get to the
bathroom, right? You're okay." ELLEN BERGH

"It must be nice to have so much time for yourself. I wish I could
take time off from work, but I'd go crazy doing nothing." ANONYMOUS

"This is all in your head! Your condition doesn't really exist."
ANONYMOUS

During one hospitalization, my abdomen was swollen out like I was
seven months pregnant, and I had unbearable pain. A new friend
came waltzing into my hospital room and flippantly said, "Well, you
know Marcia, all things work together for good." In my heart, I
believe Romans 8:28, but I didn't want to hear those words, as I
couldn't think of too much good about my present situation. People
need to be careful how Scripture is used and in what tone of voice it
is quoted. Using a soothing Scripture where God is portrayed as a
loving, caring God who hurts with us when we hurt is a much better
approach. MARCIA VAN'T LAND

"You must focus on your healing, be healed, and then that could be
your ministry." LISA COPEN

"What did you do to make God so mad at you?" LISA COPEN

"I know this man that has the same condition you have. Of course,
he's dead now. But he got it because he was always so busy and doing
so much. Maybe, if you slowed down ..." LISA COPEN

"Snap out of it!" "If you come with us, you will feel better." "Stop
taking all your medication. You'll get better." CINDY LYONS-HART

"Just remember, we all have bad days sometimes." When you have a
chronic illness, you don't just have "bad days sometimes." You have
bad weeks and months and begin to lose sight of any times when you
were not extremely ill. Those of us who are ill need to know that
those close to us may not understand the illness, but that they respect
us enough that they would not trivialize our symptoms. Having a

chronic illness has really opened my eyes to the fact that we are put on this earth to help and support each other. Many of us just don't know how to do that or what to say. Churches seem to be especially lacking when I would have thought I'd find most of my support there. BETTY VOLKART

Be aware of the fact the illness is not just a matter of attitude. Don't say, "When are you going to get rid of that cane?" or "Did you know illness is caused by stress?" **

Avoid giving "God balm." If you say, "God will heal you," or "All things work together for good," your hurting person will believe you don't really understand and will avoid sharing his or her feelings with you in the future.**

Don't feel compelled to share every cure you've heard of for this illness. Your friend is probably constantly bombarded with cures and needs you to be his or her refuge from that.**

Respect your friend's limitations and be sensitive to them. Don't say, "A little walk might do you good," or "No pain, no gain!" Only your hurting person knows his or her limits, and these limits will likely change from day to day depending on many factors. What he or she could do yesterday may not be possible today. Don't question that.**

WHAT HELPS ME

"I don't know what to say, but I'm here for you."

"I'm sure this will take a lot of adjustment. I'll be with you every step of the way."

"I've never heard of that condition before. Tell me more about it." Then listen and ask about the diagnosis. Find out what symptoms and effects it has. Ask enough questions that you will know how you can help. JUDI REID

"God is really using you through this experience. I know this sounds strange, but part of me really envies what God is revealing to you and how He is using you. You have a passion for what you do." LISA COPEN

"I don't know how you do it all." LISA COPEN

Ask specific questions. Don't be afraid to address the illness by name. Ask if the medication is helping, if your friend is getting some relief, and if there have been any changes. LINDA GILDEN

I sought the counsel of another dealing with my same condition. He asked me one simple question: "What kind of control would you like to achieve?" He somehow triggered hope in me. He empowered me to set my own attainable standards so that I wasn't perpetually defeated by attempting to reach standards that were out of the question for me. PEARL T.

WHAT I WISH PEOPLE UNDERSTOOD

Remember my limitations. I need people to understand I cannot always keep up with their schedules and to not take it personally when I have to cancel plans. LISA COPEN

A lot of life's traumas and problems are far from simple and require more than pat answers and superficial responses. Please listen and give attentiveness rather than answers. Let hurting people know you are there for them—to just give your heart. LOIS BYERS

God heals in many ways and is refining me to be who He wants me to be through my illness. I have days that I want to feel well and normal. But, overall, I feel honored that I am able to reach out to those who are hurting and say, "I understand—truly." LISA COPEN

I think the key to helping anyone through a crisis is to realize there is not a quick fix. It can be hurtful when people continually try to find solutions in a situation where there really is not a solution. JILL COODY

Hope, joy, and peace seem like lovely thoughts, but they seem just out of reach when your body is consumed with pain. You try to hope for relief, yet you know this pain all too well, as it makes its appearance frequently. You long for joy, yet the simple pleasures of life are now harder to grasp, as your mind focuses on your affliction. Peace seems like a distant dream, and simple tasks now seem like monumental jobs. How do we achieve our heart's desire when our illness is demanding all of our attention? DEBBIE FARMER

It was easier to tell people that I was fine because I looked fine— except looking haggard and tired from fighting pain all the time. KATHY KORHONEN

The hardest thing for me is the loss of all my friends. I can no longer do what they want to do, so I guess you would say I'm out of the picture. When people do come to see me and see the change in my life, I am treated like I have leprosy. CINDY LYONS-HART

I need others to be sensitive to the day-to-day frustrations I live with. I like to show by my life's example that life doesn't end when you need a wheelchair. Please don't presume to swoop down on me in my situation and have all the answers to my complicated needs.
MARCIA VAN'T LAND

I found help from a polio survivors group. Many had been in wheelchairs since youth, yet had broad, constructive lives. I had always feared and pitied disabled people until I was inducted into this army. They taught me how to be a black-belt health-care advocate. Their style of humor helped restore my love of life. They invited me to write in their newsletter. I started a Roses and Rutabagas award for stores that were sensitive or insensitive to the disabled. With curtailed activities, my downshifted lifestyle helped me focus on the good days and on sharing what I learned with other fledgling writers one morning a month. God will raise up what we need. ELLEN BERGH

I wish people understood how painful it is going through everything alone and having no social support. Having hearing and vision impairments and a brain disease makes it very difficult to cope with day-to-day activities. There is no reason to feel scared or fearful to help someone like me. We just have disabilities. If you are willing to help us, both of our lives are brighter and happier. DENNIS TROGLIO

We need to feel and express our grief to get through it. My experience has taught me to quit trying to make people fast-forward through their pain just because it makes me uncomfortable. Grieving is natural and will take time, but it is healthy. If you suppress the pain, it will manifest in worse ways. ELLEN BERGH

Pain and suffering now require me to seek help with the chores, take naps when I am weak, and seek medical attention when the symptoms of illness get the better of me. DEBBIE FARMER

Berating someone experiencing a chronic illness does no good. It only serves to bring about discouragement and rebellion, focusing on areas of weakness. Those of us weighed down with health problems need to feel less like victims of the disease or condition and more like the one in charge of our treatment and our choice to feel better. PEARL T.

When our health fails us, we often find ourselves questioning if the Lord really cares and worrying that our future seems so bleak. We need to be assured that we have not been abandoned. DEBBIE FARMER

I am making choices about my treatment based on research, practicalities, and prayer. Any change in my treatment could cause me to lose my abilities forever. To take an herb or try the new popular drug is not an option I can choose lightly. My treatment is very personal to me. Please respect that I am making the best choices for me. LISA COPEN

I began to be left off invitation lists. Some people didn't want to be friends with a cripple. Others spoke to me like I was hard of hearing or nervously looked away. Some even suggested I was "faking it." I wanted to regain my personhood. I am more than the label "disabled." ELLEN BERGH

Sometimes the nights seem to be the hardest when someone suffers from pain. The agony seems more intense, the hours seem long, and despite ourselves, we can feel so very alone. So many times I've lived this scenario, yet my faith seemed to be the only thing between despair and hope—hope that the morning will come. I need hope. DEBBIE FARMER

Treat me just as you would like to be treated. I don't want pity or to make people sad when they are around me. Be proud and rejoice with me for the courage with which I face the challenges in my life. Don't leave me behind and not invite me to go places because I'm extra trouble.

Don't assume that I cope with things the same way you do. Don't tell me I should be handling this differently. I may rebuild my strength when I'm alone, while being alone may make you depressed. LISA COPEN

WHAT YOU CAN DO

Offer to go with me to one of my appointments or treatments to keep me company and maybe even make me laugh (which admittedly is difficult in this situation). JUDI REID

The caring cards have helped a lot. These cards let me know that there are people who still want to be a part of my life. I so appreciate those who help me without being asked. A person with a chronic illness loses so much of his or her self-worth that constantly having to ask for help is hard. CINDY LYONS-HART

Just walk alongside your friend and hurt with him or her. It is important that people acknowledge the pain and not pretend that it isn't there. People tend to get uncomfortable not knowing what to say, but the key is not saying something magical. It is just saying you care and that you are there. JILL COODY

I've been hospitalized, often for long periods of time, forty-nine times. The most important thing people did for me and my family was to help take care of our children when I was too ill to parent. My children were included in family trips to the beach, Disneyland, and the circus. Others helped by doing our laundry, providing transportation, bringing meals, and most importantly, covering us in prayer. I have special friends who allow me to have a pity party every now and then. They let me cry and carry on until I'm over it. They cry with me, then we dry our tears and go on with life as it is. MARCIA VAN'T LAND

A friend helped me find an apartment where she and her husband were living. This was my first time living on my own, and I needed a lot of support. She brought me frozen bags of homemade turkey stew. Her husband brought me home from the hospital after I had suffered an injury. DENNIS TROGLIO

I am a part of a church-sponsored chronic pain support group. It is helpful to share information and have people pray for me when I am at my worst. It's good to talk to others who are going through the same things that I am. It is helpful to realize that I am not alone. DEBBIE FARMER

Last Christmas I was in so much pain I couldn't do anything. Some wonderful friends came over to do whatever I needed. They brought along a fabulous meal, complete with dessert. They cleaned my living room and put up my Christmas tree and all my decorations. What a great blessing that was. It lifted my spirits and made such a wonderful Christmas for me. JANIS KEEHN

Someone arranged for me to have a "card shower," where everyone sent me a card on the same day. The Lord really used that to minister to me on a tough day. JILL COODY

I had one dear friend who would call on me and encourage me daily. She had suffered from chronic pain and knew what I was going through. She prayed for me, offered to drive me to the doctor, and helped me with my laundry. She often invited my family and me over for dinner. KATHY KORHONEN

Sometimes just listening is the best kind of encouragement a friend can give us. Keeping this in mind, perhaps your ear can cheer the one in pain more than words. I prefer empathy over sympathy. Empathy feels the pain with someone, while sympathy feels sorry for him or her. Can you share your ear with someone hurting today? DEBBIE FARMER

Don't make your offers to help vague like, "Oh, we'll have to get together sometime." If you make an offer to help me, please follow through. Take me to something with you. Ask if there is something in my home bothering me. Ask questions like, "Could I help you with that?" "How about if I help you pack away your summer clothes and reorganize your closet?" ELLEN BERGH

As I create events to raise awareness and/or fund research, join me. Send me a card. In the stack of bills and junk mail, it is so comforting to receive a card. Leave me a quick message on my answering machine. It helps enormously to know that someone cares and that I have not been forgotten. God's timing will allow the simple act of caring to come on just the right day and at the perfect moment— guaranteed. JUDI REID

I have had incredible support from one lady who does my weekly grocery shopping, prepares five meals a week, and helps clean my house. These are wonderful tangible ways to lighten the load of someone who is in the midst of a crisis. JILL COODY

When my condition worsens for weeks at a time, I get very depressed. During one of these times, my friend Rachel called me every morning at about 11:00 to talk briefly and to find out how I was doing that day. I began to try to think of good things to report and gradually felt better. She had an illness, too, but was always taking time and energy to encourage others. It meant so much to me that someone would make the effort every day, rather than call once and sympathize and then disappear for another several weeks. BETTY VOLKART

Offer specific ways you can assist your friend. Say, "I'm going to the drugstore. Can I pick something up for you?"

Look around your friend's home and see where he or she might need some help. Does the shower need to be scrubbed? Do the leaves need to be raked? Does the carpet need to be shampooed? Offer to take care of these things.

Volunteer to pick up some groceries rather than do the cooking. Many times people with illnesses have restrictive diets, so they may prefer some fresh fruits and vegetables rather than a casserole. Ask what meals your friend is enjoying eating, then freeze some of those meals so he or she can have them on hand.

Accompany your friend to places where he or she may need assistance. Get your haircut at the same time or have the oil changed in his or her car while you're having lunch.

Bring an uplifting personal little gift when you come to visit: some fresh-cut roses, a new book, a funny movie, some cookies for the children, a blanket, or a candle or potpourri to make the house smell nice.

Remember that your friend's spouse and children have needs, too, and these often concern your friend. Take the children out for a while, planning something special for them. Before you drop the children off, pick up a small something that will make their parent smile, like fresh flowers or an ice cream.

Ask your friend what his or her concerns are and how you can address these concerns. One woman who was ill said that she would like a friend to make sure her children made it to Sunday school and church when she couldn't go.

Treat your friend as though he or she is still a whole person, despite his or her limitations. Your friend wants to feel capable and in control. Let him or her make the plans.

Ask the person's spouse how you can help the family. One spouse was appreciative of gift certificates to local fast food restaurants so the children could occasionally have quick meals and his wife didn't have to worry about making dinner.

ALL CONTRIBUTIONS ABOVE ARE USED BY PERMISSION FROM
LISA COPEN AT REST MINISTRIES, WWW.RESTMINISTRIES.ORG.

WHAT TO WRITE IN A CARD

Consistency is the most important aspect about writing a card to someone with chronic pain or a chronic illness. Contact should not be a single effort, but instead, should continue in the weeks, months, and years to come. When you have prayed for your friend, drop a note to let him or her know. When you see something that reminds you of your friend, send a card saying so. When your Bible study or choir meets, circulate a card for everyone to sign—just so your friend knows he or she is loved and not forgotten. It is *not* helpful to make reference to your friend's pain, such as "I'm praying for relief of your pain," "I understand your pain," or "I'm sorry for your pain." Your friend is all too keenly aware of his or her pain and doesn't want to be reminded of it. Avoid comments that focus on the future or a get-well type comment, such as, "I hope you feel better," or "Tomorrow is another day." Instead, offer hope for comfort today.

May God give you comfort and rest today.

I am praying that your day brings you comfort and strength.

You are God's good idea! Though life is sunlight and shadow for you right now, you are precious to many.

I know you face daily struggles. Please know that I pray for you every evening that you will have a good night's rest and awaken refreshed.

How I want to wrap you up in love and take the hurt away. I am praying for you.

May the loving thoughts of those who care strengthen you to face another day.

PRAYER

Ask what your friend would like you to pray about, and ask if he or she would like you to pray with him or her.

Lord, I come before You with (<u>name of hurting friend</u>) right now. Father, You know the constant discomfort and pain that he/she lives with daily. Sometimes (<u>name of hurting friend</u>) feels as though he/she cannot go another day. Please pour out Your grace and mercy, and ease (<u>name of hurting friend</u>)'s discomfort and give him/her hope in place of discouragement. Help (<u>name of hurting friend</u>) to know that You are with him/her and You will carry him/her through. Give (<u>name of hurting friend</u>) Your peace and rest amidst this pain. I thank You for Your presence and compassion. Amen.

CHILD with CRITICAL ILLNESS

No critical illness is easy or comfortable to be around, but to see a child suffer is even harder. The difficulty of the situation makes it all the more important for you to visit, spend time with the family, and show you care. Much of what appears in the Chronic Illness chapter applies here as well, so be sure to read that chapter. There are, however, some special considerations when the patient is a child.

WHAT HURTS ME

Don't offer clichés or pat spiritual answers. They are not welcome. Don't tell your friend to "Have faith" or ask, "Is there sin in your life?" SHARON GLASGOW

"You know she's in God's hands."

"Oh, I'm sure everything will be fine." That comment made me want to scream! If they could have seen my baby plugged into every monitor and machine in creation, they wouldn't have been so glib. DENISE SPRINGER

Don't try to spiritualize what happened. People would listen to my woes and depression and would say, "You know, God is going to use this someday to help others." All the while I was thinking, *Oh, that's wonderful. I've prayed all my life that I could be someone's bad example.* SHARON MARSHALL

WHAT HELPS ME

When I visit a young person, I like to ask him or her questions. It lets the child know that I am interested in him or her and what he or she is facing. It also helps get the conversation going. I ask questions like

❖ "What have you done today?"

❖ "Did you have to have any tests?"

❖ "What schoolwork have you done?"

❖ "Did you eat your lunch?"

❖ "Who else has come to visit you?"

❖ "What are some games you like to play?"

❖ Whether talking to the parent or the child, let them both know that you are there for them.

❖ "I'm so sorry for what you are going through. I'm praying for you."

❖ "I'm here for you." Then live out that statement in practical terms.

❖ "How are you holding up?"

❖ "What can I do to help?" Then offer suggestions of what you can do.

We were always appreciative when people said they were praying for us. REG EPP

WHAT I WISH PEOPLE UNDERSTOOD

Jason has had three brain surgeries, thirty-five radiation treatments, and fifteen months of chemotherapy. The months during his treatment were very difficult, with multiple hospital stays, lots of infections, and blood transfusions. It seemed Jason's life was on the line many times. Family life was far from the normal life we had been used to. REG EPP

My son was underdeveloped because of his surgeries and the fact that he couldn't keep anything down. Total strangers would ask how old he was, then make cutting comments about how much bigger their child or grandchild was. The comparisons hurt because they had no idea how strong Drew was to have made it through all he had. A man laughed at Drew's size and told me his three-month-old was bigger than my son. I just snapped and said, "That's great. How many surgeries has she had?" I know that was not a nice reply, but it quieted him. DENISE SPRINGER

I didn't really appreciate it when people came up with alternative things we could try in Jason's cancer treatment. Sometimes it seemed like mental overload to process more than we were already doing. There were a lot of things about diet, but sometimes Jason wouldn't eat anything, let alone drink some kind of herbal remedy or "green tea," so this added to our stress. We tried some kind of vitamins, but his reaction to chemotherapy was worse than ever. I did a lot of reading on the Internet to check on some leads people were giving, but we never had any peace about going off in another direction. We felt we should continue with the accepted medical model. I would say that every time someone came with a bit of new information, they were tactful and sensitive to our needs. Never did anyone say that conventional cancer treatment was all wrong. REG EPP

Phone calls can be draining in the midst of a crisis. People need to understand that the exhaustion level is very high. Sadness, anger, and confusion are normal and acceptable. Most people don't want to see us expressing negative emotions. We need to have a few select friends we can express these human emotions to. SHARON GLASGOW

We needed some privacy so we could try to live a normal life. But at the same time, we really liked to talk about what was happening, especially when we knew people were praying for our situation. I did appreciate people asking how we were doing and how we were holding up. REG EPP

Troubles often come in bundles. My son was born hydrocephalic, lived four and a half months, had five major brain surgeries, and died. Within thirteen months, I had four deaths in my immediate family and lost my home, virtually everything I owned, and my husband. I received food stamps for a short period of time. It still embarrasses me. I can't begin to tell you how humiliating that was.
SHARON MARSHALL

My son is in the hospital. Our church is a half hour away. I think it is strange that no one from church has made the effort to visit him. I was told that if he were in a local hospital, things would be different. I don't get it! He serves on the children's ministry team, is active in the youth group, and the list goes on. He gives hours to the church weekly! I guess time is precious, and my child is not top priority. The sad part is that my son's roommate in the hospital is also a half hour away from his church. I think that his entire congregation has stopped by. They are the ones who have prayed with my son. What a blessing! ANONYMOUS

I wish people understood the time and effort it took for me to care for my daughter. I was unable to leave the house for any length of time, and I spent many days and weeks home without a visitor. I would have loved a visit. LESLIE WAGNER

It was always encouraging to meet people who had had the same type of experience and gone through the same sort of "valley." REG EPP

WHAT YOU CAN DO

My son was born critically ill, and I had experienced complications during my emergency C-section and was not bouncing back as rapidly as women normally do. My mother came each morning to drive me to the Neonatal Intensive Care Unit, took me to lunch, took me home for a nap, cleaned my house, did my laundry, and took over calling loving friends and relatives when I was too drained to do it. Each evening Mom and Dad met my husband and me at the hospital for an evening visit and then took us to dinner. I don't know how we would have made it through without them. They really put their lives on hold to keep us going. DENISE SPRINGER

Jason really appreciated having his youth pastor and others from church come to visit him and pray with him. REG EPP

My son Bryan was always eager to rent or bring one of his own video games to Jason. They would play games together, and Bryan taught him many special maneuvers he could try. This seemed to help Jason change his focus and escape the reality of his pain, even if only for a short time. LAUREN

Our church family brought our son, Andrew, homemade gifts, gift certificates to a bookstore, cards, and travel games. ANDREA VERNON

Don't expect us to entertain you when you come to see us. I realize it takes a tremendous effort to visit a child who is dying, but I was too devastated myself. We need to be encouraged and supported. Remind us that God does not forsake the suffering. CLAUDIA WARD

Many people brought Jason things in the hospital, including balloons, books, stuffed animals, and even CDs and video games. One family packed a bag full of surprises for Jason. Pamela phoned to ask the hospital if she could bring it over. It was already past visiting hours, but she told the nurse that these things just had to be given to Jason that evening. The nurse agreed to let the family come. When they left, Jason opened the package with a CD player and a Veggie Tales CD. He put on the headset and started singing (very loudly). The nurses poked their heads in the room to see what was going on! I hadn't seen Jason having so much fun for a while, and it brought tears to my eyes to see so much joy that had been clouded by pain and nausea! That's one example of how people brightened his day. Visits were usually enjoyed very much, except for when Jason was in a lot of pain. REG EPP

A dear woman brought her children and others to sing outside my daughter Hannah's window, and they left gifts at the front door. The most memorable part was the sight of a group of children gathered outside our window singing encouragement to us weary insiders. It just so happened that we were depleted of every ounce of strength that day. We didn't have to entertain our guests or even talk to them. They just ministered to us. Sometimes we didn't have the desire to interact because we were so empty. SHARON GLASGOW

There were so many people praying for us, we were amazed! We really appreciated all the e-mails, cards, and phone calls from concerned families and individuals. Often, each evening, we would receive more than thirty e-mail messages, assuring us of the prayers of our friends. Many people whom we did not even know responded, explaining how they had heard about Jason and our family and how they were praying for us. REG EPP

The hospital my daughter was in had no companion meal trays for parents. Since I wouldn't leave her side, I was looking to spend lots of money in the cafeteria. A care package arrived from co-workers filled with microwave food and snacks that I could prepare and eat in the nurses lounge area. It was such a thoughtful gift, in lieu of flowers. LESLIE WAGNER

A special friend, Steve Springsted, came to pray with the three of us before Jason's last surgery. He sat with us in the waiting room sharing his own tears with us. Jane Adams also sat with us in the waiting room and called the operating room to get an update during the surgery. She was there with us to share tears of joy when the surgeon came in to give us good news. REG EPP

A MOPS (Mothers of Preschoolers) group from our church made meals for us for an entire month. Paper plates, cups, and forks were a great bonus. All the meals were delivered in disposable pans. They truly ministered to us. SHARON GLASGOW

People from the church that I grew up in, but had not attended in years, wrote us letters and sent us cards, many with touching and meaningful thoughts. DENISE SPRINGER

A friend took our car for some much-needed routine maintenance and a car wash. That was something we would never have been able to do. SHARON GLASGOW

I wanted to show my appreciation to the nurses and staff at the hospital for their tremendous care of my daughter. I mentioned this to my mother, and the next day, she arrived with a homemade cake and a blank thank-you card. I was able to write my own personal thank-you to these great caregivers and give them the cake in my appreciation of them. LESLIE WAGNER

Videos were brought to us weekly for entertainment. SHARON GLASGOW

Call the family home and ask to speak to the child so he or she knows you called just to talk to him or her. LAUREN

Elders and families came and prayed over my daughter but didn't stay any longer than to pray. SHARON GLASGOW

We were home on furlough from the mission field in Africa when Jason's symptoms began. Once we knew his diagnosis, we knew we could not return to Africa but would need to move to Mission Aviation Fellowship headquarters in Redlands, California. I could then work at headquarters, and Jason could receive his treatments and surgeries at Loma Linda Medical Center. After renting for a year, we decided it would be more practical to buy a home in the area. Friends recommended Lauren Briggs to help us with the buying process. Lauren was a great realtor and let us do the looking at our own pace, working us in at any moment when Jason was well enough. When we found a house that we could afford and was right for our family, she helped us understand the process and all the paperwork.

It had been Jason's wish to meet Sammy Sosa of the Chicago Cubs baseball team. The Make-a-Wish Foundation made that wish come true for Jason, with a trip to Chicago for the whole family and a visit to the dugout, where we met not only Sammy Sosa but many other team members. We were in Chicago when the escrow on the house actually closed. Jason was facing a third surgery when we returned, so our stress level was definitely quite high. The thought of setting up a home when we had virtually no possessions was quite overwhelming.

We flew home to Redlands quite late and were picked up by a good friend. On the way home, he turned in the opposite direction of our rented home. Instead, he turned onto the street of our new home. He said he just wanted to take us by there on our way home. As we turned into the driveway, we noticed the lights were on. We were greeted by Randy and Lauren Briggs and their sons at the door. As we walked in the front door, we were shocked to see our home completely furnished. The place was set up with furniture in every room, a table set for five in the dining room, and a new refrigerator complete with an ice maker. All beds were in place, with pillows, sheets, and blankets. Draperies were hung, pictures were on the wall, our family portrait was on the mantel, lamps were on end tables, dishes were in the china cabinet, silverware was in the drawers, and food was in the cupboards and refrigerator. The lawn was freshly mowed, and the whole house was cleaned. There were so many details, I couldn't list them all, including chocolates on our pillows. The house was set up so completely that we didn't even need to go to our rented house at all that evening. We just unpacked our suitcases and we were home. What a wonderful feeling. A huge burden was lifted. Without our knowing it, Lauren had been fund-raising on our behalf, organizing work crews, and scouring garage sales. We thank God over and over again for how He used such lovely and willing people to reach out to us in such a practical way! REG EPP

WHAT TO WRITE IN A CARD

It is too difficult to include specific phrases to write in a card because of the wide variety of ages of the children and range of possible illnesses. Read what is included in the previous chapter and use what you feel would be appropriate for the age and need of the child. Send separate cards to both the family and the child unless it is for an infant. The cards for children should be bright, colorful, and cheerful, as well as age appropriate. Include a little game or puzzle the child can do like a maze, tic-tac-toe, or word search. A whole book or magazine might be overwhelming, but send one page of something fun to do in every card you send. Let the child know that you are sad for what he or she is going through. Offer to come by and bring an ice cream bar or pizza.

When Samuel was born with a life-threatening disability, I received dozens and dozens of wonderful cards. Treasured friends searched for the perfect "new baby" card. Their cards did not contain the typical "congratulations" so common to baby cards. One card was inscribed with, "God Bless Your New Baby." My friend wrote, "Dear Shawna, Steve, and Sarah, What God has given you is a beautiful and precious blessing. I rejoice with you that God has given Samuel to you, even as I weep with you over the short time you will be together here on earth." Another card read, "Your child is a gift of God. With His love may you grow together in faith, peace, and joy." My friend wrote these precious words inside: "Shawna, Steve, and Sarah, Little Sam will only know *love* and *joy* here on earth and in his life with *God forever*." While this may be hard to understand, these cards helped me feel a little bit more normal. SHAWNA MARIE

PRAYER

Father, I don't understand the reasons why this little life must endure such trauma. I ache for the pain, the anguish, and bewilderment I see in his/her eyes. You, better than anyone, know what it is to see Your child suffer. This is so hard, and these days are so uncertain. Father, wrap this family in Your arms of love and protection. You know our hearts. You know our struggles. Enable us to come into Your presence and rest in You. I ask that a special measure of grace be given to this precious child. Help me stand with him/her as he/she faces each new day. I give You the honor and the glory. Amen.

Ask the child if you can pray with him or her. If he or she is comfortable with that, pray a very simple, comforting, affirming prayer.

God, You know how hard this is for (<u>name of hurting friend</u>). This isn't where he/she wants to be. Please help him/her get a good night's rest. (<u>name of hurting friend</u>) is very special to You and is loved by all of us. Help us through this very hard time. Amen.

CHILD with SPECIAL NEEDS or DISABILITIES

A parent's life changes forever with a child who has a special need. Life will never be the same. This family needs continued, long-term support and understanding. Even the seemingly easy daily tasks can become more complicated and more difficult. It may seem as if their joy has been replaced by constant fatigue. As comforters we are never to forget them; stay in touch, and provide respite and diversions if possible. Realize that the medical condition or special need never diminishes the parents' love for their child. This precious life is no less loved or cared for than a child without special needs.

WHAT HURTS ME

"What are you going to do with her?"

"If you'd taken better care of yourself, this wouldn't have happened."

"At least you still have one healthy child."

Well-meaning friends offered to help in any way they could. "Call me if you need anything," they would always say. I never called anyone or asked for anything, even though I desperately needed help.
SHAWNA MARIE

People told me to "accept it," to "act like a Christian," to "get over it." Words such as these should never be uttered. IRENE COSTILOW

Don't bring up long-term care with us when the diagnosis is fresh. The last things we want to talk about are future medical needs, group homes, or institutions. This topic shouldn't ever be brought up by others. If I initiate the discussion, that means I now need to talk about it. FRANCINE TORO

When I arrived on this earth without legs, the obstetrician told my father, "Your daughter is going to live, I am sorry to say." My dad's congregation told him, "Rev. Rieder, you and your wife must have sinned to cause such a calamity." JUDY S.

I was asked by one of the hospital staff if I planned to take Gabe home or if I wanted to give him up for adoption since he was so deformed. I was shocked that anyone would even think I would do such a thing. I was told it was standard procedure because many people do in fact abandon such afflicted children. That made me very sad. GIGI MURFLITT

When a friend heard about the testing results and the psychologist's diagnosis, her comment was, "Well, I don't know why she's so upset. She knew they had problems." Our children played together, and this hurt deeply. She showed no compassion or understanding for what I was going through. IRENE COSTILOW

"Nathan was given to you because you are such a great mom. He needed a mom like you." "God sent him especially to you!" One person gave me a poem about "Special Moms." I did not find encouragement being a "Special Mom." FRANCINE TORO

My son was born prematurely. One person said, "If only you could have held on a few weeks longer and not given birth so soon." It sounded like I could have crossed my legs and held on! These words made it seem as if I was somehow responsible for the timing of the birth. JANET LYNN MITCHELL

A friend of my brother's is an attorney. He called and asked if there was anyone I wanted to sue over Gabe's birth defects. I asked him if he had a direct line to God! I was very angry that he would even think about a lawsuit at a time like this. If I bring the question up, that is different; but never suggest a lawsuit in a situation like this. GIGI MURFLITT

One of the doctors, during the initial visit to determine the extent of Gabe's birth defects, point-blank told me, while chuckling, "Well, you'll never have to buy this little guy shoes, because he'll never walk." This was before I even knew there was anything wrong with his legs that could not be fixed surgically. It was very cold and made me sad. GIGI MURFLITT

WHAT HELPS ME

"Your daughter has beautiful eyes."

"Your son is so loving and precious."

My friend's words of tenderness were so helpful as she tried to reassure me. She said, "Irene, somehow, some way, God will get us through this." I wasn't sure I believed her. I was terribly angry with God at that point. IRENE COSTILOW

The pediatrician in the hospital took extended periods of time to talk with us about what she thought was going on with Gabe. She was digging through her medical journals and literature to provide us with information. She was supportive but realistic and did not try to cover anything up. GIGI MURFLITT

WHAT I WISH PEOPLE UNDERSTOOD

Sometimes I want to talk, but sometimes I don't. Please be understanding when I don't. Sometimes I get really emotional; please bear with me. FRANCINE TORO

The pain, the anger, the disappointment—to me, this was the death of a dream for my children's perfect, normal life. I was grieving, and no one would understand or let me grieve. Their observations of me were based on my outward appearance. They seemed oblivious to the fact that I was dying on the inside. IRENE COSTILOW

Very often when we are out with Gabe, young children will curiously come up and ask him questions about why he looks so different. Many times the mothers of these children will yank them away and tell them not to ask questions. I often stop the mothers and encourage the interaction with Gabe. I remind them that if they tell their children not to interact with my child, that will make him feel weird, and he doesn't need to feel that way. GIGI MURFLITT

After the car accident that injured my daughter and left her permanently disabled, we became the church tragedy. Many of my friends avoided us because they didn't know what to say, even years later. It was the friends who treated me as if I hadn't changed who meant the most. It was these friends who called me on the phone just to chat, who took me out to lunch, who accepted the fact that though I

hadn't changed, my life had changed, and loved me anyway.
LINDA EVANS SHEPHERD

Several years after Nathan's diagnosis, when I had a realistic perspective on his needs, I knew I was his advocate. I am going to fight and conquer anything that comes into my son's life. It does take a special mom to do this. FRANCINE TORO

I was at my breaking point. We took our children home from the hospital on Sunday. Monday, my husband started a new job, and I was left home alone with three children and was scared to death. I was on my own to give four insulin shots a day and needed to be prepared to give CPR at any moment. I also had an active four-year-old who wanted to play! I was riding an emotional roller coaster and needed another adult just to talk me through my day.
JANET LYNN MITCHELL

People don't realize the grieving process is a natural part of having a child with disabilities. We grieved the child we anticipated and did not have. We grieved the future for him. We grieved with guilt in trying to figure out if we had done something wrong to our bodies to cause something like this. We needed to be allowed to grieve. It is okay to talk about the issues. GIGI MURFLITT

WHAT YOU CAN DO

I had two children in the hospital at the same time, yet in totally different areas. I also had a four-year-old, healthy son at home. My family and friends knew that I did not want to leave my children alone. Due to their love and creativity, they worked out a schedule so that my husband could work, I could spend time with each of my children, and not one of them would be alone during a twenty-four-hour period. I had been a victim of medical fraud, so my family and friends knew my fears and planned accordingly. They loved me and covered my fears by being where I could not be. JANET LYNN MITCHELL

Some friends did not come visit me at the hospital. I'm sure it was because they didn't know what to say or do. Sometimes, just being there is enough. No words, nothing to do, just be there. GIGI MURFLITT

One friend volunteered to spend the Sunday school hour to teach disabled children. This was the only break I had from taking care of my child all week.

My daughter has been in the hospital for the past five days. I am completely out of milk and other essentials. Being at the hospital all day and then coming home tired is tough. My kids know how to order pizza, but if someone wanted to really help me they would check to see if I had milk and check to see if I had fruit and things to make my kids' lunches with. The weekends are usually when I do my shopping. This weekend was different. I spent it in the emergency room and then sitting at the hospital. After five days there, my laundry has mounted. I've given my eleven-year-old instructions to lower the mountain and do some wash this afternoon. I'll see when I get home how it turns out and what colors my whites become! JANET LYNN MITCHELL

Samuel needed to take medication thirty minutes before feeding to help him keep his formula down. Tube-feeding him took another thirty minutes. Because he needed to be fed every two hours, the whole routine would begin again in an hour. By the time I had done this for ten days, I was completely exhausted. A friend of mine who was a nurse, showed up that very day with her husband. She told me that I could trust her to care for Sam. How did she know I was afraid to let anyone else care for him? She told me if I didn't get some sleep, I wouldn't be able to care for him. She told me to go over to my mom's house for a good long nap. How did she know I wouldn't be able to sleep with my son in the other room? I didn't have the strength to argue. If she had called and offered, I would have declined. She provided me a much-needed break. SHAWNA MARIE

How I wished someone would stop by with a café mocha or a big soda and offer to stay with me. JANET LYNN MITCHELL

The greatest gift when dealing with a child with a disability is down-home friendship. The natural response is for one to withdraw because "I don't know what to say" or "I don't want to say or do the wrong thing." But what the parent and the child need most is inclusion, not exclusion. Pray for ways to stay close to the parents and make ways to include the child in normal activities like birthday parties, sleepovers, and trips to the movies. Worse than the disability is the loneliness, the empty calendars, the absence of a circle of friends. Pray that God will make you a friend and make your kids friends. JUDYANN SQUIER

When I received Nathan's diagnosis, everyone encouraged me with kind and positive words. They wanted to know more about his condition. They wanted to talk about it. No one brushed it under the carpet. When a television special or newspaper article came out about his diagnosis, they contacted me or mailed me a copy. They knew that knowledge is power! Many encouraging prayers were sent forth on Nathan's behalf. FRANCINE TORO

I had a family member who, each time she came into my house, would check my washer and dryer. I was constantly starting a load and forgetting it. I had too much on my mind. JANET LYNN MITCHELL

The day we received the testing results, the psychologist said our twin sons were profoundly retarded. Driving home from his office, desperate thoughts raced through my mind: *Don't go home. Run away. Drive into the brick wall. End it all.* When I pulled into the driveway, my friend's car was there. I didn't expect her. "Irene, I don't know why I'm here. God just told me to come and wait for you." She was an angel sent by God. I collapsed into her arms and cried on her shoulder for hours. IRENE COSTILOW

For the first year of my son's life, my husband and I never had any time alone. How I wished someone had brought a picnic lunch over and volunteered to watch over my son. I could go out in the backyard with my husband and relax, knowing that I could be with my baby if he needed me. JANET LYNN MITCHELL

You could take up a collection to hire a nurse to provide your friend with some respite. I would have loved for someone to offer to sleep in my son's room for an evening. For the first year of his life, I slept in my son's room and listened to each of his heartbeats on the heart monitor. I was sleep deprived. If only someone else would have taken a shift and allowed me to sleep with my husband and get some real sleep! JANET LYNN MITCHELL

I had two friends who would accompany me to every doctor's appointment with my sons at a time when no one else wanted to be near me. FLORENCE LITTAUER

WHAT TO WRITE IN A CARD

I was praying for you today and wanted to let you know that you are loved.

May you find strength in the knowledge that we love you and that we care.

I wish you a day filled with the gift of peace.

You are special to me, and I treasure our friendship.

PRAYER

Dear Lord, You know how much we love this precious child. While there are special needs, nothing could diminish our love for him or her. Please give my friend, (name of hurting friend), the strength needed to provide for (child's name)'s care. Show me ways I can help and support (name of hurting friend) as he/she cares for his/her child. We come to You with an ache in our hearts that won't go away. We trust You for our tomorrows, one day at a time. We ask for Your guidance and strength for the days that lie ahead. With grateful hearts, Amen.

DIFFICULT DECISIONS

I'd just walked in the door after taking Randy Jr. to school. My husband was hanging up the phone. "It's bad news." He said, "Grammy was found unresponsive in her bed this morning and is being rushed to the hospital." Leaving our two-year-old son, Jonathan, with a neighbor, we hurried to the hospital.

My eighty-five-year-old grandmother had lived with us for three years and battled melanoma cancer for five years. Just two months before, she'd moved to a retirement home two miles away from us, where she could be looked after twenty-four-hours a day.

Is this the final hour? we wondered. Or was it a minor problem that would be resolved with medial treatment?

They were taking Grammy out of the ambulance when we arrived at the emergency room. She was whisked off to an examination room while I filled out the necessary forms. Then we were told to wait in an adjoining room. Moments later her doctor called us in to speak with him. His first statement left me feeling helpless. "I need you to tell me how aggressive you want us to be."

Of course I wanted her to be treated and cared for, but how could I determine how "aggressive" they should be? The doctor became more specific. "If she stops breathing, should we put her on a respirator? If she experiences cardiac arrest, should we try to stimulate her?"

Grammy didn't want to be kept alive by machine; I knew that. But I had to make a decision—one we'd always thought God would make. At that moment, Randy and I had to respond the way we felt Grammy and her children would want us to.

I had a peace that if Grammy were standing between us, she'd say, "Let me go! I'm tired of fighting. I'm ready. Please let me go."

Randy and I knew we were speaking for Grammy and her children when we said, "No respirator, no heart machine, no extraordinary measures to keep her alive."

"I'm sure it's for the best," her doctor told us. "Her struggle with melanoma would only be a downhill road. It isn't controlled. She has had a stroke and is in a coma. I feel she has only hours to days, not weeks to months, to live."

I felt strange discussing Grammy's life and death so matter-of-factly and intellectually, yet we knew it was what she wanted. Once we'd decided not to sustain her life with support systems, the wait began. Although her condition had stabilized, she was unresponsive with no improvement. Throughout the day, she continued to breathe on her own but did not regain consciousness.

That evening her physician told us that Grammy probably would not live through the night. But by morning, she was still alive. Her breathing had become more labored, and we knew this truly was her final hour. By noon her son arrived from Dallas and made the final decision that no life-sustaining measure be taken. At 3:00 PM, with her son at her side, she passed away peacefully.

Scientific advances in today's world have forced us to make decisions people have never had to make in the past. If your hurting person has had to do that, you'll need to be aware of the emotions he or she experiences. Even making the right decision doesn't make it easy to do. His or her decision might be the decision you think you would make given the same set of circumstances, but none of us really *know* what we would do until we are there. Those individuals need your loving support without a hint of judgment.

TOUGH CHOICES

What kind of decisions are people facing today? They can be divided into two categories: those that affect the physical life of a loved one and those that affect their emotions. The ones that affect physical life include things like halting efforts to keep a premature baby alive, ending chemotherapy treatments, or turning off life-support systems.

It is not my position to tell someone else what to do at a time like this. It is important not to offer opinions or make judgments.

Consider the feelings of a family whose premature baby is barely being kept alive. He has severe brain damage, a weakened heart, and poor lung development. While the baby might survive necessary heart surgery, due to the other factors, he would never be normal and would probably spend the rest of his life institutionalized.

Imagine how family members attempting to make this kind of decision feel. Do they insist that everything possible be done to keep the baby alive? Or do they request that no extraordinary measures be taken and allow the baby to live or die according to his own ability?

A woman who is four months pregnant goes in for a routine sonogram of her baby and learns that the child has no brain and that he cannot survive outside the womb. She is asked to decide whether doctors should induce premature labor or if she should carry her baby for another five months, knowing he will die at birth.

A forty-five-year-old woman with two teenage children has been told that she has breast cancer and that it has already spread through the lymph system. She is given six months to live. Chemotherapy might extend her life another six months. The woman and her family must now decide whether she should take the chemotherapy, with all of its side effects, to add some time to her life. Or should she allow things to take their natural course and intervene as little as possible?

A teenage son lies comatose in the emergency room following a severe car accident. Indications are that he will not survive. However, exploratory surgery could be performed to find the true extent of the injuries. "Your son is touch and go," the family is told. "He'll never be the same." They must decide whether to consent or not.

A sixty-year-old husband and father has suffered a major heart attack and is on a respirator. The doctor informs the family that there has been extensive damage. Most likely he won't regain con-sciousness or be able to live without the respirator. How long do they want him to be "kept alive," and what extraordinary measures should be taken?

The other kind of difficult decisions affect emotional situations. Consider the wife and mother who, after two years of earnest mar-riage counseling, is served with divorce papers. She is asked to sign that she agrees with their statements. Is she to continue to live in emotional turmoil, refusing to agree to her husband's demands? Is she to face months of court battles over money and custody? Or is she to agree to something she doesn't want?

Penelope shares a difficult decision she had to face:

> I went through the difficult decision of having to place Mother in a nursing home. It was all the more difficult since I was a nurse and had said on numerous occasions, "Don't worry, Mother, you will never have to live in a nursing home." But Mother needed twenty-four-hour, seven-days-a-week total care. We couldn't do it ourselves. It was terrible to leave her. I felt that I had buried her alive. Then, when she failed so fast and her time in the nursing home was only three months, I thought, *I could have done that.* But none of us knows the future.

PRAY FOR THEM

There are many other situations like these that require a decision. Some may seem clear, but often they are painful and difficult. Rarely are they easy.

As comforters, we must uphold our friends in prayer before they make the decision, while it is being carried out, and afterwards as well. In addition, let's provide them with nonjudgmental and unconditional support. They need our prayers and our love.

HELP WITH THEIR FEELINGS OF GUILT

One of the natural reactions to making such painful choices is guilt. That guilt may be reasonable, the result of something for which the individual is responsible, or it may be unjustified. Whichever the reason, guilt is a natural response to making these kinds of decisions. The people ask themselves, "Did I make the right choice?"

Whether your hurting person is experiencing justifiable or false guilt, we need to be aware that those feelings are very real and should be discussed. As the grief process takes place, encourage your friend to share his or her thoughts.

Never respond by saying, "Oh, you shouldn't feel that way." The truth is, he or she *does* feel that way and needs your understanding and compassion. Encourage your friend by talking about God's unconditional love. Even if the decision he or she made is not what you think you would have done, don't say that. Just reassure your loved one that you know his or her heart is one of pure and loving motives.

DEALING WITH HINDSIGHT

Guilt can be the result of a person's "if only's."

"If only I hadn't said those things to him."
"If only I had called the doctor sooner."
"If only I wasn't working then, this would never have happened."

It is easy to feel guilty about some of the things we did or did not do when a loved one dies. The finality of death destroys the possibility of righting any wrongs toward the person.

How do we help such individuals? There may be nothing we can say to resolve the problem. We can pray that God will give our friend the insight he or she needs. And we can stay with him or her, communicating God's unconditional love for as long as we are needed.

PART
three

LOSS

WHAT IS LOSS?

One month at our local meeting of The Compassionate Friends, a guest speaker asked, "What is the one thing you want the world to understand about your grief?" I found the answers profound and vitally important for those who wish to be effective comforters.

Grief is my constant companion. I need to have a conversation with it every day.

Grief is a long and hard process. Even though years have passed, my pain has not.

It takes such a long time to cope with a devastating loss.

It is definitely okay to talk about the person who has passed away.

Please don't make decisions for me. I'm not as fragile as you may think. I want to be a part of the decisions that are made.

The pain continues even though it's been a year. I continue to have good days and bad days.

The pain is real and lingers even if I don't show it.

I won't "get over it" just because everyone else has.

My grief is real and in its own way is always present.

After an amount of time goes by, I'm not all better. This will always hurt; my heart will always be missing the piece that was my loved one.

I am confused. Sometimes I cry. Sometimes I can think; other times I cannot. Sometimes I just am. Please be patient.

Just because I've experienced a loss doesn't mean we can't be friends. Please don't shy away from me. I need you.

No one else can know the depth and reality of my loss.

My grief is sometimes overwhelming.

I lost my love, and I have felt so alone and empty for a long time.

It is going to take a long time to recover well enough to function.

It hurts so much that I don't have words for the hurt I feel.

I have missed my son every day in some small way all of the last five years.

Please don't be uncomfortable when I talk about my loved one and the grief I am experiencing.

To effectively comfort someone, we need to understand what the hurting person is experiencing and feeling. One of the ways to do that is to understand the descriptive terms associated with their plight.

1. LOSS. Anything that falls short of realistic expectations is loss. It is also "being deprived of or being without something one has had and has valued."[1] Both definitions show that people can experience loss at many different levels—from losing a tooth to losing a loved one.*

2. GRIEF. Grief is a deep sadness, intense emotional suffering, and acute sorrow caused by loss.

3. MOURNING. This word encompasses the external signs of grief, such as the funeral, the wearing of black, and withdrawal from public. Mourning varies according to cultural background, personal beliefs, and societal pressures.

My friend Georgia Shaffer, author of *A Gift of Mourning Glories*, likens grief to a full soda bottle that has been shaken. If we open the bottle too quickly, the contents explode and go all over. Instead, we need to slowly release the cap, a little at a time, to relieve the pressure that is built up inside. In the same way, it is best for us and those closest to us if we do our grief work slowly, dealing with a little of the pain at a time. Otherwise, the pain we are feeling inside can explode, creating quite a mess around us.

TYPES OF LOSS

There are two types of loss: predictable and unexpected. With a loss of any kind, a person will experience the normal stages of grief.

Whether that sense of loss is only momentary, as in a missed phone call, or long lasting, as with a death or divorce—any loss results in grief. It's the severity that differs. With a predictable loss, like the anticipated death of a terminally ill person, some of the grieving— known as anticipatory grief—begins before the person dies. If the person is elderly, the death may be expected and may even seem benign.

When the death is unexpected—like one that is the result of an accident or that of a stillborn child—it may seem especially unfair. If any loss is connected with past experiences, the current event will seem even more extreme.

Once a person suffers a loss, he or she feels vulnerable. *It happened once; it could happen again.* Your husband doesn't come home from work on time, and you think, *He's been in an accident.* You remember how it was when your father died. *Maybe it's happened again.*

Everyone who loves is vulnerable to the pain of grief. I found a sympathy card that said, "Grief is the purest evidence that we have loved and loved well." We hurt because we love. Love means attachment, and all human attachments are subject to loss. I often say, "We hurt much because we love much." If we didn't love so much, our pain would not be as great. I often affirm a grieving person that the depth of their pain is an indicator of the depth of their love. Our responsibility as comforters is to be sensitive to those experiencing loss and to the ways each individual reacts to that loss.

In the following sections, you will find a wide variety of things you can do to help a friend following the death of a loved one. It is divided into specific types of loss. I encourage you to read all of the sections, as many of the suggestions will be appropriate for any loss.

LOSS *of* PREGNANCY *or* INFANT

A miscarriage, premature birth, stillbirth, or death of an infant is the loss of a much-wanted and loved baby. A baby's death is not only a tangible loss, but with the baby, the parents' future—their hopes and dreams—died. People often underestimate the significance and impact of this loss. Those of us who have experienced an infant or pregnancy loss have few or no memories to hold on to. One of the reasons we grieve so deeply is because we miss our child's entire future. As comforters, we need to validate the significance of this kind of loss.

When my first son, Randy Jr. was two-and-a-half years old, I became pregnant. Five months into the pregnancy, I lost the baby. My time in the hospital compounded my grief. Every two hours a nurse came in to my roommate, turned on the fetal monitor, and listened to her baby's heartbeat. I cringed in pain. That mother-to-be complained constantly about her discomfort and said she regretted getting pregnant. *Why did I have to lose the baby I cherished when she doesn't seem to care about hers?* Continual hospital mix-ups intensified my misery. A nurse came in and asked, "Did you have a boy or girl?" *Hasn't she read my chart? Doesn't she know my baby died?*

A nutritionist asked, "Will you be nursing your baby?" An aide popped in and said gaily, "Your baby will be coming to be nursed soon." *How can such heartbreaking errors be made? Doesn't anyone know why I'm here? Doesn't anyone care?*

The day I went home, the realization hit me that I was leaving empty-handed, without a baby in my arms. Devastated, I tried to be strong and not show how upset and angry I was.

Even focusing my thoughts on Randy Jr. and the joy he gave us couldn't compensate for the child I'd lost. Everything seemed to remind me—from my overweight condition to the boxes of baby things I had to pack away.

Some of the things people said only made me feel worse, like "Just be thankful you have Randy Jr."; "At least you can always try again"; and "Maybe it was all for the best." No one, not even my family, understood how deeply I was hurting. No one understood what a major loss this was for me.

WHAT HURTS ME

"You can always have another one."

"At least you never got to know it."

"Be thankful you already have two children."

"It's all in God's plan." "Your baby is in heaven." What a grieving mother-to-be wants is a baby in her arms. These comments appear extremely insensitive. "You can have more children." After a miscarriage, couples fear that another pregnancy could be impossible for them, and another baby would never replace the child they lost. "It wasn't God's timing." "It happens all the time." "You're young. You can try again." These remarks minimize the couple's loss. DENA DYER

People tried to console me with pat answers of "It's okay; you can have another." Others said something insensitive like, "Well, if God wanted you to have this child, it would have been born." Or "There must have been something wrong with the baby; that's why you miscarried. Be happy you don't have a deformed child." LECIA SEEGARD

When I saw the doctor he told me, "Don't consider this as your losing a child because a child was never formed." I can still hear his voice and see the cold expression on his face. CARRIE CARVER

The nurse in the hospital told me not to cry; I was waking up the other patients on the floor. My husband implied that it was my fault and turned away instead of comforting and giving me support. LEONETTE DIMURO

When we lost our daughter, the worst things people said were, "You have other children." And "Maybe your child would have not been a good person later in life, so God took her now." ANONYMOUS

Don't say trite things like "cheer up" or belittle my loss with comments like, "It was not a real baby." "Are you sure you want any more children?" ANNA HEBB

"He's in a better place." We wanted him here with us.
LYLE AND DANA CASTELLAW

After we lost our two-year-old following a three-week battle with a rare condition, one friend commented, "When you two get through this, you are going to come out like pure gold." We didn't want to be gold; we wanted our child to survive. PAUL SEARCEY

"It's all for the best." "It's God's will." "Is it just the miscarriage thing?" "You already have three healthy children." "You wouldn't want to have an abnormal child." "That's original sin for you!" "You know what is really sad? My friend just lost her baby at eight months." Right away, people suggested that I take Prozac, as though my grief was abnormal or unacceptable. MELANIE WILSON

There were people who kept telling me, "It's okay." Because I am a Christian, God would make it okay, and I would not have to suffer. One woman said, "If God wanted you to be a mother, He would not have let her die." STEPHANIE DAVIS

One awful comment came from Christians, saying, "This is God's way of dealing with your sin." I was not married at the time. How horrible to tell someone it is her fault that her child is dead. I had already dealt with the Lord about my sin, and I know He loves me and was holding me during that time. He was not out to hurt me. If I had believed that, I would have never survived that time, nor would I be a Christian today.*

"You're lucky that your son died so young. Imagine how much worse it would've been if he'd been seventeen months or seventeen years instead of seventeen days when he died." I couldn't begin to imagine it being worse! At that time I would have given my own life in exchange for even one more day with my son. SHAWNA MARIE

"I know just how you feel!" No they did not. They had never lost a child, and even if they had, they did not know how I felt. Just as I can never know just how other people feel when they lose a child. I may be able to relate to some of the things they share or emotions they express, but I cannot walk in their shoes. DONNA ANDRE

WHAT HELPS ME

"I'm sorry for your loss."

"Do you want to talk about it?"

"How are you feeling?"

"I know how much being a mother means to you."

"We love you, and we will pray for you."

"I'm sorry you have to go through this."

"Your faith and strength inspire me."

"I know it hurts."

"I don't know what to say."

"I know how much you wanted this baby."

"I'm so sorry. Don't be afraid to grieve. This is a real loss."

I will never forget one thing that a friend shared with me. She said, "Don't let anyone rob you of your grief." What she meant was not to try and rush through my grieving process because other people thought I should be over it. Everyone is different and deals with grief in different ways, at different levels. DONNA ANDRE

WHAT I WISH PEOPLE UNDERSTOOD

I wish people understood that this was my child. While it may not have been fully developed, it was fully loved from conception. There is a grieving process that a mother goes through after the loss of a child, born or unborn. It is okay to cry; it's okay to have feelings of loss. While the loss of the child may have been due to medical issues or physical problems, it is not the fault of the mother or father.
LECIA SEGAARD

A miscarriage is the loss of a child and hopes and dreams, even if you have other children. You still mourn the loss of that child.
LESLIE WAGNER

Don't ignore my pain. I had the desire to talk about my loss. I wished people would call me to talk about it and ask questions, take me out to lunch and listen to my thoughts no matter how crazy they were—just listen. I needed people to pray with me. ANNA HEBB

Kyle lived for six weeks before dying of congestive heart failure. Many people expected that the grieving process should end after thirty days. The church I pastored made it clear that I'd better not take too much time off work. Others treated us like we had some sort of disease. We were in a young-married fellowship group at our church, and people didn't know how to relate to us, so they just avoided us. Sometimes when a person is going through hard times, others stay away, thinking they may get "hit by the shrapnel" when the bombs drop. LYLE AND DANA CASTELLAW

I really needed to be with someone and to talk about what I was going through. I felt that most people were very uncomfortable hearing about it and just wanted me to stop being sad. I wanted people to understand that miscarriage at any stage is incredibly painful, both physically and emotionally. The hormonal changes are extremely powerful and complicate the grief. My friends withdrew from me hoping I would "get over it" on my own. MELANIE WILSON

Say something! Don't just ignore me or pretend that my loss didn't happen. Identify that you know I am hurting and going through a very tough time. Use my child's name. Talk to me about my baby.

Knowing that the baby I was carrying had a fatal birth defect, the only time I had with her was during my pregnancy. I wanted to enjoy that time. Others made that hard because they were depressed when they approached me. They did not smile or allow me to enjoy my pregnancy. STEPHANIE DAVIS

I just wish people understood that I needed to talk, talk, talk, all about my beautiful daughter. Some of the best friends I had are those who allowed me to talk often about Lyndsay. They let me cry, get angry, or whatever emotion I needed to vent, and they never judged me. They loved me and didn't even have to say anything. They sat and cried with me and held my hand when I needed it. I needed someone to listen to me, to just be my friend. DONNA ANDRE

WHAT YOU CAN DO

People gave me memory-type baby gifts. One gift was a pillow with my baby's name and birth date on it. Another friend sent me a card of encouragement every week. STEPHANIE DAVIS

My daughter, Lyndsay, died twenty-four hours after her birth. One friend took pictures of me with Lyndsay after she was born. I had numerous photos of her first eighteen hours of life. Another friend took those photos and made a picture board that we displayed at the memorial service so that anyone who had not seen Lyndsay in person could at least see her beautiful little face. It was so special and made everyone feel so much more a part of her life. DONNA ANDRE

A male friend of ours who lost his first baby through a miscarriage arrived at our door just as my husband and I were fighting about how we were grieving differently. He brought with him a book on miscarriage for men and some chocolates for me. He hugged me long and hard and mourned with us. His tears were so comforting to me, and we talked about the day we would see our children in heaven. My best friend came to stay with me and just rubbed my arm when there weren't words. The doctor at the hospital told me it was a baby, and it was okay to be sad. MELANIE WILSON

One friend gave me an angel as a symbol gift that meant "hope," and another gave me a daffodil pin. Someone sent a card that stated my husband and I would make great parents and God would certainly bless us with another child one day. This gave us encouragement, because somehow we thought that maybe the reason for our loss was that we would not be good enough parents. Others sent encouraging e-mails. People really prayed for me, cried with me. ANNA HEBB

I encouraged my cousin's daughter to get on the Internet to find support groups and web pages she might find helpful. We have been able to stay in touch by e-mail. MARILYN HEAVILIN

A girlfriend of mine did something I will never forget. She called and said, "Shawna, I'm on my way to the grocery store and want to pick up some items for you while I'm there. Is there anything you need?" I thanked her and told her I didn't think I needed anything. Then she said, "Do you have any milk?" I didn't know. She told me to go look in the refrigerator. I was surprised to discover that I had no milk. Then she asked, "Do you have any eggs?" Again, I responded negatively. For several minutes my precious friend asked at least a dozen specific questions. Only then did I notice the empty condition of my refrigerator. Another friend didn't ask what she could do for me, but came with a plan of her own. She showed up one afternoon and said, "Shawna, you look exhausted! Why don't you take a nap, and I'll take your daughter to the zoo?" Within minutes they were gone, and I was sound asleep. Crying helps! Please let me cry, and don't worry if you cry. I'm used to it! I had a friend walk up to me with open arms. She didn't say a word, but her unspoken invitation to cry on her shoulder did me a world of good. SHAWNA MARIE

Be present, go to the memorial service and graveside. Be proactive. Pray and ask God to reveal ways to help, and then go to the hurting person and say, "This is what I want to do for you." Our church family cleaned our house and prepared meals. A group of men noticed that I needed a sprinkler system for our yard. They put together a team to work with me to install the system. Not only was it good therapy for me to be outside working with my hands, it gave me a chance to connect with these men. LYLE CASTELLAW

Encourage your friend to consider ways of memorializing the baby, such as naming the baby, holding a memorial service, creating a memory album, or planting a tree. MELANIE WILSON

After our daughter's death, friends gave us a gift basket filled with tea, chocolates, candles, crackers, and books. It made me feel that we were special and worthy of a tender-care basket. ANONYMOUS

I have worked with many bereaved parents. I make sure they know they can help dress their baby and can hold the baby prior to the viewing. If a picture is available, I try to make up a special program folder with a picture of the child on the front. MARILYN HEAVILIN

After my third miscarriage, this last one of a twin, my pastor's wife hugged me and reaffirmed her love and the love of God for me. She followed that by a prayer over the child that I was still carrying. The words were heartfelt and eloquent in their sincerity of heart. We held hands as she prayed for protection and safe delivery of the remaining twin. To this day I cannot think of this time of prayer without awe at the incredible way God answered the very specific and sincere prayer of Sister Jean Bell. LECIA SEGAARD

Remember the anniversary of the pregnancy loss and the due date. When the baby's estimated birth date arrives, it brings a flood of memories, reminding the parents of the hopes and dreams destroyed by the miscarriage. Why not send flowers, offer to cook a meal, or call the couple and assure them that you're thinking about their loss? Churches can realize the impact Mother's Day has on infertile women and those who have suffered the loss of a child. A beautiful gesture would be to have a special Mother's Day corsage or single white rose available for women who have suffered these tragedies. If a couple you know has suffered a pregnancy loss, ask the Lord to give you sensitivity to their situation. The exact words you say are not as important as the heart from which they come. DENA DYER

When my sixteen-month-old son, Isaac, died in the hospital, I was quickly whisked out of the room. Months later, I felt a need to revisit that room. Marilyn Heavilin made arrangements with the hospital and took me to the same room where my son had died. I took a tape recorder and a camera so that I could remember that day. We took lots of Kleenex. Marilyn brought a gift; it was a figurine of a little boy being held in the palm of God's hand. That was a very important day for me. SUZANNE AGUIRRE

When there has been a pregnancy loss, often parents don't feel they should name their baby. It was years after my pregnancy loss when I felt the desire to name my baby. I knew it was a girl. I always had two girl names picked out, but since I only had boys, they were never used. I decided to name her Christina Luise. Luise is my middle name, and I wanted to pass that on. I encourage parents to name their baby, even if their loss was mid-pregnancy. It is a tangible way to remember the baby's existence.

WHAT TO WRITE IN A CARD

There is no perfect formula to communicate just the right thing. Here are some examples of what you might include in a note:

Words cannot express my sorrow.

I know how much your baby meant to you.

I can hardly imagine what you are going through right now, but know that I am praying for you.

Nothing I can say can ever bring your baby back, but know that I love you and that I care.

It must be hard to understand. I don't understand, either. I send you my love.

I can't believe this has happened. You were so looking forward to her arrival.

My heart goes out to you at this very sad time.

Encourage the parents with your love, your concern, your support, and your prayers. Make sure that nothing you write in any way minimizes or trivializes their loss. Share a memory of watching them with someone else's baby and how you know they wanted to be parents. If you got to see their baby, share a special feature the baby had and how precious the baby was to you. Something like, "I remember holding her little fingers"; or "He had such soft skin; I loved having his face touch mine." Validate that you know they loved their baby.

PRAYER

When our lives are touched by tragedy, we often don't know how to pray. We're not sure we can connect with God at all at the time. Dena Dyer wrote, "I couldn't find the words to pray, so knowing others were interceding for me was truly comforting." Ask if you may pray with your friend now. When you pray with your grieving friend you might say,

> Dear Lord, we come to You now with sad and broken hearts. We don't understand why this has happened, but we do know how deeply it hurts. You know how much (name of hurting friend) wanted this baby, loved this baby. Please wrap Your arms of love and compassion around us. Let Your presence be known during this very difficult time. We ask for Your comfort and peace. Amen.

LOSS *of a* CHILD

W hen my mother held her dying son in her arms, she soon realized that nothing else mattered. Her wall-to-wall carpeting, color television, and beautiful landscaping were of no value in the face of her son's death. Her priorities changed, and she became focused on her grief. I watched as my mom grieved for the loss of one son and then the second. These tragic events changed our lives dramatically. Mom and Dad became members of a group that no one wants to be a member of—bereaved parents. We plan for the death of our parents. We even plan for our own death, but we never expect our children to die before us. It is not the natural order of things.

The following is a letter published in The Compassionate Friends (Redlands Chapter) Newsletter that encourages the newly bereaved family to share with family and friends. The letter is a brief outline of what a bereaved parent is dealing with, and perhaps it will help you get a better understanding of how to help.

Dear General Public, Friends, and Relatives,

Allow us to share with you a little of what we are feeling and how you can help and support us. First of all, we have suffered a tremendous loss, and we need to grieve. Even though this may make it uncomfortable for you to be around us, it's something we must do. We won't be "over it" in a few weeks or months, as you might expect. Hopefully, we will learn to "live with it" and cope with it. If, in the first stages of our grief we seem to talk incessantly about our child, how much we loved him, and all the details of his death, just listen to us and "be there." It is one of the kindest things you can do for us. Even in the future, would you give us the freedom and pleasure to talk of our dead child? Please mention his name from time to time or relate something you remember about him. It makes us feel good when someone else remembers! Some of the problems bereaved families face as a part of their grief are:

Restoring emotional balance

Deciding what to do with our child's belongings

Lacking motivation

Dealing with guilt and anger

Feeling the intensity of the hurt

Knowing the individuality of grief

Handling anniversary dates—birth and death

Delaying major decisions for at least a year (moving, job changes, etc.)

Experiencing marital discord

Remembering the child in special ways

Feeling that we are "different"

Dealing with the question, "How many children do you have?"

Grieving is work. It's something we must do for our health's sake. A meeting of The Compassionate Friends is one of the few places where we feel at ease talking about our child—where we do not feel so different and alone, and where tears are not intimidating to those around us. If we sound a bit selfish, I guess grieving is selfish. Only after we resolve the many feelings that we have and accept the fact that our child is dead can we reach out to help others, experience growth, and live life again in a full and productive way.

We try not to be critical of you. After all, before our child died, we were the General Public, Friends, and Relatives.

Thanks for the opportunity to share some of our feelings. We do need your help and support!

Sincerely,
A Typical Bereaved Parent

WHAT HURTS ME

I found that people tried to come up with reasons why this happened. Don't quote clichés or Scripture. I found that if I used the Scripture it was comforting, but if someone else applied it, the timing was wrong and it irritated me. LANA FLETCHER

After my nine-year-old daughter, Mallory, died, I was told, "You are still young enough to have another child," and "You could adopt." Just because I have an empty bedroom does not mean I need to fill it. No other child could replace Mallory. "God needed another angel in heaven." Don't suggest that God inflicts or allows hurt to meet His own needs. God didn't need Mallory. "If you could have just gotten her to the doctor sooner, don't you think it would have made a difference?" This suggests that, as a mother, I had failed my daughter. TERESA GRIGGS

Connie Holly died from injuries sustained in a bicycle accident. People said things like, "She's in a better place." Such comments made me feel unworthy to be her parent. "You'll see her again." "Just think; she doesn't have to go through any of this junk in the world." One friend told me that she hurt just as much as I did. There is no possible way she hurt as much as I did, for she had not experienced the death of her child. Another person told me, "You have to go on for your boys." I would go on, but I also needed to grieve for my daughter. JANET PATE

People need to process their own grief. One friend asked a question that puzzled me: "How can you not be mad at God?" It was a very good question, but I didn't know the answer. I remembered talking with my husband, and he said very emphatically, "This is not about God. He did not kill Meredith." I knew I agreed completely. LANA FLETCHER

Often parents will have the opposite reaction and will be mad at God. "Why did He allow this to happen?" "Why didn't He step in and prevent this tragedy?" "Where was God when my child died?" That is okay, too! Our God is big enough to handle both our love and our anger. He already knows how we feel. He patiently comes beside us and wraps us in His unconditional love.

Don't say, "I know what you are going through," or "I know how you feel." That is the worst! An elder of our church asked, "Did you thank God for this?" I was taught that we thank God *in* everything, not *for* everything. ANNA RICH

I was talking to an acquaintance and was telling her about my son's death, and she said, "God only does what's good for us. You should be happy your son is in heaven." I never spoke to her again. Please don't blame God for our loss. Realize that there is nothing that will ever make us "happy" that our child died. MICHELLE KILIAN

Don't minimize or correct feelings. Don't tell the person that he or she should or shouldn't feel a certain way, such as mad, scared, hurt, sad, or guilty. Emotions are not right or wrong. They just are. Don't set your own time frame for the other person's grief or loss process by making callous remarks such as, "You should be over that by now. It happened a long time ago." "Just put it behind you." Don't provide false reassurances. "It'll be okay." "You'll get over it." "You'll forget about it soon." SHIRLEY GIBBS

WHAT HELPS ME

"I'm sorry for your loss."

"Do you want to talk about it?" Be willing to wait for an answer.

"How are you feeling?"

"We love you and we will pray for you. What are some specific prayer needs?"

"I'm sorry you have to go through this."

"Your faith and strength inspire me."

"I know it hurts."

"I'm so sorry. Don't be afraid to grieve. This is a huge loss." Stick around and allow your friend to grieve in front of you.

If you don't know what to say, say that. "I don't know what to say, Anna. I'm at a loss for words, but we love you. We loved your daughter too. We are praying for you. We are so very sad for you and your family." ANNA RICH

WHAT I WISH PEOPLE UNDERSTOOD

So many people came to our home, at times it was completely overwhelming. I wish my family had kept me from some of that. There were times when I thought I was going to die emotionally, yet I found myself entertaining. They meant well, but it was hard and exhausting.

One thing that bothered me was people who told me, "You can't handle this" or "can't handle that." They underestimated me, and it upset me. I was far stronger than anyone thought possible, and no one was going to tell me what I could and couldn't handle. For example, it was very important to me to see my son and kiss him good-bye. Some of my friends didn't want me to do that. I insisted, and I am glad I did. My advice is, let the person set the pace as to what he or she can or can't handle. Be at your friend's side to help him or her handle what he or she wants to do. JUDI BARKMAN

We do find a new normal. I will never be the same, but it does get better. JULIE CHRISTENSEN

The loss is great, the pain is horrendous, and the despair is often immeasurable. Parents who lose children like to know they haven't been forgotten. To suffer alone is definitely the pits. ANNA RICH

Just having someone sit with you, holding your hand, perhaps praying with you, crying with you, and listening is a tremendous help. It helps to have someone to do your thinking for you and remind you of things needing to be done. People are afraid of a grieving person and don't know what to say or do. All they have to do is sit quietly and not even say anything. Just listening to the person really helps. Let the person talk about his or her child. Don't hurry the person. If your loved one wants to just sit and reflect, let him or her. Don't put your friend on a time schedule. SUSAN SHELLEY

Every person grieves differently. This is so important to understand. You must let each person grieve in his or her own way. There were many beautiful flowers at the funeral, but I didn't want a single one of them in my house afterwards. My sister offered to distribute the flowers to special friends. I told her she could do that, but I wanted nothing to do with it. BETH BLANCHARD

One thing that surprised me was that—for me—the second year was more difficult than the first, as I'd started coming out of the fog. I thought after the "magical" one year, I would be okay. It wasn't like that for me. I survived and am now living my new normal. I learned guilt and anger are a part of grief and that having these emotions is entirely normal. I was angry at God. I was guilty because I could have been a better mom. The list goes on and on, and it's different for everyone. JULIE CHRISTENSEN

When dealing with a loss, a person can't make many decisions or reason very well. He or she is consumed with getting through the day. It is helpful for someone to see a need and just meet it. Don't stay away because you don't know what to say. You can go and just sit. Nothing needs to be said. Don't ask; just go. If you don't want to visit, write a note. Write notes to remember special days. One friend sends a card on the anniversary of Jackie's death, her birthday, Mother's Day, and Father's Day. Write down a special memory and send it to us. We can read these things over and over.
BETH BLANCHARD

Our friends will go on with their lives, and so will we. However, we will never get over the death of our daughter. This is a loss that will go with us the rest of our lives. Don't expect us to "get over it." TERESA GRIGGS

When my son died, the people who shared their own vulnerability and pain as they listened to mine were the most helpful. ANONYMOUS

While our child's life has ended, our love for him has not.

I lost faith in the God I thought I knew as I watched my daughter dying of leukemia for nine months. We ran out of money for the transfusions, hospitalizations, and the daily medical assistance.
CLAUDIA WARD

The first year after a child dies, the parents will often grieve in the extreme of their personalities. People need to give them some leeway. I am an extroverted chorus teacher. I did some offensive things to other teachers in order to make my choirs bigger—not because I was trying to steal students from them, but because I wanted to feel better. I would have done anything to make myself feel better after losing my son. It took a while to mend those relationships. PAUL SEARCEY

I wish people understood that the pain never goes away. We will never forget our child. Nothing or no one will ever take the place of our child. A COMPASSIONATE FRIENDS PARENT

I need to talk about my daughter. Please do not be afraid to bring her up in conversation. If you have a memory with my child, please take the time to share it with me. If you have pictures of her, please make me copies. They are now so precious to me. The best thing you can do is talk about the child who is gone. Don't avoid the subject; don't ignore my loss. I need to be able to talk about my memories, the fun times, and even the bad times. TERESA GRIGGS

The fact that grief hits anytime, any place, surprised me. A special song on the radio, a memory, a conversation, a variety of things, would set me off. I could be driving in the car and just start crying. This is normal. Even after eight-and-a-half years, a special song, movies Angie loved, or a movie that reminds me of Angie or my grief will make me cry. The good part is that now it also often makes me smile to think of her—and remember. JULIE CHRISTENSEN

WHAT YOU CAN DO

My cousin called about one month after Mallory died. She said she had asked God to give her a portion of my pain so that I might not carry the whole burden alone. That touched me, and I will never forget it. One lady in our church made it her job to call me at least once a week and send cards almost daily. She would share little words of encouragement and send gifts that would remind her of me or Mallory. TERESA GRIGGS

The Granillos lost their son in the same accident that killed my son, Shane. I was frantic and screaming when they called to tell me about the death of our sons. It wasn't long after I got off the phone that I looked up, and the entire Granillo family was at my house. They had come to pray with me! We prayed, and their presence brought me so much comfort. Their eighteen-year-old daughter, Dione, held me and prayed. She said, "Let's not forget to pray for the family of this drunk woman as they have lost their loved one in this tragedy, too." I was awed and moved by the heartfelt wisdom of this young girl.
JUDI BARKMAN

"How can I help you?" "Can we take your daughter with us? We'll take care of her until you get the funeral arrangements settled and your family arrives." "Can I drive you into town?" "Can we pick anyone up at the airport for you?" "Do you have out-of-town relatives who need a place to stay? We have homes ready for anyone coming in." "Can we feed your dog?" "Is there anyone you'd like us to call for you?" "Can you stay at our house tonight? You're welcome to stay as long as you need." Just knowing there were people ready to help was a tremendous blessing. SUSAN SHELLEY

A twenty-one-year-old young man came to our door two days after our daughter died and gave us a boneless turkey to serve when people arrived in our home. He said, "For the next twenty-four hours I will fast, and each time I have hunger pains, I will pray for you and your family." Our next-door neighbor came by and said, "It's times like this that the devil is near, and I will be by your side to pray and keep him away from you." PHYLLIS LAWSON

Since Jackie died, I will cry sometimes when we talk about her, but please say her name, talk about your memories. It is important to me that I know she will not be forgotten by those who loved her. A college freshman had to write a college entrance essay. She wrote it about Jackie, printed and framed it, and gave it to us. What a treasure. BETH BLANCHARD

My friend Natalie came to my house and helped me find memorable pictures of my son, Shane. She then spent three days prior to the funeral making the most amazing memory boards in his honor. Many people commented on how touching it was to look back and see Shane's life—his smiling face, his relationship with his family, his friends. I still have the boards under my bed and take them out from time to time to cherish the memories. JUDI BARKMAN

When my friend's ten-year-old son died, I not only prayed for her daily, but every two weeks or so I would send her a card. Some were store-bought, and some were just simple note cards telling her I was praying for her and letting her know I cared about her as a friend. I was a mother whose heart hurt for her. I did this for one solid year. Short notes and cards are so helpful because sometimes people can't or don't want to talk. Many times it is hard to verbalize feelings during a crisis. EVELYNE TIMBERLAKE

The sound of my child's name may bring tears to my eyes, but it is music to my ears. A COMPASSIONATE FRIENDS PARENT

Everyone went to other family members to ask how we were doing. These family members received all the encouraging words, hugs, and phone calls. Very few came to me. I felt very alone. It felt like I was their greatest nightmare, and they were afraid to get too close to me. People told my sister-in-law that they didn't want to bring it up to me. They didn't want to remind me. Did they think I had forgotten my daughter died? TERESA GRIGGS

One lady would come to our house every morning and encourage me to walk the track with her. We continue to do this daily. I had a woman call every night at ten o'clock for one year straight to pray with me. My niece attended all the support groups with me until I was able to attend on my own. If only people knew how good it makes us feel when they speak of our child, even if we cry. JANET PATE

What helped was when people hugged me, had tears in their eyes, cried with me, sat with me, and reinforced my love for my child. Even twenty-three years later, people still tell me what a wonderful little girl Danah was. Just last month, one of her friends visited me and gave me some photographs of my daughter. She said, "I had this printed from my pictures at home. I thought you might like to have these." ANNA RICH

A man who had taken videos of many high school activities of his children filled a tape with every scene where Meredith even flashed by, and then he sent us that video. What a treasure that he took the time to show he cared. LANA FLETCHER

Our minister's wife drove me to the hospital where my son had been taken after he was shot. She stayed with me all that day. Later that night several women from our church went to my house, washed all my dirty dishes, took the clothes in off the line, packed a bag for both my daughter and me, cleaned the area where the tragedy had taken place, and took us into their home. These precious people fed us, gave us a place to sleep, drove us around town to take care of business, baby-sat my daughter, took turns feeding my dog, brought tons of food to us, and organized a huge meal for us after the funeral. SUSAN SHELLEY

So much food was brought to the house, along with flowers and gifts. My mother set up a book in the kitchen and took care of writing down the name of every person who brought something or came by to visit, so that I could see later all the many wonderful people who came or brought something. I was in so much shock right at first, I didn't really comprehend everything that was going on around me. Anything that is practical is helpful. A local lawn-service company came by and mowed our yard for the next couple of weeks. Someone took my ironing. Others came by to clean the house. Friends took me out to lunch to get me out of the house and to make sure I ate. For the first weeks, the practical things of everyday life escaped me. TERESA GRIGGS

Try to avoid bringing us things that must be returned. Or, if you bring something, come and retrieve it in a short while. One person dropped off some tapes and wanted them back when we were trying to move things out of Jackie's apartment. I don't think we ever found them. Don't bring food in dishes that must be returned. We can't keep track of who brought what, let alone return them to you.
BETH BLANCHARD

My friend Shann came in and completely took charge of my house. The accident happened early on a Sunday morning, so things were not tidy and beds were not made. She stepped in and made sure all that was done. She set up a table in our living room and filled it with flowers, candles, a picture of each child who died in the accident, and a book for all the guests who would arrive over the next few days to write their thoughts in. It is something I still cherish to this day. Shann and another friend Lynn provided us with a housekeeper for a month in lieu of flowers. It was a welcome treat as we were just so shocked and distraught over the tragedy we couldn't even think.
JUDI BARKMAN

A helpful and priceless gift was photographs and letters friends saved to send us years later. We shared dreams we would have about her. It's been twenty years, and we still receive cards and telephone calls on her birthday and death date, along with notes in Christmas cards about her. PHYLLIS LAWSON

An issue bereaved parents have to deal with is if or when to clean their child's room. When should they sort through the child's clothes? Do they leave his or her room as it was? Do they give everything away? The decisions about what to do and when to do it are different for everyone. I personally had my sister help me go through Angie's things several weeks after her death. We laughed at the ugly shoes she used to love. We cried. We got through it together. I gave most of Angie's clothes and belongings to her precious cousins and friends. I kept the things that were special to me. JULIE CHRISTENSEN

Jackie's husband could not deal with cleaning out their apartment. I could do most of it, but I couldn't pack up her clothes. We asked two special friends to go in and do that without us, which they did. Everyone has his or her limitations on what he or she can and cannot do. BETH BLANCHARD

A Creative Memories album consultant came to my house instead of me going to a class and taught me how to make a memory album. I spent three years putting three albums of my daughter's life's pictures together. It was great therapy for me. LANA FLETCHER

My pastor, Roy, was a godsend. He came to the house immediately and began talking to me about the arrangements. I didn't know the first thing about what to do or where to go. He walked me through the funeral every step of the way and was so helpful and comforting, I couldn't believe it. JUDI BARKMAN

A teacher at our school who was also a bereaved parent called our friends until she found someone with a picture of our two-year-old son, Adam. She made a copy of the picture and mounted it in a large frame. Under it she put the words:

> Some people come into our lives,
> And leave tracks in our hearts,
> And our lives will never be the same.

Then she hired a local artist to make a large portrait of our son from the picture. It now hangs in our living room. Only a bereaved parent would have known what to do. PAUL SEARCEY

My sister overheard my husband, Bill, say that he'd never have another family picture taken since Angie wasn't there to be in it. She took a picture of our current family to a photographer and had Angie's picture superimposed in the clouds above. Oh, what a special gift she gave us. One thing that Bill does is always make sure there is a white rose in any bouquet he buys for me. The white rose is "from" Angie. JULIE CHRISTENSEN

A boy from our school gave our name to a local charity. The charity provided a Thanksgiving meal, toys for our remaining son for Christmas, and a Christmas meal. It's not that we needed it financially, but it helped our emotions through that first holiday season. PAUL SEARCEY

Many of the young people who came to the house had no idea what to say or how to handle the situation. They just came, in spite of their discomfort. We talked about Shane. People think you can't mention his name. I wanted them to talk about him. I wanted them to tell me stories about Shane. One friend of Shane's shared that a week before Shane died, she and Shane had stayed up late talking about their love for the Lord. What a relief it was for a mother to be told that her son is in the kingdom of heaven. I felt sure he was a Christian, but that girl's story blessed my heart more than words can say. JUDI BARKMAN

A friend sponsored the day in our daughter's memory on our local Christian radio station on the one-year anniversary of Meredith's death. LANA FLETCHER

One thing I did was complete a special picture album of Angie. All of the pictures in this album have Angie in them. It starts from infancy and ends with the last night we spent together before the coma. Everyone enjoys looking at the album, even people who never knew Angie. We still go through it often. JULIE CHRISTENSEN

WHAT TO WRITE IN A CARD

When I learned that Nathan Heavilin had been killed by a drunk driver, I went to the store to find a card I could send to Glen and Marilyn. At the rack labeled "Sympathy" I read one card after another. None of them came close to expressing the intensity of this family's loss or my deep compassion for them. The cards were filled with empty platitudes and hopeful euphemisms. These messages wouldn't comfort Nathan's parents. They might even be offended by references to the "flowers of the future" or "a better home beyond."

Finally, I stopped searching for a sympathy card and looked for a plain note card where I could express my own sorrow and concern. I chose one that said on its cover, "The words we most want to say are difficult to find sometimes. Their journey begins far, far away in the heart" (Flavia, Roserich Designs). On the blank inside page I wrote some comforting words of my own. Yes, they were difficult to find, but they'd come from my heart.

The card you send is very important and will serve as a demonstration of your love and support. The parents will probably read your card many times for years to come. While the printed message will bring comfort, so will the personal note you add. Offer an acknowledgment statement that indicates you are aware of their loss.

If you are not a close friend of the family, be sure to include how you know them:

Our sons were in fourth grade together.

We were in the prenatal class with you.

I'm the nurse at your doctor's office.

I sing with you in the community chorus.

Include a way that their child touched your life. Share something that you will always remember about their child:

I remember the first day you brought her to my Sunday school class.

I will always remember the twinkle in his eye.

She loved playing dress-up with my girls.

His solo at the Christmas concert was beautiful.

Include a special memory or experience you shared with their child:

I can remember holding her hand on the field trip we took.

He always had a hug for me whenever I arrived.

We had a long talk last year about what he should major in at college.

She was the first one to help another student with his schoolwork.

If you happen to have a photograph of their child, it is good to include it.

Some comforting phrases I like to use are:

I'd like to wrap you up in love and take the hurt away.

I wish I could be with you to hold your hand, but know that my heart and prayers are with you.

You are in my thoughts and in my heart.

Immediately messages came pouring in. Memories of her beautiful smile, her inner beauty, her kindness, unconditional acceptance, friendliness, love for children, her listening ear, and friendship to many were included in the cards. It helped when people mentioned specific memories about Meredith in a card and let us know they were missing her, too. LANA FLETCHER

PRAYER

At a time of such devastation and loss, bereaved parents may not feel they can relate to God. Your strength and support will be a source of great comfort to them. When you have some private moments with them, ask if you may pray for them. If they prefer not, respect their desires and assure them that you will be praying for them. If they would like you to pray with them, do so. I can remember many times when I didn't want to pray, but I was certainly thankful when someone else prayed for me. Here is an example of what you might pray:

> Our heavenly Father, You know our earthly pain. This grief is more than we can bear. Please come beside (<u>parents' names</u>) and let them feel Your presence and know Your comfort. Surround them with people who love them and share their pain. This is a loss of immeasurable sorrow. While we find comfort knowing that (<u>name of child</u>) is with You, oh, how we wish he/she were still here with us. Please bring beautiful memories to our minds as a soothing balm. We ask Your special mercy on our aching hearts. Amen.

Remember to pray for the family as the reality of their loss becomes more real every day. Your prayers, love, and support will make a difference.

LOSS *of a* SPOUSE

I will never forget the look of shock, panic, and anguish that flooded my mother's face as I told her Dad had died. She was in the middle of her speech when someone located my sister and me and informed us that Dad passed away at home that afternoon. Marita and I had about twenty minutes to absorb the news and devise a plan of how we would deliver the news to Mom. Should we interrupt her speech and tell her immediately? The decision was made to let her finish her message and then have her brought to our hotel room before she could speak to anyone else. As she entered the room, she knew something was wrong but had no idea what it could be. "Mom, it is the worst it could be—Dad has died," I cried.

"No! He can't be dead. I just talked with him this afternoon!" Mom uttered in disbelief. Dad died less than five months before their fiftieth wedding anniversary. He was her constant companion, her soul mate, her ministry partner, and her best friend. How could she go on without him? I can still hear her saying, "He did everything for me! What will I do by myself? Three meals a day! We were together three meals a day. I'll have to eat all by myself, alone at the table."

When a spouse dies, the sense of loneliness and separation is overwhelming. Your friend will need your presence, your time, and your companionship. Include him or her in new activities and offer to accompany your friend to appointments. Try to understand the enormity of the loss.

WHAT HURTS ME

"You were so lucky to have had him for thirty years."

Do not say you know what I am going through. No! You don't. You don't know what I'm going through. You can't, because you did not know what Linda's and my relationship was like, what our marriage was like, what our family ties were. Each person who goes through this experience is different. JOHN DUDDING

"You're young; you'll remarry." BRENDA BROWN

"You can't manage that dog the way your husband used to." Don't make any comment that makes your friend feel vaguely incompetent. SYLVIA DUNCAN

"Here's my number. Call me if you need something or when you're alone." I needed everything, but I couldn't remember the person's name and wasn't about to call her up sobbing. LANE DOLLY

Shortly after John's wife died, a customer in our store said, "I know just how you feel; my dog just died." I was outraged that someone would be so insensitive. Fortunately, John knew how much this single, older man cared for his dog and was not completely offended.

Don't tell me when I should be "over it." What people don't understand is that this process is not linear. You have good days and bad, good weeks and bad. After seven years and a very happy remarriage, there are still things that I see and hear that grab me and remind me of what a sad loss this was. MARGARET WINTER

When I had finally mustered the nerve to eat alone at a restaurant, a friend saw me and said, "Why didn't you call us?" LANE DOLLY

When asked, "How are you doing?" most grieving people don't think they can say "terrible," so they give a weak or disingenuous response. In fact, we are doing terrible. I learned to not say, "I'm fine," because I wasn't. A friend taught me to say, "I'm about the same," or "Quite frankly, I'm terrible." LANE DOLLY

Don't ask if a widow or widower is dating. If we start dating right away, it's viewed as too soon. If we don't start dating soon enough, people wonder what's wrong with us. We can't win. Unless I bring it up, please don't ask. MARGARET WINTER

What really bugged me and still does is when people find out Linda passed away from cancer, they immediately start telling me about so-and-so who has cancer or someone else they know who has recently died from cancer. I think it is because people want to show they understand my hurt. I am sorry that their friend or loved one has cancer, but it does me no good to know about it. I'm in too much pain to care about that. Just say you are sorry for my loss and let it be. JOHN DUDDING

WHAT HELPS ME

"I'm sorry for your loss. I could see how precious he was to you."

"I could see what a special relationship you had; I know you miss her."

"Do you want to talk about it?"

"How are you feeling?"

"We love you and we will pray for you. Every evening, while I'm fixing dinner for my family, I will be praying for you."

"I'm sorry you have to go through this. I will stay close."

"I know it hurts. I want to be available to you as you face the days ahead."

"I don't know what to say. No words can ever ease your loss, but I pray that it will be helpful to know that I love you and that I care."

The best is people telling me how special Linda was. Of course I knew that all along, but it is nice to hear it. JOHN DUDDING

"You can call me during the night; I'll leave the phone by my bed." "I'll call you every day at a certain time, so if you want to talk you can." SYLVIA DUNCAN

"I haven't experienced what you are going through. Can you help me see it through your eyes?" "I know I can't change anything, but can I spend time helping you do something or just fill the empty room?" "I'm not a great cook, but come over and let me feed you anyway." "We feel terrible too. Why not come over, and let's at least feel bad together." LANE DOLLY

WHAT I WISH PEOPLE UNDERSTOOD

There is not much anyone can do. The loneliness is terrible—an empty chair, an empty bed. It's hard to take. JOHN DUDDING

I was in shock, which is a definable physiological condition. When associated with grief, most people think it is a passing emotion. I started to shake; I hyperventilated; I forgot people's names. My memory was terribly compromised. The exhaustion was intense. Shock is embarrassing, scary, painful, and frustrating. LANE DOLLY

There is absolutely no time line for our grief. MARGARET WINTER

My Uncle Jim indicated that one of the hardest things to adjust to after my Aunt Katie's death was the loneliness. He was used to coming home after a long day and talking with Katie about the day's events. They would sit for hours and just talk. Now when he comes home, the house is empty. No one calls down, "Hello, I'm glad you're home," or "I'm in the kitchen." His children are very caring and supportive, but they have their own families to care for. LAUREN

I wished people understood that I want to be treated normally and have normal conversations with the name of my husband included. I hate the awkwardness and the tiptoeing around me.
SYLVIA DUNCAN

I still like it when people tell me funny or wonderful stories about my husband. Especially at the beginning, the best conversation anyone could have with me was telling stories about him. My kids love hearing about how great their dad was. It was that kind of interaction that got them to talk. MARGARET WINTER

I had to remove my husband's things from his office less than two weeks after the plane crash. Someone approached me and asked, "Did you like the meal we brought over?" I was a total blank. I couldn't remember his name and had no memory of the meal. I felt he was confronting me in search of appreciation. I attempted to thank him warmly and asked his understanding of my tardiness in follow-through. Afterwards, I cried for hours. LANE DOLLY

The need for friendship does not stop after the memorial service. If anything, it increases because you have to go back to your usual life and figure out how to do all the things you used to do together, by yourself. MARGARET WINTER

My ex-husband was killed in a motorcycle accident when our son was a teenager. We had shared every celebration in our son's life even though we were divorced. Don't diminish this loss in my son's or my life with comments like, "At least you weren't together when he died." ANONYMOUS

WHAT YOU CAN DO

My friend Becky left a bag on my doorstep. It was filled with energy bars, raisins, and easy-to-eat but nutritious food. I found that much less daunting than casseroles or heavy food. SYLVIA DUNCAN

When you provide food for a widow or widower, be sensitive to how many people are living in the home and how many people will be around. Is he alone? Does he or she have children? Will family be staying with him or her for a while? When Aunt Katie died, their six children, spouses, and grandchildren all arrived at the family home. There was a great need for food. When the memorial service was held, more of us arrived, flying in from all parts of the country. We wanted to be together, but feeding that large a clan was a daunting task. Church friends brought what seemed to be an unending supply of food. LAUREN

My house was full of unmarked dishes from lots of people. Don't take a good dish to a grieving person. Always use disposables. Because I was alone and had no children, food sat on the counter of my kitchen until it molded and had to be thrown away. LANE DOLLY

The visits, cards, and flowers were special. They showed me that people cared. People asking how I am and inviting me to be with them means so much. JOHN DUDDING

One friend called and said, "I'll stay with you for a few nights." Another offered support by walking with me on a regular basis. SYLVIA DUNCAN

This is a great example of using your gifts to help someone else. Becky is an art teacher and has experienced a loss of her own. Several months after my husband's death, she invited me over for dinner. She said, "After dinner, we're going to paint and cry." After dinner, all the art materials came out. She understood how to teach children and to encourage them—and she applied that to me and my grief. "Do you want to paint a chicken or a fish?" she asked quietly. I'm no artist. I picked the chicken and began a very rudimentary painting. It was a new focus, and it calmed my mind and heart to paint. In a loving, encouraging voice she looked for the good and would say things like, "Oh, you're mixing your colors so well!" As we painted, she gradually asked me questions, and in responding, we both began to weep. That release was vitally important because I was bottling the grief, hating the sound of my own sobs. LANE DOLLY

Good friends stay in touch, invite you out, encourage you to talk, don't act uncomfortable when you do, and don't make you have to be fine when you aren't. Make room for us in your lives. Don't make us feel like a third wheel in our new and different circumstances. Please make us feel as welcome as we ever were. MARGARET WINTER

One of the most important things friends can do is to not abandon us once our spouse dies. There are three couples who have been great personal friends to me. They have been there for me since the day Linda died. Yes, I am single, but to them it doesn't matter. I am included in just about everything they do. We have even vacationed together. JOHN DUDDING

After the immediacy of my husband's death had passed, it would have been nice to have been invited by my friends to join them for dinner or to go to a movie. They soon forgot and left me experiencing lonely weekends as they got on with their lives, at a time when I was just starting to want to circulate again. ANNIE VANCE

Two different groups of friends went together and had two meals for fifteen people catered and delivered to my home after Fred's death. This was one of the most helpful things that was done for me and my family. FLORENCE LITTAUER

My house was full of flower arrangements that were going bad. Several friends came over with ladders. They took all the flower arrangements out to the garage and removed the flowers that could be dried. They hammered nails along the rafters in the garage and hung the removed flowers for preservation. The flowers that were good but would not dry well were reorganized and turned into all new flower arrangements for my home. A few weeks later, these friends returned and made beautiful dried arrangements for me to keep. They saw that I needed something—anything—to hold on to. LANE DOLLY

On what would have been my parents' fifty-ninth wedding anniversary, I met my dad at Mother's grave. He came bearing flowers, and I came bearing balloons. My dad and I launched the balloons, and with each balloon we uttered an "I love you," or an "I miss you." My favorite memory of my dad was when he waved after a balloon and said, "Say hi to Berti for me!" MARILYN HEAVILIN

One of the greatest difficulties is deciding what to do with the spouse's belongings. Be sensitive and don't push your loved one to do anything he or she is not ready to do. Offer to come over and sort through a few things at a time, one drawer at a time. Identify family heirlooms. You might even write a story or remembrance connected with the item. When it is appropriate, this can be very therapeutic. One person reports, "My friend, a young mother of four, died of breast cancer. The week after the funeral, I heard some of the ladies from church were planning to go over while her husband was at work and take all her things out of their bedroom so he would not have to be reminded of her death. I caught them just in time and prevented them going over." ANONYMOUS

WHAT TO WRITE IN A CARD

I needed to find a sympathy card to send to the family of a customer. I went to our local Christian bookstore and scoured card after card. I could not find one card that addressed the depth of sorrow I wished to communicate. When I returned to our store, I asked our partner John, "During Linda's illness and after her death, what cards did you receive that were helpful?"

He responded, "They didn't come from a Christian bookstore, I can tell you that much."

Stay away from cards that refer to "loved ones beyond the gate," "now found rest and peace," "joy in God's presence," or "now in God's garden." The card is not for the deceased, but is intended for those of us still here. The spouse needs you to acknowledge the sadness and pain of his or her loss.

When Dad died, loving and caring cards flooded in to Mom. Mom quickly noticed that she read every handwritten word, but only skimmed the printed content. She was especially blessed when comments were included about Dad, how he'd helped the person, what he meant to them, or special qualities that impressed them about Dad. Clear, readable penmanship is important. It is laborious trying to decipher difficult handwriting. Be sure to sign your last name to the card, since the family may know more than one person by the same name, and the card often gets separated from the envelope.

If you are not a close friend of the family, be sure to include how you know them:

> *I knew your wife from Bible study.*
>
> *We were in Rotary with your husband.*
>
> *Our children went to high school together.*
>
> *I sing with you in the community chorus.*

Include a way that the spouse touched your life. Share something that you will always remember about the person:

> *I will always remember her beautiful smile and welcoming heart.*
>
> *I loved watching the way he treated you.*
>
> *His face lit up whenever you walked into the room.*

Include a special memory or experience you shared with the spouse:

> *I can remember sitting with him at a church dinner.*
>
> *She was the one person who made me feel special when we met for Bible study.*
>
> *We had a long talk last year about your grandchildren and their dreams.*
>
> *He was always the first one to offer his help at our meetings.*

If you happen to have a photograph of yourself with the spouse or them as a couple, it is great to include it with a caption of where and when it was taken.

Some comforting phrases I like to use are:

> *I wish I could soothe the empty place inside your heart.*
>
> *I'd like to wrap you up in love and take the hurt away.*

I am hurting with you. May the knowledge of my love bring you comfort.

There are no words to express the depths of my heartache for you.

All that we love deeply becomes a part of us. _____ will always be a part of your life.

I know this is a difficult time for you. I'll stay close.

PRAYER

Dear Lord, we come before You with an emptiness and an ache in our hearts. You know how precious (<u>name of spouse</u>) is to (<u>name of hurting friend</u>). His/Her loss leaves a monumental hole in (<u>name of hurting friend</u>)'s life. There is a loneliness that can't be described and a pain that seems endless. We know You understand his/her pain. We pray that (<u>name of hurting friend</u>) will feel Your presence enveloping and sustaining him/her. May he/she feel wrapped in the support and prayers of those of us who love him/her. We ask for Your comfort in his/her life at this most difficult time. Amen.

LOSS *of a* PARENT

*The reason we are so devastated when a parent dies
is that the audience we've fought against and tried to please
all of our lives has suddenly left the theater.*

AUTHOR UNKNOWN

L ittle did I know when I began to write this book, I would have a personal example to offer in this chapter. As I mentioned in chapter 23, while my mom, sister, and I were away leading the Glorieta Christian Writers' Conference in October 2002, we received word that my dad had passed away. He was alone and sitting peacefully at his desk when he breathed his last breath. He had been to his cardiologist only hours before and was told he was doing fine. As the oldest daughter, the organizer, and planner of the family, I began to make all of the necessary arrangements. Our lives were put on hold as we faced the enormity of our loss.

Since I am an adult child with a family of my own and live an hour away from Mom and Dad, my loss is different from a younger person losing a parent while in the formative years, but the grief and pain are no less real. Not only did I experience my own heartache, but I needed to meet tangible and emotional needs for my mother as well. I am the one who manages my parents' finances and pays their bills. Immediately after flying back to California, I needed to sit in the very office where Dad had died in order to work on financial matters and mortuary arrangements. It was surreal to sit at his desk, go through his files, his projects, and his papers, and realize he wouldn't be coming around the corner any minute. Dad was always there, always available—but now he was gone.

Before this experience, I think I underestimated the impact of the loss of a parent. After all, intellectually, we know our parents will die, and presumably before we do. But I don't think we are ever prepared for the enormity and significance of their loss. They have been a part of our lives longer than any other person. When that relationship is gone, the grief is powerful. We need your understanding, compassion, and support.

WHAT HURTS ME

"It must be such a relief now that it's over."

When my father died, we were told to be happy that he was in heaven with Jesus. At that time, we were mourning our loss, and I couldn't possibly find comfort in the idea that he was gone and in heaven. That kind of peace and comfort came later. At the time, it is downright annoying. LESLIE WAGNER

My mom died unexpectedly when I was thirteen and she was forty-five. People told me it was God's will or that God needed my mom in heaven. DONELLE WEST

"I know just how you feel." No you don't! You don't have my history and my experiences with her. ROBB DENNIS

I was twelve when my dad died. People said, "Don't worry, you still have your mother." Mom and Dad played different roles in my life. Besides, when one parent exits as fast as my dad did, you know that it's possible to lose the other parent just as quickly. ANNA NAPOLI

The things people said that hurt were the all-too-common sayings: "She's better off now"; "She's had a good life." PENELOPE CARLEVATO

At the time of a death, it is not comforting to hear that time heals all wounds. Sometimes a hug and an ear to listen, instead of senseless words, comfort much more. LESLIE WAGNER

When my mom died, I was forty-two, and people would say, "Well, at least you had your mom for forty-two years, so move on. Your poor sister only had her for twenty-six years." I wanted to yell at them, "It doesn't matter. She was my mom, and I just lost my mommy!" When your mother dies and she is your best friend, it doesn't matter if you're twenty, forty, or sixty. She is still your mother, and it hurts. I just needed to hear how sorry someone was, not platitudes or "move on" stuff. EVELYNE TIMBERLAKE

"Well, at least she lived a long life." Age is irrelevant; you still grieve.
ANNA NAPOLI

At the funeral viewing, a well-meaning cousin said, "You should not be sad. This should be a time of celebration. Your dad is in heaven!" I knew that, but I wanted to scream, "I want him here on earth! I will miss him!" How could I celebrate losing my father until eternity begins for me? RAELENE PHILLIPS

It did not help me when, while at the viewing, people said, "Your father looks so natural. He looks so good." I just wanted to scream, "He doesn't look good. He looks dead." I wish, instead of trying to encourage me, people would have commiserated with me and understood how horrible it was that he died. EMILY WHITE

The worst thing I remember was a minister from my brother's church who came to the emergency room and talked nonstop. I actually had to leave the room because his chatter was so offensive. I have no idea what he was saying; he just talked too much. SUE ROBERTS

"It's a good thing your dad didn't live with you. You hardly saw him, so his death is not so much of a loss." ANONYMOUS

A few weeks after my dad's death, my friends told me that they were tired of my being sad, and if I didn't stop it, they didn't want to be around me. I wasn't fun anymore. ANONYMOUS

WHAT HELPS ME

"I'm sorry for your loss."

"Do you want to talk about it?"

"How are you feeling?"

"We love you and we will pray for you."

"I'm sorry you have to go through this."

"Your faith and strength inspire me."

"I know it hurts."

"I don't know what to say."

"Even though he needed a lot of your time, I know you'll miss his company."

The chaplain at the hospital was very helpful. She spoke directly but softly and kept telling us that everyone was going to handle this crisis differently. SUE ROBERTS

One thing that was said to me that was most helpful was spoken one time when I was crying with my brother. I said, "I just wish things could get back to normal." Johnny said, "Raelene, things will never be normal again. But we will have a new kind of normal someday." He was right. It took a fairly long time to develop, but there is a new kind of normal. What was so helpful is that he told the truth, gently, in love. He did not say, "Oh, we will be back to normal before long." It gave me hope to look for that new normal. RAELENE PHILLIPS

The best things said were from the neighbors, friends, and former students and their parents who shared how my mother's life had made a difference in their lives. PENELOPE CARLEVATO

I want to hear my dad's name used.

WHAT I WISH PEOPLE UNDERSTOOD

After being at the hospital every day for four months, my emotions were raw, and all I needed was love and tenderness, not sermons or advice. RAELENE PHILLIPS

When a parent dies, it makes you face your own mortality. I moved up to my mother's place in the family. I became the matriarch. I am the oldest daughter, and I guess that was the natural progression of things. EVELYNE TIMBERLAKE

The most important need for me was to talk honestly about all the confusing emotions. Both of my parents were ill in different and difficult ways. I had essentially lost my parents long before they died, and I had become the parent. Even though the burden of their care was lifted, there was a void in my life. With both of my parents gone, I had no one to take care of but me, and that was the strangest feeling of all. SUE ROBERTS

The best input anyone gave me was from my mother. She said, "There is not a right or wrong way to grieve." I did not need to feel guilty for my feelings, no matter what they were. She gave me permission to handle my grief in my own way. Later that night, I couldn't stand to stay in the house and focus on the tragedy. Mom let me go to the movies with a friend. That was the best thing she could have done. EMILY WHITE

I think it's important to remember that time becomes suspended in the early days after a trauma. So much happens so quickly that it is hard to absorb the flood of cards and calls that come immediately, so let some time pass and communicate again. SUE ROBERTS

I wish more people understood the long-term effects of grieving. I cried more in the years following my father's death than in the weeks following. I got a lot of attention after he died, but people fail to realize the loss I felt when my father wasn't there to see me graduate from high school or college, to see me get married, or to meet his grandchild. I wish people would sympathize with me over the long-term effects of having a parent die. EMILY WHITE

I wish people understood the loneliness I felt as the only child still at home. My dad worked two jobs, so he was gone a lot in the evenings. DONELLE WEST

Losing a mother is one of the hardest things for a daughter because there is no other relationship like this one on earth, and nothing prepares you for losing her. No matter how old we are or how old or sick she is, it hurts. PENELOPE CARLEVATO

Understand that the seemingly silliest thing may trigger an emotional response. When I was young, my mother often played Teresa Brewer songs on the piano while my sister and I sang and danced. Several years after Mother's death, I attended a Dino concert, and when he began to play a Teresa Brewer selection, I fell apart. It caught me, and those around me, totally off guard. LINDA GILDEN

Grieving is individual and personal. No two people grieve alike. We need to accept and love people where they are. EVELYNE TIMBERLAKE

My mom told me, "Whatever the relationship and respective ages of the father or mother and the child, it's always hard to lose a parent." If the relationship is good, the child will miss the parent's continued companionship and good counsel. However, if the relationship is strained or the parent has been abusive, the child is left with no hope

of ever reconciling with his or her parent in this lifetime.
LINDA JEWELL

I "lost" my mother to alcoholism and mental illness, something that can damage a young girl or an adult of any age who still needs a mom. But, as He promises, God brought another woman into my life to replace the "years the locusts had eaten." This woman saw my need and, as Christ would have done, she has loved me, encouraged me, laughed, cried, and shared her wisdom with me. God gives us many parents in life. Although no one can take the place of our natural children, I thank God that Florence Littauer has chosen to take many in as her daughters, including me. ROSE SWEET

WHAT YOU CAN DO

I was caring for my father, husband, and three children. For an entire week after my mom died, our church delivered home-cooked meals to our home every night. I didn't have to think about feeding anyone; just knowing the meals would be brought was a blessing. It was a wonderful way to show love and support. I also knew by all the cards that people were praying for me. Words at a time like that are inadequate, but the "hands on" said it all. The old saying "Actions speak louder than words" is so true. EVELYNE TIMBERLAKE

After my father died, I most appreciated those who just hugged me, patted my back, perhaps cried with me, but said nothing.
RAELENE PHILLIPS

The most helpful food item was a basket that arrived the day before the funeral filled with breakfast foods, bagels, and yogurt. It was all consumed and was different from anything else. When providing food, be aware of how many people will be around and for how long. More than one person brought expensive hams. I know it was very thoughtful, but they required preparation. A small tray of prepared sandwiches is more helpful than a huge ham. SUE ROBERTS

One friend spent about four hours just sitting on one sofa while I sat on the other. His presence meant the world to me. My friends found things to do I never knew had to be done, like staying in the house to receive food during the funeral. Friends of different faiths came to the memorial Mass. Parish members I didn't even know came to pray.

Later, one friend helped me empty my mother's apartment and brought sons to haul things. ANNA NAPOLI

Three friends from church came over as soon as they heard we were home from making arrangements at the funeral home and did two things: They brought a ham and two loaves of bread so that we could make sandwiches anytime without having to open cans or mix ingredients, and they sat with me, sometimes talking, sometimes listening, and remaining silent the rest of the time. They were just there, not acting as if they had to entertain, distract, or comfort me. They were available if I felt there was a need I had that they could help meet, but no one was pressured to do or say anything in particular. Their "withness" was their witness to me in my time of sorrow. MARY LIBBY PAYNE

Members of my choir sent me money when my ex-husband died. He had been providing child support for our son. They answered a practical, immediate, and tangible need. Two members helped us above and beyond what we could have wished for. They provided the funds for my son to be a kid for a while and go snowboarding with his friends. Their gifts also allowed him to get some much-needed new clothes. ANONYMOUS

After my mother and father died within eighteen months of each other, there were some out-of-town friends who were unable to attend the funerals. I invited them to come to my house for a "Mel and Bertha Willett weekend." I used my mom's recipes and cooked the foods my mother was most known for. I showed off the wooden pieces my father had made for me. We shared favorite stories about my parents and looked at picture albums full of memories for all of us. Finally, we went out to the cemetery, talked some more, and then we prayed as we all stood holding hands. MARILYN HEAVILIN

My parents were divorced, and my dad died before I was sixteen. One family, consistently and without being asked, invited me to dinner in their home almost every week. I was able to laugh or cry there. I could just fall asleep on their couch or get help with my homework. It was a place where I felt God's love and support. I wasn't being pushed to "get over it" while I was there. ANONYMOUS

Friends from church provided for my needs. They took me to their home the night my mom died. The pastor's wife came to clean our home a few times. People showing up was a great comfort. Just having them there, even when they didn't know what to say, and having warm bodies around was helpful. DONELLE WEST

My mother and a friend had started a Bible study twenty years ago. They had met every Tuesday for the past twenty years. They invited me to attend one week. The ladies shared many things about my mother—what she had done and how she blessed their lives. PENELOPE CARLEVATO

What we do as parents has an impact upon our children. We can remove the stigma or worry about being around someone who has just experienced the death of a loved one. When we live out our words in actions, our children remember, as demonstrated in the following story.

I had just walked into the house when Mother said, "Don't take off your coat. We have to go next door. Miss Howard's mother just died, and she needs us." Miss Howard had been my fifth-grade teacher; now I was a high school senior, and I was sure Miss Howard did not need me. I had no idea what to say. Daddy was the wordsmith. Why couldn't we wait until he got home? I was going to feel like a fool. Surely I would be a liability, not an asset, in this situation.

But my mother, my timid mother, would have none of it. *She will expect me to do the talking, and I am at a loss for words,* I thought. In moments, we were across the driveway and headed upstairs to Miss Howard's apartment. Miss Howard answered the door and just fell into Mother's arms sobbing. Mother didn't say anything. She just hugged Miss Howard, patted her on the back, and wept with her. They stood there a long time in silence until Miss Howard's sobs subsided. Miss Howard introduced us to the other people in the room. Miss Howard hugged me and thanked me profusely for coming and then went on to tell someone that I was not only her neighbor, but also a star pupil many years before.

I didn't have to say a word. After a while, Mother told Miss Howard that we would have to be going but to call on us anytime and we would be right over. My mother, not my eloquent daddy, had been the best ministering angel in that room. That which I dreaded most—not knowing what to say, or worse still, saying the wrong thing—never presented itself. We took nothing except our love, but it had been enough. Now, even decades later, when I hear of the loss of a parent, I know that God does not require us to know what to do or say. He just says, "Go!" He will take care of the rest.

A friend of mine talks about Christians being "Jesus with skin on." My mother was a very smart woman, usually underappreciated, but it was her love, not her intellect, that educated me that day.

MARY LIBBY PAYNE

WHAT TO WRITE IN A CARD

When my dad died, I received almost one hundred cards in the first few weeks. In the midst of making funeral plans, caring for Mom, my own grief, and visiting with family, I found I did not take the time to read the printed part of the sympathy card if there was more than a sentence or two on it. I did however, read every word that was handwritten. I was especially blessed by the cards that included kind words and special remembrances written about my dad. One of my favorites said, "My memories of your dad are of a dashing man with a charming smile and twinkling eyes." A smile grew in my heart as I thought about my dashing dad, his charming smile, and twinkling eyes. Another wrote, "Your father has left a dynamic legacy." My cousin Deirdre, wrote, "Your father had the unique ability to fill a room with joy and make each person in it feel special." Two other people referenced Dad's graciousness when they wrote, "Your father was a special man and always gracious and kind to us;" and "I was impressed with his gentleness and caring."

I have kept all of the cards that were sent to me, and I will make a scrapbook with them and include photos taken during that week, the program from Dad's service, the e-mails we sent out to everyone, and the obituaries from the various newspapers. One of the important aspects of receiving sympathy cards is that I can reread them later, when time is not at such a premium. I was unable to absorb much of what was said at the time, but as I look over the cards now, I am bathed in a sense of compassion and love.

If you are not a close friend of the family, be sure to include how you know them. Include a way that your friend's parent touched your life. Share something that you will always remember about his or her parent. Include a special memory or experience you shared with the parent. Mention a good quality that the parent had that is shared by your friend. Be sure to sign your last name to the card, unless you are a very close friend.

I encourage people to put something in writing. One of the most precious remembrances were letters that people wrote to me telling of memories of Mom in earlier days. They wrote notes telling her good qualities and of happier days. I saved all the notes and reread them many times. They helped me during the grieving process.
SUE ROBERTS

I just heard from Mom about your father's death. It is always hard to lose a parent. Mom speaks highly of you—I know that you are precious to my mother. LINDA JEWELL

PRAYER

Lord, we come to You today with heavy hearts. (name of hurting friend) has lost his/her mother/father. Lord, You know the deep grief that comes with this loss no matter how much we've prepared for it or know it is coming. You know the emptiness that remains. We thank You for the life of (name of hurting friend)'s mother/father. Help (name of hurting friend) to grieve through the loss and to work through all the various emotions that may need expression. Thank You that Your Word promises that You will be near those who have a broken heart and who need comfort. Please be with (name of hurting friend) today and in the days to come. Bring peace to the places of unrest and healing to the emptiness. Thank You that Jesus came to bind up the brokenhearted. Amen.

LOSS by SUICIDE

No death is ever easy, but to lose a loved one because of suicide is an especially complicated, devastating kind of loss. Don't shy away because this is an awkward situation. Your friend will need you now more than ever. Lovingly and prayerfully reach out quickly by paying a visit, phoning, or sending a card. Once you have made the initial contact, your following interactions will become easier. Suicide is often inappropriately shrouded in shame for the family. Be supportive of them and their loved one by releasing them of any guilt or shame they may feel. They couldn't have known. They were loving and supportive to their loved one. Your nonjudgmental, unconditional love may be the only light they have in this dark and long tunnel of loss.

WHAT HURTS ME

"I'm so sorry for your loss. It's a shame Jay committed the one unforgivable sin when he took his own life." My friend couldn't show me where it says that in the Bible.

"How does it feel not knowing if your son went to heaven because he committed suicide?" Jay accepted Jesus Christ as his Lord and Savior in May of 1995. That is the way into heaven. He died only three months later.

"Jay was so intelligent and had everything going for him; how could he do such a stupid thing?" Not one of us escapes foolish or inappropriate choices in our lifetime.

"Did you ever feel it was wasted time and energy on your part to raise him since his promising life was barely beginning?"

"How could you not know something was wrong with your son?" Jay was a successful young businessman who lived apart from us. The only times he came to our home were when he was "up" or happy. It is easy not to know about a person if he or she chooses not to let you know.

"Did you ever blame yourself?" I did at first, but now I have come to understand suicide is a personal decision. It is an escape from pain, despair, or hopelessness. Suicide is a permanent solution to a temporary situation. This situation cannot be changed or lightened by blaming myself or anyone else. As much as we may want to, we cannot make other people's choices for them.

ALL CONTRIBUTIONS ABOVE ARE FROM BJ JENSEN

It's been thirteen years since my father committed suicide. Invariably, after people find out my father is no longer living, they ask how he died. The conversation always turns awkward when I have to tell them he committed suicide. I've even had people ask how he did it. These people didn't know my father or me at the time. I wish they would say, "I'm sorry you lost your father," and leave it up to me to reveal the details if I want to. EMILY WHITE

Do not imply that the person who committed suicide is going to hell. We are not God and do not know anyone else's spiritual heart. ANNA RICH

"I can't believe your loved one did this." [1]

"We always knew she seemed a little off-balance or a little crazy." [2]

"I know your children are horrified by this terrible death." [3]

Avoid questions like "Didn't you know?" "Couldn't you stop him?" "How are you going to live with this shame?" [4]

WHAT HELPS ME

Instead of misguided inquiries, I would have been more comforted by words of encouragement on what a good person Jay was, how we had done a good job raising him the best we could, or the fond memories about how our son had positively impacted their lives. BJ JENSEN

One of the best responses to a suicide that I have ever heard came through a sermon delivered by the pastor of a young man who shot himself. With great eloquence, his pastor was able to convey tremendous hope through these words: "Our friend died on his own battlefield. He was killed in action, fighting a civil war. He fought against adversaries that were as real to him as his casket is real to us. They were powerful adversaries. They took a toll on his energies and endurance. They exhausted the last vestiges of his courage, and only

God knows how this child of His suffered in the silent skirmishes that took place in his soul."[5]

WHAT I WISH PEOPLE UNDERSTOOD

One of the most devastating times imaginable in the life of parents is the death of a child. In our case, the loss was compounded because our son committed suicide as a young adult. The totally unexpected and shocking blow that this loss was to our family was excruciating to us for months, if not for years. BJ JENSEN

I realize it is awkward to comfort the parents of a suicide victim because there is no protocol to follow. Just know that it is a difficult loss, and all loss is painful. BJ JENSEN

A suicide is no less emotionally difficult than an accidental or illness-related death. That person is still gone, and the family still misses him or her terribly.

My husband was really angry with Danny for hurting me. His anger and outbursts didn't help me with my grief process. After six months, he thought I should be farther along in my grief and should have come to terms with Danny's death.

Danny was an adult and made the decision to commit suicide. My attempts to help my son didn't make a difference to his ultimate decision. The mind-set of someone contemplating suicide is not the same as someone who is not depressed. His or her mind is not working the same as ours.

I wish friends and family would talk about Danny and mention his name.

CONTRIBUTIONS ABOVE ARE FROM VICKI SMOLA

Suicide exploded into my life when I was nine years old and forever changed my world. Following my father's suicide, I was immediately whisked away to another state to stay with relatives. No one ever mentioned my father or the circumstances of his death again. That silence signaled to me that suicide was a subject you didn't discuss. I felt great shame and anger regarding my father's death. By the time I was a teenager, I was experiencing suicidal ideation myself. More than anything, suicide survivors—those left behind—need to talk about what they are thinking and feeling. Otherwise, the grieving process will be agonizingly delayed. I know from personal experience. [6]

I wrote this poem after almost a year of sleepless nights following my eighteen-year-old brother's suicide.

Another sleepless night.
I guess I am trying to figure out why, Bart, why you left us.
It must get easier.
It has to get easier, but almost a year, and it just seems more
*   painful.*
I never knew you were in such incredible pain.
Why couldn't you share it? Did I fail you?
Why did you go? Wouldn't you miss me?
How could you leave me?
If you saw our pain, I know you wouldn't have left.
I miss you, little brother. Life was so hard for you.
Did you ever really have a chance?
Why did I make it, and you didn't?
How difficult life was for you.
I guess you must be at peace. Now, finally.
I know Jesus understands your heartache like no one ever
*   could.*
He's taking care of you now, but I miss you.

SUZY RYAN

WHAT YOU CAN DO

A long-standing and dear friend made sure I had a flower arrangement waiting for me when I returned home the first day after learning of my son's suicide.

Let me talk and tell my story, even if you've heard it before.

My brother arranged for and took me to a counselor that specialized in suicide counseling.

My sister went with me the next day to the neighboring state to get my son's ashes and help me deal with his estranged wife.

ALL CONTRIBUTIONS ABOVE ARE FROM VICKI SMOLA

While I navigated through the healing process, it lifted me when people telephoned but didn't talk too long.

I didn't like being asked, "How are you doing?" Naturally, I was not doing very well at all. However, when they asked, "What are you doing?" or "How is work?" I felt the freedom to share my anguish or just talk about something not so painful.

A couple of friends called twice a week during the first year just to let me know that they hadn't forgotten about my grief. This kindness carried me through many dark days.

I savored reading and rereading notes of sympathy. Unlike phone calls, there was no pressure for me to respond or explain how I felt in the midst of my nightmare.

The greatest gift a person could give me was permission to deal with this tragedy in my own time and in my own way.

CONTRIBUTIONS ABOVE ARE FROM SUZY RYAN

Treat a suicide death like any other loss of a loved one. [7]

Hug the survivors. Some people act almost like suicide is "catching" and touching the surviving family members will contaminate them. [8]

Mention positive qualities about the suicide victim. Remember the victim by the good things about him or her, rather than the act of suicide. [9]

Allow the survivors to talk about their grief, even if they are upset to the point of anger. [10]

Be aware of the fears and anxieties of surviving children. If possible, provide a fun activity for surviving children like a movie, a trip to the mountains, or an opportunity to play with other children. [11]

WHAT TO WRITE IN A CARD

Pick cards of sympathy for suicide carefully. Read them all the way through, and be certain the sentiments are appropriate for this loss. What if your father or sister had just committed suicide? What do you want said in a note? Always write positive things about your friend's loved one. Don't reference depression, struggles, or negative qualities in your note. Share your shock, just as you would with any sudden death, without any inference of judgment. When someone loses a loved one to suicide, making the initial contact by sending a card is crucial to opening up future lines of communication and reassuring him or her of your continued support. Use the suggestions in the previous chapters for the appropriate relationship:

❖ If you are not a close friend of the family, be sure to include how you know the deceased.

❖ Include a way that your friend's loved one touched your life. Share something that you will always remember about their relationship.

❖ Include a special memory or experience you shared with your friend's loved one.

❖ Be sure to sign your last name to the card, unless you are a very close friend.

PRAYER

Lord, we come to You with heavy hearts, filled with confusion and unanswered questions. We don't understand. This grief is more than we can bear. You know our pain and our sorrow. Please bring peace to the places of unrest and healing and forgiveness to places of hurt and brokenness. We ask that You wrap Your arms of compassion and comfort around (name of hurting friend) right now. May we rest in Your presence as we look to You for peace amidst our unrest. Amen.

LOSS of a FAMILY MEMBER or SPECIAL FRIEND

Grammy Chapman had been the quiet, gentle nurturer in my life. As a child, when I was sick, she would come over and stay with me all day, fix cream of tomato soup, sit by my bed, and put cold washcloths on my forehead. When I was a teen, she was always available to listen to my stories and tales of woe. When I became a parent, it was Grammy Chapman who had time to read stories—seemingly nonstop—to my young children and play endless games of Go Fish, Chutes and Ladders, and Candyland. It was my privilege to have Grammy spend the last three years of her life living with me. When she died, it was not the loss of a distant relative, but that of a treasured lifetime companion.

As the support community, we do not always know the depth of the relationship when a family member or special friend dies. Take time to learn about your friend's loved one. What role did the loved one play in your friend's life; what relationship did they have? You will then be able to provide support, comfort, and compassion. Much of what is in the previous chapters on loss will be appropriate here as well. You may want to go back and reread those sections to give you additional input.

WHAT HURTS ME

"She had a long and happy life." Although Grammy Chapman had a full life and is with the Lord, we still miss her. I still expect to see her sitting in her chair by the window reading a story to my son, hulling strawberries, or crocheting an afghan.

"You shouldn't feel that way." Don't correct or minimize feelings. Don't tell the person how he or she should or shouldn't feel.

Don't use clichés or pat answers such as "Time heals all wounds"; "Life goes on"; or "Just put it behind you." These expressions trivialize the person's loss. SHIRLEY GIBBS

"Be glad he didn't suffer." "Be happy she had such a good life." These types of comments are said in an attempt to "cheer us up" or have us "look on the bright side." We don't want to be cheered up, and we don't see any "bright side." We are sad, and we want you to share our loss with us.

WHAT HELPS ME

"I know you had a very special relationship with _____. I'm sure you will miss him or her." Acknowledge the special relationship they had and that you know the loved one will be missed.

"I am so sorry to hear of your loss. Was it sudden, or had he or she been ill?"

"He or she was always such fun to be around. I'm sure this is hard on you."

"I want to stand beside you as you move through this difficult time."

"I always enjoyed your _____. I will miss him or her too."

WHAT I WISH PEOPLE UNDERSTOOD

After a series of deaths in my family, I felt numb. My world seemed out of sorts, as if it were a dream or a bad nightmare. The worst part of the ordeal was sharing this with Christians and having them say absolutely nothing. Not even one of the five pastors of our church said anything. Their silence was a killer. I learned how to comfort because of the compassion and comfort I did not receive. There are some simple words like, "I am so sorry to hear that," or "May I pray for you right now?" Even the simple gesture of a genuine hug would be more meaningful than silence. JACQUELINE CROSS

WHAT YOU CAN DO

I was approaching the one-year anniversary date of my brother Laird's death. My friend Karen called and asked if I wanted to have a "Laird" day with her. She invited me to lunch and asked me to bring some pictures of Laird. At first, I was leery about it because it seemed so intimate, and I didn't know if I could talk about him without coming apart at the seams. But on that morning, I woke up with an excitement about the day. I grabbed all the pictures I could find and met Karen. She had set a table with her finest linens and dishes. She served me lunch and asked questions about my precious brother. As we shared, I told her that the one issue that bothered me the most was not that he died, but that I wanted to know what purpose there had been in his life. As I talked, I began to see a pattern; Laird was always bringing home stray and unlovable people. Suddenly, there was a knock at Karen's door. This was very unusual because we were out in the country. When we opened the door, there was an unkempt and distraught young woman. She asked if she could talk to us. We let her in, tried to calm her down, and asked about her life. She was grieving the death of her daddy. When I asked her when he had died, she said, "January 10, 1996." It was five years ago that day, and the exact day as Laird's death! We spent more time with her, and when she left, I felt the Lord had shown me that Laird's life had not been in vain. Laird had indeed been a friend to the friendless and had served his purpose on earth with dignity and grace. Peace settled over me, and I have been celebrating his life ever since. Karen's great sacrifice of time with me meant more than we ever dreamt it would.

SHARLEEN THORNBERRY

When I lost my brother in a tragic accident four days after Thanksgiving, I was unable to face the Christmas season. I felt robbed of my joy and wondered if I would ever again feel the excitement at the season of Christ's birth. We had two young daughters, and I knew they needed something to look forward to, but it just was not in me. One night I received a call from my new pastor. He said he couldn't help but notice we didn't have a Christmas tree up. He wondered if I minded if he took our girls to pick one out. They were so excited that I let them go. Not long after they left, the doorbell rang. It was the pastor's sister with a lasagna dinner, complete with salad, French bread, and dessert. She explained that when her father died, a friend had done the same for her, and it had been a big help.

Soon the kids returned with the most beautiful tree. My pastor and his fourteen-year-old son helped them string the lights and decorate the tree. I was touched beyond words by these acts of kindness, knowing how busy everyone is during the holidays. As I sat by the fire long into the night, which I had been doing for weeks, I could not help but feel my spirits lifted and my heart aching a little less. We had never experienced this kind of generosity from people we hardly knew, and I was overwhelmed by their unselfish gestures. That act of Christian love meant more to me than I can ever express.

As I surveyed the room that night, my eyes fell on the nativity scene and the beautiful lighted star our pastor's son had painstakingly mounted above it in the window. An incredible sense of peace entered my heart as I realized for the first time the true significance of the Christmas season. The greatest present I could ever receive was knowing that Jesus had come to offer us the gift of eternal life, and that several years before, my brother had accepted that gift. While I know life for our family on earth will never quite be the same without Tim, I have the assurance that he is in heaven. One day we will have a joyous family reunion! SHERRI VILLARREAL

WHAT TO WRITE IN A CARD

When my grandmother passed away, I received many touching cards. One friend wrote, "I have always admired you for the caring and patience you have shown in taking care of your grandmother. I'm sure being a part of your home enriched her life." It was special to know that my friend saw the effort it took to have Grammy with us, but she also knew the special relationship we had.

Another friend wrote, "Having lost my grandma, I can relate to the loss you are feeling. No one can take the place of a dear grandma." If you have shared a similar experience, share that in your note. Your friend does not, however, need to have all the minute details of your tragedy.

It is wise to include what the individual meant to you. One mother in our church wrote, "Grammy was always cheerful and interested in my baby Jacob. I will remember her fondly. Grammas are such precious gifts. (I still miss mine after fourteen years.)"

My grandmother's sister wrote me a letter shortly after Grammy's death and said, "Thanks to you for being such a caring granddaughter to her. She said so many times you were the one person who seemed to care what happened to her. Needless to say there were many others, but you had the knack of letting her know your feelings." That comment from my great-aunt made all my efforts on Grammy's behalf worthwhile. What a blessing a few sentences can be to an aching heart!

As with other losses, be sure to identify yourself and tell the family how you knew their loved one.

Share a special quality that you admired about the deceased, how he or she made an impact in your life, or an interesting experience you shared.

All that we love deeply becomes a part of us. I know how much you loved _____. He will always be a part of you. May the precious memories of the wonderful times you shared be a comfort to you.

If you did not know the person who died, say so—but add, "I wish I'd had the opportunity to know _____. From what you've told me, I know she was a special person."

PRAYER

Dear Lord, we come to You today with broken and sad hearts. This very special (<u>uncle, grandmother, friend, etc.</u>) has died and leaves a real void in our lives. Please wrap (<u>name of hurting friend</u>) in Your arms of love and comfort. Help us to remember the blessing he/she has been to us. May we rest in the memory of the joys they shared together. Come beside (<u>name of hurting friend</u>) and his/her family at this time of loss. Amen.

LOSS *of* HOME *or* POSSESSIONS

The loss of a home or possessions is often viewed as a materialistic loss, and we tend to minimize its significance and impact. Often overlooked are the irreplaceable family heirloom-type items that are lost and the huge amount of time, effort, and money it will take to rebuild after such a loss. A trunk full of baby clothes, a box of school memorabilia, photo albums, and baby books are the kinds of things no one and no amount of insurance can replace.

My mom lost her *Good News Bible* on an airplane. It was the first Bible she purchased when she became a Christian, and she had been studying and speaking out of it for over twenty years. It had all of her original markings she had written as she made spiritual discoveries for the first time. She said, "I've never studied and marked up the Bible the same way since I lost that Bible."

There are emotional connections to our things that make a dramatic impact on us when they are lost. I lost the onyx stone out of an antique ring my Grammy Littauer gave me. A few years later, the beautifully filigreed mounting was crushed. I looked in antique stores for twenty years before I found a ring that was similar. I now wear that ring almost every day as a precious reminder of my grandmother's love, even though it is not the same ring.

WHAT HURTS ME

"Call me if you need anything." I never asked. I was all alone.
PAT LINK

"I bet it would be fun to get to buy all new things and start fresh."

"This time you'll get a new house built from the ground up instead of having to remodel."

"Remember, our home is really in heaven."

"Store up treasures in heaven, not here on earth." Don't try to spiritualize an earthly loss.

"You'll probably have a nicer house than you had before." I didn't really care about what I might have in the future. All I could think about was what we had lost. BARBARA BUELER

WHAT HELPS ME

"I've been a part of many wonderful times in your home."

"I can't begin to imagine what this must be like for you. I want to help you." Make a specific offer of what you can do to help.

"Nothing can undo this tragic loss, but I want to work with you to rebuild your life."

"I can see how precious that _____ is to you. Nothing can ever replace it."

"I have been praying for you ever since I got the news. How may I help you?" Offer some ideas of what you are willing and available to do.

WHAT I WISH PEOPLE UNDERSTOOD

Once we moved into a rented house, it seemed as if most of our friends stopped calling. People had been so helpful immediately following the fire, but then it seemed as though they thought their job was done. I desperately needed people to stay close and be my friends. When I did receive the casual, "How are you doing?" I knew all they wanted to hear was, "I'm doing just fine." I didn't feel free to tell those people how lonely I was, how overwhelmed I was by the things I had to do. I needed people who would keep me involved, help me move, and see what they could do for me. BARBARA BUELER

We had to purchase everything new with little money to our name. PAT LINK

I had to face the fact that all my possessions were gone. There were family heirlooms and personal things that meant so much to me. I had a trunk filled with the children's baby shoes, clothes, and special things I'd saved to give them when they got married. It is still hard to believe that in ten minutes, it was all gone. There is nothing fun about this devastation. BARBARA BUELER

WHAT YOU CAN DO

A crew of friends arrived to help clear the debris. Just when the crew was getting hungry, a woman I had met only once pulled in the driveway, dropped down the back of her station wagon, and announced, "Here's lunch." She'd cooked several big lasagna casseroles and made garlic bread and a salad. There was enough food for everyone.

Knowing that we had nothing but the clothes on our backs, Lauren volunteered to buy some essentials, if I would just write down our sizes. When she arrived, I realized that I was stalling. I hadn't thought about what we needed, let alone the sizes. "Barbara, I know you'll need underwear, shoes, cosmetics, nightgowns, and much more. I want to help you." We went to the department store to shop. There, among the racks of clothes, reality suddenly hit me. I don't even own a single nightgown! Totally overwhelmed, I sat in a chair in the shoe department while Lauren shopped throughout the store, gathering the essentials my family needed. I was so thankful to have a friend who cared enough about us to shop for me and start me thinking about the future.

As word got out about the fire, bags of clothing of every kind, color, and size—from fuchsia polyester pants to black mini-skirts—began arriving. Some things people knew would fit and were appropriate for our family, but many others were their castoffs—old and worn out.

Ladies from church held a starting-over shower for me. Most of the things they brought were very practical, like appliances, linens, and tableware. But it was also fun to get some nonessentials like a beautiful crystal bud vase and a set of delicate stemware.

I truly appreciated those who invited us over for dinner, especially since I couldn't reciprocate.

ALL OF THE ABOVE WERE CONTRIBUTED BY BARBARA BUELER

Purchase a journal for your friend. When you are together, record memories of special things that happened in that home, items that were lost, and sentimental stories that went with the things that were destroyed.

Because of my loss, I know to just "do" for people. I make suggestions of what I can do when I check in with them, but I don't leave the ball in their court to call me to help them. PAT LINK

All of our photo albums were destroyed. All the pictures of our children were gone. Friends went through their photos to find pictures of our family. They made copies and gave them to us. We began to compile new albums with the pictures we were given.

My principal drove me out of the glowing ashes that were the remains of my home. That evening, there was a knock on the door of my motel room. There stood one of my teacher friends. She hugged me with all sincerity, handed me a peanut patty, sat by my side in silence, and then left me to my solitude. Often, we had shared one of those hard, red, sugary, peanut-filled delights when we had a difficult day at school. It brought such joy to my soul. It was a ray of sunshine. It conveyed to me that she shared in my pain and the importance of the little things in life. That was twenty-six years ago. To this day when someone suffers a great loss, I am reminded that just my presence and something as small as a peanut patty speak all the words one needs to hear. CYNTHIA THOMAS

WHAT TO SAY IN A CARD

I can't believe this happened! I will be with you, and together we will work to rebuild your lives.

You are in my heart and in my prayers. I would like to spend every Monday with you, helping you _____.

I'm praying for you today, and tomorrow, too. I'm sure tomorrow must be frightening. I will be here for you.

You are a precious friend. May you find the courage to face tomorrow as you rest in the knowledge that we care.

May the love of those who care deeply surround you during this difficult time.

May you sense God's presence touching all that lies before you.

PRAYER

Lord, You know what a major loss this is for (<u>name of hurting friend</u>). The job before us seems overwhelming. We don't even know where to start. Help us to move forward, one day at a time, trusting You to supply all our needs. I want my friend (<u>name of hurting friend</u>) to know that I am here for the long haul. I will walk beside him/her as we begin to rebuild what has been lost. Father, You know the magnitude of this tragedy. You know all the special memories and family treasures that are gone. Bring comfort to (<u>name of hurting friend</u>)'s heart. We rest in the knowledge that You care and are ever-present in our lives. Amen.

LOSS *of a* PET

It is stronger than most marriages today, that union between

man and dog. Trust and honor, and at least one partner

that can keep your secrets, all bonded by unconditional love.

AS SEEN AT JACK'S IN MT. VERNON, OHIO, AUGUST 2002

When a much-loved pet is lost or dies, the resulting grief is very real. Moni was our first dog. One morning she began having convulsions, and we rushed her to the veterinarian. She survived for three days; then her liver failed, and she died. When Moni died, I cried for days. I kept hearing her bark and would expect to see her sleeping on the couch when I walked into the family room. Months later, we purchased a new miniature schnauzer who looked just like Moni; she even had some of the same champions in her pedigree. We looked at her and expected her to be Moni, but she was not. She was a new and different dog. When humans let us down, we can always depend on our pet to provide us with unconditional love. While I am away writing this chapter, I have a plush-toy miniature schnauzer sitting on the table to remind me of the three I have left at home. Our pets are a very important part of our lives.

WHAT HURTS ME

"Why are you so upset? He was only a dog!" A comment like this attempts to minimize the loss your friend is experiencing. You need to validate how special and loving the pet was and what a significant role he played in your friend's life.

Our two dogs died within a few months of each other. My dad said, "You should have put Puddles to sleep a long time ago. She's been looking 'pitiful' for a while now." He also said maybe it was good that

Mickey died while we were gone so we wouldn't have to see him die. I wanted to be with him, to comfort him and make sure he wasn't suffering any more than he had to. Other people tried to ease the pain of my dogs' deaths by telling me that they were old and had lived good, long lives. So what? I loved them and wanted them to live longer.
LUCY SEAY

"Don't worry, you can just buy a new cat." Each pet has a special spot in a person's heart, and getting a new pet will never replace the one that died.

WHAT HELPS ME

"I'm sorry for your loss. He or she was always a faithful companion."

"I know your pet was important to you."

"I'm so sorry. Don't be afraid to grieve. This is a real loss."

Share a happy or special memory you have of your friend's pet such as, "He was always there to greet me at the door." "I can still see her fetching that stick, time after time." "I loved watching you play with him." "She always wanted to sit right at your feet and would follow you wherever you went."

Several friends assured me that Mickey knew I loved him and that he appreciated how I had cared for him during the months he was sick.
LUCY SEAY

After I put my dog to sleep, my vet said, "I applaud your efforts." As I think about it later, his comment took away some of the guilt of having to make that decision. AES

WHAT I WISH PEOPLE UNDERSTOOD

An emotional response to the loss of a pet can be increased if there have been other significant losses in the family's lives already. When my pets died, it brought back all the other hurts I'd had in my life. This just added one more to them. Be sensitive to your friends' sadness when they've lost a pet.

People do not realize that pets need to be properly mourned, too.
ANNA NAPOLI

For Christmas, I gave my mom a miniature schnauzer puppy that I had bred. She loved little Sheba and doted on her. Somehow, Sheba was lost to the coyotes. For weeks after her disappearance, Mom thought she could hear the dog crying at the back door. She awoke in the night and went to the door thinking she had just heard the dog. She would start to fix Sheba's breakfast, only to remember she was gone. When we lose a pet, we keep expecting her to come around the corner. We keep seeing her, wishing for her.

My dogs are very important and precious to me. They are like our children. They are members of the family. They are a daily, sometimes hourly, part of our lives—and not having them anymore is a big change and leaves a big void in our home. LUCY SEAY

WHAT YOU CAN DO

A colleague sent a thoughtful card. Another friend helped me celebrate Nicodemus's life and dug his grave. It helped for people to acknowledge the importance of Nicodemus to me. He had been my cat for seventeen-and-a-half years, which is longer than many human relationships and marriages. ANNA NAPOLI

Many people sent sympathy cards. Two sets of neighbors came over to the house after they learned that Mickey had died. The women cried with me and hugged me. One woman brought me flowers. These sensitive friends treated me, and my feelings, with dignity and respect even though the death was that of an animal. My best friend, Sarah, called me regularly for several weeks after Mickey's death. LUCY SEAY

Portia had lived to be over sixteen years old. She was Ron and Karen's only "child." Her health and happiness were of great importance to them. She died, following a lengthy kidney problem. I continued to call to check on Portia's health, and when she died, I ordered a memorial brick with Portia's name, birth date, and death date on it. I didn't give it to them right away, but when I felt they could handle it, I presented them with the brick. They have placed it in their garden right where Portia loved to sun herself. It reminds them of the joy they had with her and how precious she was to them. Many mail order catalogues have memorial stones or plaques that you can order to honor a special pet.

Our choir director's miniature schnauzers died within one month of each other. The first Christmas after the deaths, I purchased two brass, doghouse tree ornaments with a place for a picture in each. On the card I wrote, "In memory of Anna and Mogford." I still buy him a miniature schnauzer calendar each year, even though he has chosen not to get another dog. Our schnauzers are a connection we share.

After having put Nicodemus to sleep, I received a sympathy note from my vet saying that a donation had been made in his name to U.C. Davis for the "Visiting Pets Program." Today, there is a pet visiting in Nicodemus's honor—bringing love. ANNA NAPOLI

We shared a funny experience with our friends, Fred and Linsey. On New Year's Eve, we were in the process of preparing some extravagant canapés and pouring our beverages in the kitchen. We heard some "chomping" coming from the living room. We discovered that their golden retriever, Gabe, had forty dollars' worth of foie gras in his mouth. We yelled, and Fred yanked the fois gras out of his mouth. Not willing to let such a delicacy go to waste, we washed and trimmed the foie gras and put it back on the serving dish. We have laughed about that moment for years. When Gabe reached the end of his life, we invited Fred and Linsey to our home. We honored Gabe by eating foie gras and toasting to his years of faithful companionship. "To Gabriel!"

Our friend's giant schnauzer died from eating snail bait that the gardener had left in the yard. The husband had just come home following some surgery. He was unable to bury their dog, Velvet. My son Randy, who was sixteen at the time, volunteered to dig the grave. Because Velvet was so big, he had to dig a hole 6' by 6'. I will never forget coming home that afternoon and seeing Randy's muddy shoes sitting on the front step. I knew he had finished burying Velvet. It was not easy or comfortable for Randy to dig that grave, but he stepped outside his own comfort and pleasure to help someone else.

WHAT TO WRITE IN A CARD

There are now many great cards honoring the life of a pet as a faithful companion. Be sure to add a personal note about your loved one's pet, a cute or funny memory you have, and a way you know the pet will be missed.

I know how special (<u>pet's name</u>) was to you. I always enjoyed seeing you walk him each evening.

Our pets are a beautiful demonstration of unconditional love. (<u>pet's name</u>) surely loved you.

All that we love deeply becomes a part of us.

I know you'll miss (<u>pet's name</u>). She always brought you such joy. I especially enjoyed watching her play with your children.

His deep brown eyes always had such love in them.

PRAYER

Dear Lord, You know how important our pets are. Please come beside (<u>name of hurting friend</u>) and bring him/her comfort at this very sad time. I can still see the love in (<u>pet's name</u>) eyes as he/she welcomed me whenever I came to the house. Our pets are such a beautiful example of unconditional love. Thank You for showing us love in that way. We will miss (<u>pet's name</u>) but are so thankful for the joy he/she brought to the family. I pray that memories of his/her life will bring comfort to (<u>name of hurting friend</u>) at this time. Thank You for caring about our every need and heartache. Amen.

WHEN YOU HEAR
the NEWS

W hen a family is facing the death of a loved one, there are so many things to tend to that it is a perfect time for friends to mobilize and put their love and concern into action. You'll have to take the initiative, because often the grieving person is too confused to judge what needs to be done. One person can't do everything, so it's a good idea for one friend to coordinate the project and see that all needs are being met.

Many churches have a family services ministry that springs into action whenever someone in their fellowship or community has a need. Usually one person serves as the coordinator and then calls volunteers to help with meals, baby-sitting, transportation, and other needs. Meeting a family's needs at a time of crisis is an ideal way for a church to minister, both to its own flock and to the community as well.

PROVIDE FOOD

The family will need meals before, as well as after, the funeral service. Find out approximately how many people will be with the family. This number will probably change daily. Check on dietary restrictions or preferences. Ask volunteers what they're bringing, or make suggestions to reduce duplications. Make sure there will be enough food as well as a variety of food. Suggest that the food be provided in disposable containers. If that is not possible, be sure the dishes are labeled to make them easier to return.

Because Mom, my sister, and I were out of state when my dad died, we flew home to an empty home with a virtually empty refrigerator. The first meal we had together, we ate out. The second evening, with nine people present, we went out to dinner as well at significant expense. Dad's service was one week after his death, and we needed meals for all seven days. The numbers we needed to feed continued to increase, as all four of his siblings and spouses flew in to be there, Mom's two brothers and their spouses arrived, and several of my cousins came as well. Toward the end of the week, we were serving twenty to thirty people at every dinner. The greatest tangible thing that was done for us at the time was to have fully-catered meals arrive. Groups of friends went together and arranged for a local caterer to provide meals for us. Each meal was large enough to feed us for two nights. My Uncle Bill and Aunt Virginia have a home in the same development as my parents, and by midweek, they hosted all the dinners there so Mom would not be involved in the preparation and cleaning process and could get needed privacy and rest.

Don't expect the bereaved to remember what you brought, even if you're a close friend. There is so much going on, and his or her mind is on overload. It is helpful to have a guest book in the kitchen to record what was delivered.

Following the death of her mother, Martha said, "Because people were preparing the meals, Dad ate. If he'd had to cook, I know he wouldn't have eaten."

Even though you may have arranged for meals to be prepared, see that there are staples on hand such as milk, cream, butter, coffee, and paper goods.

When Nancy's twenty-year-old daughter was killed in an auto accident, her home was nearly bombarded with family and friends. As we were cleaning up after the reception in Nancy's home, she said, "Guess what was the most useful thing that was brought here over the last few days?"

"The group-sized coffeepot from the church?" I asked.

"No," she said, "though that was good. The most useful thing was a bag filled with toilet paper, paper towels, paper napkins, paper plates, and plastic utensils. I would have been very embarrassed at the lack of toilet paper in this house had someone not done that."

Now, whenever someone dies, I run to the store, pick up lots of paper items, and head over to the family's home. I learned my lesson.

EVA MARIE EVERSON

MAKE PHONE CALLS

Many people will need to be called and informed. Ask family members whom they need to contact personally. (They may need someone with them when they make these calls.) Offer to call the rest of the people for them. Only make calls with the family's permission. Write down the basic information in order to be accurate. Say something like:

"This is Lauren Briggs. The Johnson family has asked me to call to let you know that their son, Robert, was fatally injured this morning in a car accident. Funeral services will be held at the Greenspot Mortuary, Tuesday at 2, and visitation will be there from 3–8 on Monday."

Offer to call the church prayer chain. If the family agrees, ask prayer chain members to pray for something specific. It might be "that Christ be glorified at the service"; "that the family will experience God's protection and strength"; "that Uncle John can be reached in time to attend the service."

MAKING ARRANGEMENTS

See if the family would like you or someone else to go with them to the funeral home to make final arrangements or to the cemetery to pick out a plot. They will want to make these decisions themselves, but having a friend for support who can be objective may be very helpful.

Do they wish to see their loved one? Be sure someone goes with them if they do. Did the death take place out of the area? Would they like someone to accompany the body?

Before the funeral, make yourself available to help the family prepare for the service. "I didn't know how to plan a funeral. My pastor suggested we do things that the deceased would have chosen.

We played a favorite CD instead of using the organ. That helped so much." LANA FLETCHER

What music is fitting? Are there some favorite verses to be read? Is there someone in addition to the minister who would want to share? Do they have a favorite poem? Does anyone wish to write a letter to the loved one to be read at the service?

When Miriam died of breast cancer, I went through her home and gathered things that I knew were important to her. I decorated the communion table at the front of the church with the items, including her favorite portrait, some of her artwork, and a piece of her unfinished embroidery. I draped it over the table and put the threaded needle in place as if she were making another stitch. Miriam had requested that our community chorus sing at her service because she had sung in the chorus for many years. We sang "His Eye Is on the Sparrow" and her favorite song, "Ubi Caritas," which says, "Where there is charity and love, God is there. … From a sincere heart, let us love one another."

ARRANGE FOR TRANSPORTATION

Family members may be flying in for the funeral, and they'll need to be picked up at the airport. Although the family may want to go themselves, they may be relieved to have you do it for them.

If they need an extra car for their visitors, see if you can find someone who has a car available.

FIND LODGING FOR GUESTS

Some relatives may stay in the family home, but there is proba-bly not enough room for everyone. You can help make other lodging arrangements. Find hotels or motels in the area. If everyone can stay at the same place, that is the best. Your community might even have a bed-and-breakfast that could accommodate visiting family.

Some may need a place to stay but are unable to afford a hotel. This might be just the time for an anonymous gift, or there may be a church family willing to have them as guests. Be sensitive to what the family wants and try to facilitate their wishes as much as possible.

PREPARE FOR CHILDREN

Will young children be arriving? Does the family need a portable crib, high chairs, car seats, or toys? Use the church's resources to find equipment or baby-sitters.

Children often sense the tension of a crisis and need special attention and love. Offer to baby-sit. Be creative with your care of the children. Depending on their ages, children often enjoy a trip to the ice cream parlor, the park, or maybe a pizza outing with other children.

Watch for special needs that arise. Offer to bathe the children and wash or set their hair before the service. For their emotional security, though, children should be with their parents at bedtime.

DO NEEDED HOUSEWORK

In the days following a death, many people will be visiting the bereaved family. See that some of the everyday household tasks are done, such as cleaning the bathrooms, making sure there is toilet paper, changing the sheets on the beds, vacuuming the floors, doing the laundry, and watering the plants. It will be comforting to know that when Aunt Edith arrives, she'll be sleeping on clean sheets.

In an effort to help her friend, Joyce took her cleaning lady to tidy her friend's house before the family started arriving. When she got there, Joyce realized that due to the deceased's lengthy illness, many things had been left undone. Joyce decided to stay and work with the cleaning lady to make sure everything was ready for company.

CHECK ON CLOTHING

Has your friend decided what she'll wear to the funeral? Does it need to be dry-cleaned? Does she want to go shopping? Does anyone need pantyhose? Do shoes need polishing?

As Bill was dressing for the funeral, he realized the shirt he always wore with his suit was still in the ironing pile. That was one more last-minute tension the family didn't need.

PROCESS THE OBITUARY

In times of stress some people can't write a simple sentence. They'd appreciate your help preparing the obituary. Be sure to include some special aspects of the person's life, checking to make sure what you've written is accurate. Help select a photograph. Phone it in or deliver it to the appropriate papers, including any out-of-town papers that should carry the notice. The mortuary can be helpful in providing a form to fill in for the obituary and placing it in the newspaper.

MEET UNIQUE NEEDS

Linda's son was three weeks old when her mother died. As a nursing mother, Linda was extremely grateful when a young woman she barely knew arrived at her door. She presented Linda with some of her frozen breast milk. "I pumped this in case you get low or need to leave Stephen for a while."

Linda said, "What meant even more than the milk was that somebody understood some of my concerns and took time to meet them."

Does someone need a wheelchair? Are there dietary needs to be met? Are there appointments that need to be canceled? Do hair or nail appointments need to be made?

When Karen's dad died, her husband's mom was in a wheelchair and needed assistance. I was asked to stay with her and take care of her needs while the rest of the family went to the graveside service. My husband drove family members to the graveside service while I stayed with Karen's mother-in-law.

PROVIDE SPECIAL TOUCHES

When my husband's mother died, we decided to have a picture of her at the memorial service in place of a casket. I suggested that we use one taken at our wedding, which was a special day for us all. I had it enlarged, framed, and then displayed, surrounded by flowers at the altar. I later used that picture as the first page in a memorial scrapbook. In it I put all the sympathy cards, floral cards, and letters we received. It clearly represents the love others expressed toward us at the time of our loss. Since they never had the opportunity to know her, it will help my children understand what their grandmother was like.

When my dad died, Mom chose a casket that looked like a silver box. She had a large floral casket spray bursting forth with red roses, topped with a huge, beautiful silver bow. We placed a copy of her book *Silver Boxes* on the casket beside the roses. The final quote on the service program was from Mom, saying, "You have always been my Silver Box, a giver of encouraging words. *Silver Boxes – The Gift of Encouragement* is one of Mom's most popular books and is a mainstay of her ministry. The book teaches how to lift up others through the giving of encouraging words like "little silver boxes with bows on top." Marita had prayer cards made to be given out at the visitation and the service that read,

> *Let no corrupt communication proceed out of your mouth, but that which is good to the use of edifying, that it may minister grace unto the hearers.* Ephesians 4:29 KJV

While our mother is the one who is known for the "Silver Box" concept, it is truly our father who originated the idea. Ephesians 4:29 was one of our family memory verses, drilled into our minds by our father. In his honor, we encourage you to carry this card with you, memorize this verse, and put the principle into practice in your life.

Please use this card as a prayer reminder. Pray for Mom and the entire Littauer Family.

THE LITTAUER CHILDREN

The day I came home from the hospital after losing my baby, my mom gave me a scrapbook and said, "It's so easy to remember the negative things and keep a record of wrongs. Use this book to keep a record of all the thoughtful things people are doing for you, such as bringing meals, watching Randy Jr., sending flowers, calling to say they're praying for you, and writing you cards." That book is a reminder of the light that shone in my darkness.

Ask if there are special remembrances the family would like to have on display such as a family Bible, a baby picture, or a special trophy.

CREATE MEMORY BOARDS

It is becoming quite popular to have photographic memory boards at the funeral home, church, or reception. When Aunt Katie died, her children had many family photographs all sorted out by time period. I arrived two days before the service and was able to help lay out and decorate the boards. We put them on easels in the reception hall with flowers decorating the easels. We reminisced as we put them together, and the people enjoyed the photographic memories of Aunt Katie's life.

I did a similar thing for our partner John, when his wife died at the age of fifty-three. His daughters prepared the boards, but I embellished them with silk flowers and beautiful ribbons. I also arranged the front of the church with the flowers and several family portraits. I saved the silk flowers and ribbons and made a floral arrangement for each daughter with the flowers I used for the memory boards.

BE AVAILABLE

Chris told me about a family whose son had died. She arrived shortly afterward and found the family so distraught they couldn't make any of the necessary arrangements. She'd worried all the way over about what she'd say when she got there, but she soon realized that she didn't have to say much. Just giving the family members a hug and telling them how sorry she was and how much she liked their son was enough.

After that, she did things to meet their physical needs. In the midst of their crisis, she had food on the table at mealtime, washed the dishes, and arranged for meals to be brought in.

Since the family hadn't started to make their phone calls, Chris asked whom they wanted notified. When they couldn't decide, with their permission, she began going through their phone list. She called their friends and let them know about John's death and the time of the funeral and encouraged them to visit the family.

Chris was there from eight in the morning until midnight for four days helping to meet the family's physical needs. During that time, she called the pastor and led her friends through the funeral arrangements. When it was over, the family told her thankfully, "We could never repay you for all you've done for us."

Chris responded, "Next time you have a friend in need, go to them and do the same thing for them. That's all the thanks I want."

As news of my father's death spread, family and friends began to gather, eager and willing to help. This is just a small sampling from my mother of the unusual things people did to help:

> Cal and Carolyn Walker flew in from Connecticut to be at my side. One day, they organized and cleaned the garage!
>
> Bob Barnes washed the kitchen floor.
>
> My son Fred planted those pots of flowers and did constant errands and needed repairs.
>
> Virginia bought new kitchen towels and pot holders. Every time I turned around, something new was happening.
>
> Marita had our phone switched to her office so we could have the business calls handled away from the house.
>
> Pat Knox made an emergency run to the store when Lauren had a run in her black pantyhose. FLORENCE LITTAUER

You can't follow every suggestion I've listed. Be sensitive and willing to help, and you will discern which needs you can meet. Use your talents, and do not put yourself under pressure to perform a task that is difficult or undesirable to you. Function within your gifts. Do things that you naturally enjoy. Remember, you are an extension of Christ. He wants to use you and the rest of His body to meet the bereaved's physical and emotional needs during this difficult time.

HELP *for the* FUNERAL

Why are funerals so difficult for us to attend? One reason is because they remind us of our own vulnerability. The other is we don't know what to expect or what to do. The following suggestions may help you relax and have the confidence you need to comfort the bereaved.

AT THE FUNERAL HOME

The family may set up a visitation time at the funeral home or at their home when friends can bring flowers, pay their respects, and sign the guest book. It usually occurs the night before the service and can be anytime from noon through 9:00 PM. Call the funeral home to find out whether there will be a visitation time, or look for a listing in the newspaper.

If the family is present when you visit, that means they want to be with you and want you to share their loss. Identify yourself and your relationship with the deceased and share some of your personal feelings with the family. The visitation is less formal than the funeral. Visit with the family members and share something special about their loved one. If there is an open casket, don't comment on how "natural" the person looks. Instead make reference to a special pin she is wearing; ask what it represents. Or comment on the choice of clothing. For example, "That was one of my favorite suits your mom is wearing." Even if the family has chosen cremation, there may still be visitation hours.

If there is no public visitation time, it is thoughtful to stop by the family home. Call first to see when would be a good time. Doing nothing is often seen as a lack of concern.

THE FUNERAL

Be sure to arrive promptly at the services so you have enough time to quiet your heart. It doesn't make the family feel the service was very important to you if you rush in at the last minute. As you sit there, think about the deceased and address your own feelings of loss. Remember what the person meant to you, the impact he or she had on your life, the ways God used the person to minister to you, and specific times you will miss him or her.

Express your own grief to the Lord. As you are praying, ask God to reveal what you can do to assist the family members during this time. Commit yourself to share their burdens and provide the comfort they need.

Be sure to sign the guest book. At such a stressful time, the family may not remember who attended, but they'll look over the guest book many times and thank God for the love each person showed.

When the funeral ends, you'll probably be dismissed by rows to walk by the family. If they're behind a curtain or divider, look toward them to express your sympathy; if they're seated out in the front section, be sure to greet them. You may not be able to give them a hug, but you can acknowledge them and hold out your hand to them. You may not be able to express your feelings in words, but your mere presence will be a comfort.

Often the family goes outside to wait for the casket to be placed into the hearse. That is a time you can greet them. Do you plan to be at the reception following the service? If not, let them know a specific time when you will see them in the near future. Whatever arrangements you make, be sure they know they can count on your tangible support. I find it easier to know what to say if I have something concrete in mind to do for them.

Plan to follow the family to the gravesite. Johnny Thiem was in the high school marching band with my sons. When he died of cystic fibrosis at the age of twenty-one, we went to the band room and got the school banner that usually hung in the stands at our competitions. We draped the banner along the side of my son's truck as we traveled in a caravan to the gravesite. Once we were there, we had all the band members in attendance sign the banner. I believe that banner still hangs in the Thiems' home. His mom stayed at the gravesite for a long time, but ultimately, she had to leave. My family stayed until he was lowered into the ground. My boys each took a shovel and began shoveling the dirt. When we returned to the reception, we told Esther that we stayed and made sure they took care of Johnny. I think that was a comfort to her.

If there is a reception or dinner afterward, and especially if you've come a long way, plan to stay. If you will not be staying, never leave without making some kind of contact with the family. When and how to do so will depend upon the format of the service and whether or not the family is available. Don't think that just because the bereaved are surrounded by close friends that they do not need to see you.

Other family members whom you don't know may be present. Introduce yourself and tell how you knew their loved one. Did you work together? Go to school together? Were you in the same Bible study?

When the time is right, share some special things you can remember about the deceased—some warm experience you've had that the family may not even know about. You'll give them positive things to consider and remember concerning their loved one.

Apply these suggestions to the next situation involving a loss that you face, and you'll have a greater understanding of what the family is experiencing and a deeper peace about attending the service.

TAKE FAMILY PICTURES

Unfortunately, a funeral is one of the few times that the whole family is together. While the timing may feel wrong, it is important to take family pictures. You can help by locating an experienced photographer to take the pictures. With the introduction of digital cameras it is easier to know you've captured the picture you wanted. My cousin Dwayne Littauer, used his digital camera to take pictures of every gathering we had surrounding my dad's death. Many of us had not been together in ten to twenty years. He put all of the photos on a CD for us. I can now print out the ones I want to place in Dad's memory book.

My friend Vicki told me how difficult taking family pictures was immediately after her brother, Samuel, died. No one wanted a picture without him in it. One of the grandchildren held Samuel's basketball for the portrait.

KEEP RECORDS

The bereaved won't be able to remember every detail surrounding the service, but those memories will be important later. So make sure that there are notepads and pens near each phone on which messages can be recorded and reviewed in the future.

Here are some other things you can do:

Have a guest book at the home for visitors to sign.

Record deliveries, food, and gifts that arrive.

Save the local newspaper from the day of the death.

Clip the obituary notices from the different newspapers.

Accompany the family to the deceased's safe deposit box and record the information that is kept there for the family.

If the family requests that donations be made to a certain cause in lieu of sending flowers, do what the family asks. During these very difficult days, you can make a difference.

FORGOTTEN GRIEVERS

LOOK, THERE'S THE CHILD'S FATHER

Look—over there in the corner.
There's the child's father.
Don't shut him out.
Don't pass him by.
He's grieving, too.
Support him.
Understand him.
Love him, too.
Look—over there in the corner.
There's the child's father.
Be with him as he mourns.

GLADYS CHMIEL

As comforters, we need to be aware that more people are affected by a crisis or loss than the immediate family or primary griever. Often these others are forgotten or ignored. My friend Vicki told me how that happened in her family after the death of her brother, Samuel. "My husband, Dwight, was probably closer to my brother than anyone else. While Samuel was in the hospital, Dwight was with him more than anyone. Even though Samuel was unconscious, he'd stand with him and hold his hand.

"Dwight told me that everyone came up to him and asked, 'How's Vicki?' 'How's her family?' No one ever asked him how he was taking it. No one took into consideration that he was hurting, too. Dwight said, 'Nobody was asking about me, because I am just an in-law.'"

As Vicki said those words, I realized that I'd done exactly the same thing. At church, when Vicki was absent from the service, I went over to Dwight and asked him how she was doing. Never once did I ask Dwight how he was. In my efforts to be sensitive to Vicki's needs, I had totally overlooked her husband. Truly, Dwight was a forgotten griever.

The following is a list of people who, like Dwight, may be forgotten grievers and need our loving comfort.

HUSBANDS AND FATHERS. When there is a crisis, we expect men to be strong. However, men have genuine, deep feelings of grief as well. Often men work through their feelings differently than women and at a different rate, but that doesn't mean they need less concern or support. I never saw my husband cry when his mother died of multiple sclerosis at the age of fifty. It wasn't until we were watching a movie years later that reminded him of his mother that he wept.

I remember wondering if Randy was sad about my pregnancy loss. It wasn't until our next son was born healthy that he dared share his feelings with me. He felt he had to be strong for me, and I interpreted that to mean he didn't care.

Husbands often feel that they must support their families and not disclose how much they're hurting. They may feel that the attention is going to their families and that no one is considering their needs. Husbands and fathers need to know that their friends are praying for them. They need friends to offer them comfort, too.

GRANDPARENTS. In comforting a family who has lost a child, we often fail to realize that grandparents grieve also. They may not react the same way or to the same extent as the parents, but they do grieve.

Their grief is two-sided. One is for their grandchild who died, and the other is the sadness and pain of seeing their own child in such torment. To see their child in pain and not be able to ease it leaves them feeling helpless and frustrated.

The death of a grandchild can bring back memories of their own past losses—a painful revival of the grief they thought was over. When my pregnancy ended mid-term and we discovered that my baby had a severe abnormality, my mom grieved, not only over the loss of her grandchild and my pain, but because it brought back the loss of her own sons.

PARENTS. When their children are facing a crisis, parents experience the loss firsthand for themselves, but they also hurt for their children and the pain they are facing.

IN-LAWS are not seen as immediate family. Their feelings are not expected to be as strong as other relatives'. That is often not the case. If they have had a close relationship with the family, their loss and grief will be just as great.

SIBLINGS. Most attention is focused on the parents' needs at the time of a tragedy, but a brother or sister may be hurting very deeply as well.

GRANDCHILDREN. Because of their special relation-ship, grandchildren have their own individual needs during a crisis involving a grandparent.

CAREGIVERS. When there is an injury or long-term illness, it is often the caregivers who are forgotten. They are the ones who have physically cared for the patient, been attentive to his or her needs, and been around to listen to the patient's cares and concerns. This may be a family member, such as a mom, or it may be professional help as in hospice care. Remember these caregivers; they are the ones who give and give and give. Ask how they are holding up.

I remember when my three sons had the chicken pox, one right after the other exactly two weeks apart. I was housebound for six weeks straight, applying calamine lotion, watching children's videos, and preparing special meals. This is all a normal part of parenting, but I was exhausted.

CHILDREN. We may overlook children's emotional needs because we think they are too young to understand and that they don't grieve. Most counselors believe that if a child is old enough to love, he or she is old enough to grieve. As I recall my childhood, I realize now that I had feelings of loss over my brothers' illnesses and resultant deaths when I was seven years old. My sister, who is four years younger and has a totally different personality than me, remembers little of the trauma surrounding my brothers' problems. A child moves in and out of the grieving process. A child can be sad and tearful one minute and tossing the football in the backyard or playing with dolls the next. Children are more prone to compartmentalize their grief than adults are.

WHAT HURTS ME

"Uncle Bob passed away." A child doesn't know what the term "passed away" means. The child needs to hear that Uncle Bob died. Using the words *die, death,* and *dead* may seem harsh, but it is much more helpful for children.

"God just needed another angel in heaven." Be careful about using references to God or Jesus when explaining death to a child. He or she may believe that death is God's fault and develop a sense of anger toward God.

"Grandmother just went to sleep." The child may think the person will eventually wake up, or the child may be fearful of falling asleep because he or she knows the person who died never woke up.

WHAT HELPS ME

Be honest with children. Explain death clearly and truthfully. Use the correct words. Depending on a child's maturity, he or she may need to know what happened to the body.

"I love you." After a death, children need to be reassured of your love. Say it often.

"Tell me how you are feeling." If the child's response is "I don't know" then say, "Let's figure it out together." Start by asking if he or she feels mad, sad, scared, hurt, or lonely.

"Do you know how Grandpa died?" A question like this encourages the child to gather information and clarifies misconceptions the child might have.

My three sons and husband had sustained a wide variety of injuries. One day a friend asked for a report on everyone. I filled her in, and as she said good-bye she said, "Ruth, you deserve a medal." Those five little words meant the world to me. Someone understood. When you see me out, ask me how I'm holding up. RUTH HAUGER

Children need open communication about death. Keep in mind, children are literal thinkers. What may be comforting words to an adult may terrify a child.

HOW TO HELP CHILDREN WITH THEIR GRIEF

Prepare the children for what will come. Explain what the funeral will be like, what changes will take place, and what feelings they may experience.

My son's friend in kindergarten was killed in a tragic accident. Almost the entire class went to the funeral. They couldn't fully grasp the magnitude of his death, but they knew it was very sad and they would not see Chris again. It was so touching to see child after child pass the coffin and leave a small toy for Chris. When it is age appropriate, or for a family member, I believe it is fine for children to attend the funeral.

My father died when I was twelve. Many of my friends came to the funeral for me. I sensed that the adults were there for my mother and each other. Kids have a need to grieve too. Children shouldn't be isolated from their friends and childhood activities during the period of mourning. ANNA NAPOLI

Share your own feelings of loss with the child.

Don't be afraid to let the child see you cry. Some adults are afraid that if the child sees them cry, it may create further insecurities for the child. Many children will believe that a loss was not significant if they do not see their parents cry. Others believe they shouldn't cry about the loss because the adults haven't cried. Don't be ashamed of your tears.

Go through pictures of the child with his or her loved one. Talk about special times they shared together so the child will have positive memories of the deceased. Encourage him or her to tell you when he or she is thinking about the one who's gone, and talk together about how much you both miss the person.

That's what we did with six-year-old Randy Jr. when Grammy Chapman was taken to the hospital. I went to school early to pick him up. As we sat on the lawn outside our house, my husband and I explained that Grammy had been taken to the hospital that morning and that she was very sick. We went on to say that she had a bad disease in her body. We told him that the doctors were taking care of her, but it didn't look like she would get better. She was unconscious—we explained *unconscious* since it was a new word and we taught him its meaning—and she was probably going to die.

I asked him if he wanted to go see Grammy even though she wouldn't be able to talk to him. He said, "No, I was with her yesterday, and we had a good talk." He was content with his positive memories of yesterday and didn't feel a need to see her in an unconscious state. He was not left out of anything, yet he was not forced to do something he didn't need to do.

An excellent way of helping kids cope with death is to make a book with them. That way the book is specific to their loss. The book can include their drawings, family pictures, or magazine clips. The text helps the child acknowledge his or her feelings and see a hopeful resolution. For example, the first page could say, "Molly is very excited because she is expecting a new baby brother or sister." A middle page could say, "Molly is very sad because her baby sister died." A last page could say, "Molly is still sad sometimes when she thinks about her baby sister, but she is happy when she thinks about meeting her in heaven."

My son had a marvelous English teacher who had recently lost her son. She shared her experience with my son. Although she didn't say, "I know how you feel," he clearly got the sense that she had some understanding of his situation. One day, she gave him a flyer for a Teen Age Grief (TAG) group on campus, and he decided to go. He participated in every activity, made new friends, helped other kids in even more difficult circumstances than his, wrote essays, and put together collages. It was great for him. I don't think children should be left to their own devices to come to terms with loss. Sometimes adults have to intervene, but I think it can be very important to provide avenues for kids to take advantage of on their own with the right support. ANONYMOUS

I made my sons "dad-books" the year after their father died. There were lots of pictures and letters and condolence notes, as well as professional programs with his photo and biography, to help them have a permanent impression of the man their dad was. ANONYMOUS

Help children understand the behavior of adults around them. Explain why Aunt Sally is tearful or Grandpa is silent. A little explanation will go a long way.

Never underestimate the impact a loss or crisis has had on a child. Children's attitudes and concepts about death and tragedy are related not only to their age, but to their maturity and experience as well. The way we deal with children must be highly individualized. On the surface, they may seem to adjust to a crisis easily, but this may be a form of self-protection. I never let my parents know how much I was hurting, because I didn't want to add to their pain. The real task of completing the grieving process may come later in life. If losses pile up on one another, resolution of a new loss will be more difficult.

When my second brother, Larry, who had been in a children's home since he was two, died at twenty years of age, I experienced all the emotion that accompanies a loss. It was much greater than I expected. I soon realized that I was re-experiencing the loss and accompanying grief from my childhood and my first brother's death.

Parental mood swings can be frightening to children if they're not discussed. I remember one morning when Mom was in a terrible mood. Everything we did seemed to upset her. I was getting mad at her for being so upset with us when Dad asked to speak to me. "Mom is upset today because it is Larry's fifth birthday." He had been in a home since he was two. He had not been a part of our daily lives, and the doctors did not expect him to live to be five. It is appropriate for a child to see his or her parent's sadness, but he or she needs to know the reason for it.

Reassure children that the death isn't their fault. Often children fear their nasty thoughts about the person caused the death. Young children have imagined powers and think they somehow made the death happen. Tell them they are not responsible. BRENDA NIXON

My son was very distressed about going to junior high school and having to tell new people that his dad had died, because he was afraid he would cry. I encouraged him to go into our bathroom, run the water, look in the mirror, and say over and over, out loud, "My dad died when I was ten," until the spoken words lost their trigger. ANONYMOUS

Watch for the forgotten grievers in your life. Your love and support will be just what they need. You can make a difference.

SPECIAL THANKS TO MELANIE WILSON, PH.D. FOR HER PROFESSIONAL INSIGHT.

PART *four*

CONTINUED SUPPORT

PRAYER

When my Uncle Jim was visiting me a few months after his wife died, we discussed the questions: What is the value of prayer? What good does it do, anyway? As soon as his wife, my Aunt Katie, was diagnosed with cancer, the news spread internationally. Having been a chaplain in the Air Force for thirty years, my uncle had contacts all over the world. With the benefit of modern technology and e-mail, hundreds of people were involved in praying for Aunt Katie's healing. Looking to my uncle for spiritual guidance, many people asked, "What good did our prayers do? Katie died anyway."

I think if we were honest with ourselves, we'd admit we ask that question often. There are times I think God must get tired of hearing me start my prayer with, "I don't know what good it will do, but Lord …" What good is prayer if the condition about which we pray goes on unrelieved, unchanged, or unabated? Uncle Jim responded by saying, "Prayer has never been a mail-order business for me—a place where I get what I order when I want it. It is a communication level with God and those who share in the love of God so that we may understand His will and act upon it as it is made clear to us. Our fellowship of prayer and hope in these trying months has not demonstrated to me the failure of prayer, but its sublime sense of presence and ultimate peace."

Should we pray? Is there any point in asking God for anything? My uncle responded, "There is nothing wrong with presenting our own wants and needs to God in prayer, but the final criterion is not our will, but God's. We test our own desires and hopes against what we come to understand to be the will of God. Do I believe in prayer? Absolutely, if prayer is the process by which we learn of the will of God. If it is by praying, that we can love God and one another, and from that love then comes the greatest blessing life can bestow: the fellowship of love with God, with our families, and with the many friends with whom we have shared that love."

I don't have any answers, and I don't believe even the most noted theologians have the answers. The Scriptures are clear, however, about many aspects of prayer. Accordingly, here's what I do know:

Jesus prayed.

Jesus taught us to pray.

Jesus intercedes for us continually.

We are to pray according to His will.

My relationship with God is nourished through prayer.

God desires for me to take my needs to Him.

God is omnipotent and is capable of doing miracles.

Following Christ's example, we pray. As an act of obedience, we pray as Jesus taught us. We are to ask for God's will. Jesus said, "Not My will, but Thy will be done." My communication and conversation with God deepens my relationship with Him. Prayer is communication with our heavenly Father. It is not a monologue, but a dialogue. Prayer isn't just talking; it is also listening. God speaks through His Word, but He also speaks through a still small voice that requires a quiet heart willing to listen and wait. I am continually reminded of God's power and remain hopeful for tomorrow.

I believe we have many misconceptions about the value, purpose, and reason for prayer. We look upon prayer as a means of getting things for ourselves or others, but the biblical idea of prayer is that we may get to know God Himself.

The notion that if enough people prayed for my husband, there would be a greater possibility of some kind of favorable outcome was difficult for me. I appreciated the friends who said, "I am keeping you in my prayers." But I was deeply offended when people said things like, "We'll just get lots of people to pray for you, and we know God will listen." I believe God is always listening. MARGARET WINTER

I think Oswald Chambers expressed it best when he wrote, "It is not so true that 'prayer changes things' as that prayer changes *me.* ...

Prayer is not a question of altering things externally, but of working wonders in a man's disposition." IN *MY UTMOST FOR HIS HIGHEST*

THE VALUE OF PRAYER FOR OTHERS

What do all of these definitions of prayer mean for us as we pray for our loved ones who are going through a difficult time? Many times people in a crisis can't pray; they need us to pray for them and with them. When praying for someone, you want to validate his or her feelings—where he or she is at the present—and offer hope for the future. Even if my hurting friends can't believe for themselves, I want to activate their faith by believing for them and praying with them. I feel it is important to help my friend realize God's heart in all of this pain. I like to use God's Word and His promises and pray them back to Him:

> *Lord, You say that You will complete the good work that You've begun in _____'s life.*
>
> *Lord, You promise never to leave or forsake us."*
>
> *Lord, You say that You love _____ with an everlasting love.*
>
> *Lord, thank You that Your mercies are new every morning.*

One day, a few weeks following my dad's death, Mom said, "Everyone must have stopped praying for me today, because this has been a very difficult day." Had everyone stopped praying for her on that particular day? Probably not, but the truth is, Mom knew she was being held up in the prayers of others, and she knew it made a difference.

When you tell people you are praying for them, make a special time when you pray for them, specifically. For me, I have prayer reminders distributed throughout my home and garden. When I see those reminders, I pray for that person or that family right then. At this moment, I have a friend undergoing cancer surgery. Just prior to her diagnosis, she sent me a sympathy card for my dad. I have her card sitting on my desk to remind me to pray for her. I have over forty-five rose bushes, and many of them have specific meanings.

When I prune or trim one of those bushes, I pray for the person or family it represents to me. For five years I have had Emilie Barnes' book *Fill My Cup, Lord* sitting to the left of my computer as a reminder to pray for her. When I see or use a gift someone has given me, I pray for him or her. Find triggers that will remind you to pray for people walking through difficult times.

My sister, Marita, has a fairly unconventional means of praying as well. "I talk to God like I talk to my best friends. While I'm cooking, while I'm doing the dishes, and while I'm driving across town, I talk to my girlfriends because that is when my brain is free. Likewise, those are the times I find I have extended conversations with God. My best friends know me and love me; they accept this means of communication. God knows me and loves me. I find He hears those prayers as well. Some people don't pray because they are afraid they won't do it right. Some of us don't know if we'll get results when we pray. Still others think it is no fun, or just plain too much work. In her book, *Come As You Are,* Marita says, "Feel free to experiment with what works for you. Trying the things that have worked for others is a great way to start. Let go of the standard system that you thought you had to fit into and relate to God through the way He made you. Remember, God is there for us, no matter how we come to Him."[1]

Is there any reason to pray? Should we pray? Absolutely. Will our loved one be healed? Will the circumstances change? Will the Lord "let this cup pass" from our lives? Possibly not. But that does not mean we shouldn't pray. This is what I believe about prayer:

Prayer is when we present our desires to God.

Prayer is the process by which we learn the will of God.

Prayer is a fellowship of love with God and others.

Prayer deepens my relationship with God.

God speaks to us when we pray.

Prayer changes me.

Prayer is a time of praise, thanksgiving, and supplication.

One prayer is as important to God as the prayers of thousands.

Prayer makes a difference in our hearts and in the lives of those we are praying for.

When we minister to those who are going through a difficult time, we become an example of faith and prayer for them. Often they are questioning their faith, the role of God in their lives, and the purpose of prayer. Through our prayers, we can help activate their faith, help them realize God's heart, and be an expression of God's love and comfort in their lives. Prayer does make a difference.

GIFTS

I have mentioned several times throughout this book that making the initial contact with someone is often the most difficult. I view bringing a little gift, food, or flowers as an icebreaker. It is a way to give purpose to your visit and a start to the conversation. As Marilyn Heavilin says in *Roses in December,*

> "I felt we should visit the family right away, but since we didn't know them well, I was a little nervous. I took a loaf of homemade bread out of my freezer, thinking, *Even if they don't want to see us, they'll like my bread.* We went to their door armed with my bread.... I stayed until late that evening making phone calls, helping with funeral arrangements, and planning meals. A simple loaf of bread had opened the door and made it possible for me to help the family in a vital way."[1]

Your gift may be as simple as one rose from your garden, a package of herb teas, a votive candle, or a brownie. The idea is not to be elaborate or expensive. The idea is to have something with you when you go to visit—something that lets the person know you thought about him or her and made an effort to bring a token of love and concern. There will also be times when you wish to purchase a gift to commemorate a special occasion or just to let your friend know you love him or her and that you acknowledge the difficult time.

Each of the preceding chapters have gift suggestions specific to that situation, yet many of them can be used in a broader manner. Read over the "What You Can Do" sections to find ideas that will fit your purpose. The following suggestions are some additional interesting, creative, and unusual gifts you may take to your hurting person.

GENERAL GIFTS

Bubble bath, luxurious body lotion, or scented body spray

Relaxing CD or cassette tape of praise songs

Personal journal

Ty Inc. makes a little stuffed bear named Faith that is praying. It is a cute way to remind your friend that you are praying for him or her.

One friend tucked a phone card in with a note of encouragement.
MARTHA

Comfort baskets, which can range in theme from breakfast foods, tea and scones, or an afternoon picnic to a romantic dessert treat

Gift baskets filled with granola bars, fruit juices, crossword puzzle books, and other goodies

Boyd Bears makes a praying bear in resin that can represent your support through prayer.

Provide stamped and addressed cards. If your friend is going to be hospitalized for a lengthy time, purchase a selection of greeting cards for his or her children, address them to the child/children, and put postage on them. With that much done, he or she can easily write a note and send love to his or her children. Another angle on the same idea is to purchase thank-you notes, put postage on them, and give them to the family. If a list has been created for who brought meals, you can even address the thank-you notes, which will save them some worries.

Whenever a crisis arises and people may be coming to the house, the most practical gift ever is a bag full of paper goods. Take rolls of paper towels, toilet paper, tissues, napkins, and paper plates.

Books of encouragement by Emilie Barnes, such as *A Different Kind of Miracle—A Story of Hope, Healing, and Amazing Grace; Minute Meditations for Hurt and Healing; Fill My Cup, Lord … with the Peace of Your Presence; A Cup of Hope—Resting in the Promise of God's Faithfulness,* and *Help Me to Trust You, Lord* will be a source of comfort and hope.

When Aunt Katie died, I went to an antique store and purchased a beautiful ladies' hankie. A soft, antique hankie makes a lovely gift and says, "Tears are expected here."

My thirteen-year-old buddy with brain cancer was given a collectible sports magazine and some rare baseball cards by one of our customers. In his thank-you note, Jason said, "Before I knew I had cancer I collected baseball cards, and now this gets me more back to normal."

A friend sent me gift certificates inside encouraging greeting cards. Others, anonymously, sent money, store gift cards, and gift certificates. ALICE

Donate blood in the name of your friend.

I was pampered with a basket of toiletries from Bath & Body Works. MAXINE

I purchased a Prayer Pal for my friend Jason just before he had brain surgery. It is similar to an autograph doll and is a soft stuffed cloth doll with yarn hair and a plain body. The card that comes with it says, "I am your special prayer pal, a gift of love that is shared, for all who sign upon me, will pledge to you their prayers." The instructions say, "Just sign me and send me to anyone who needs a prayer." Several families all signed their names as a commitment to pray for Jason. Many hospitals even allow these dolls to accompany patients into surgery.

Offer to be a bone marrow donor—let your friend know she is the reason.

Write out one of God's promises on a beautiful piece of stationary, or create a small poster on the computer with a comforting Scripture of His promise.

I was given a "Friendship Bag" in memory of Josh Robinson, the only son of Bryan and Jamie Robinson. This precious gift is perfect for anyone going through a difficult time. The card attached to the bag said

In this bag are a few reminders of Friendship.

LIFESAVER (the candy)—to remind you of the many times others need your help and you need theirs.

COTTON BALL—cushioned support of friends for the tough road ahead.

CANDY KISS & HUG—we all need kisses and hugs.

PAPER CLIP—to help hold it all together.

CANDLE—a reminder to share your light.

MARBLE—to help you keep rolling (or in case you lose one).

SWEET & SOUR CANDY—to help you accept and appreciate the difference of others.

HAPPY FACE (sticker)—smiling not only increases your face value; it's contagious.

BAND-AID—for healing hurt feelings, yours or someone else's.

ERASER—to remind you that every day you can start over with a clean slate.

RUBBERBAND—reminder to stay flexible.

These tiny items were neatly wrapped in a little pouch, tied up with a ribbon. Instead of making up the bag, you might send one item a week with its explanation in an encouraging note.

GIFTS FOLLOWING A DEATH

Following my pregnancy loss, my friend Linsey gave me a little Dreamsicle angel figurine holding a baby angel. A few years later, another friend gave me a beautiful angel from Seraphim Classics™ with exquisite wings and a flowing gown, holding an infant in her outstretched arms as if she is receiving the child. These serve as precious reminders of my daughter as well as the love of special friends.

I learned of a jeweler who makes gold pendants for bereaved parents with their child's picture etched on it. I sent a picture of my daughter off to this jeweler and ordered one. I wear it every day. It gets a lot of comments. This is so special to me that I ordered a second one with the same picture, just in case something ever happens to the current one. When wearing this charm, it provides a chance for the parent to talk about their child, which is very important to them. The "picture charms" may be ordered from Marsha Brunelle, a bereaved parent herself, by calling (718) 983-0377 or e-mail at marsh143@aol.com. They are available in four sizes and four shapes. JULIE CHRISTENSEN

I wear a gold bangle bracelet with an angel on it to remind me of my loved ones who have died. It has a blank back which can be engraved. The bracelet also reminds me that I can't always be with my children, but God's heavenly hosts of angels surround them. The bangle is available in sterling silver and 14 karat gold and may be ordered from Lauren@LaurenBriggs.com.

A guest book so the family may record who comes and who phones. This is helpful not only for a loss, but for a hospital stay or a lengthy illness. After my pregnancy loss, my mom brought me a scrapbook and said, "It is so easy to keep a record of wrongs in our mind, I want you to have a place to keep a record of rights."

Christian Family Jewelers makes a "Memorial Tear ©" to comfort those who mourn. It is a simple teardrop with a rose etched in it, a symbol of the love that never dies. It is available as a pendant, lapel pin, charm bracelet, or locket in both sterling silver or 14 karat gold. I gave a necklace to our partner's two daughters after their mother's death. For more information go to: www.memorialtear.net

Make a donation to Gideon's Bibles. Several friends did that following Dad's death. There is nothing that would please Dad more than to know there are Bibles available in his memory.

I like to give the family a rose bush with an interesting name in memory of their loved one. I have given Fragrant Memory, Unforgettable, Love, Heaven, Double Delight, and Honor. There is a wide variety of plants with meaningful names that make a great gift.

Precious Moments® made a limited edition "benefit" piece inspired by Marilyn Heavilin that is a little girl holding a few roses while sitting by a wintry gravestone. Inscribed on the stone are the words, "God Gives Us Memories So That We Might Have Roses in December." This piece benefits The Compassionate Friends, a national organization for families who have experienced the death of a child.

There is a new Precious Moments® figurine, "Gone But Never Forgotten." It is a "Chapel Exclusive" figurine that depicts a boy and girl standing at a grave marker with the girl ready to place flowers near the grave. This is a token of the grieving person's compassion for a lost loved one and a tribute to everyone who bereaves the passing of someone dear. It is available online at: http://shop.preciousmoments.com/

"Little Life" charm, in memory of a child, is a sterling silver pendant with a little handprint. The gift box says, "While you miss having that little hand in yours, may you find comfort in knowing whose hands are holding your "Little Life"—Forever. For more information visit, www.sterlinggrace.net

A little garden statue of a cherub

A "Memory Keepsake" in Memory of Our Precious Baby is a leatherette 5" x 7" double folding frame with the "Little Footprints" poem and an imprint of tiny footprints. "How very softly you tiptoed into my world. Almost silently, only a moment you stayed. But what an imprint your footsteps have left upon my heart." Little Footprints© from Angels in Heaven, Bringing Comfort and Peace in Times of Grief by Dorothy Ferguson may be purchased at: www.angelsinheaven.org/store/

When our choir director's wife died suddenly at the age of fifty-three, several of us purchased eighty tiny angel pins. On the backing of each angel pin I put a label with the words, "In Loving Memory of Maureen Rickard—1999." We gave them to each person in the choir, and we wore them on the shoulder of our choir robes.

When Maureen died, I felt the need to do something to help keep her memory alive, not only for her husband, Jeff, but for the grandchildren. I crafted a hollow gourd and wood-burned an angel on it. I asked the members of our chorus to write descriptions or humorous memories of Maureen. When I gave the gourd to Jeff, I suggested the he reach in and pick out a card on occasions when he was feeling down, lonely, or just needed a pick-me-up. ELLEN SCHOUEST (For those of us who don't do "craft gourds," we could use a decorative basket or jar and do the same thing.)

A friend brought a pillow for my daughter's bed. It was a little girl with blonde hair in pigtails sitting at a piano. The little girl is facing the piano, so we can only see her back, which has a set of wings. What a precious gift it has been to me.

If you or someone close to you has suffered a pregnancy loss, The Personal Memory Box offers a special place to hold the cherished mementos that are connections with your child. With the ribbons tied, the box is closed and the memories are kept safely inside. When the bow is untied the open box reveals the things that touched your baby's tiny life and left "footprints on the heart."

Hospital mementos, cards from family and friends, even unsent letters written to the baby may be included. The padded, fabric-covered box has a center-opening top with padded frames for a baby's prints and picture (if available) or for the verse and baby data card, which are included.

The verse card and six note cards (blank on the inside) read:

When someone comes into our lives,
And they are too quietly and quickly gone,
They leave footprints on our hearts,
And their memory stays with us forever.

AVAILABLE THROUGH SHARE.

Knowing I was hurting, my friend Sharon dropped by with a framed picture of two large hands. They were strong, muscular, bronze-colored hands cradling a little child in between. It was a reminder that Abba Father was holding me in His arms, cradling me like a little child. What a comfort. JACQUELINE CROSS

A RARE AND GENEROUS GIFT

Our dear friends had watched us raise our only son, Marco. They had come to love and adore him. Over the past year, they had seen me lose my job and, therefore, my health insurance benefits. Moving on in faith, Susan and I felt prompted by God to continue to "be fruitful and multiply," even though by the world's standards we shouldn't because we did not have any health insurance.

One morning over breakfast, my friend said, "We will be your health insurance." Over the next seven months, they paid for every medical visit and expense, as well as the hospital bill. Nicolas came into the world at their expense. What a mighty God we serve! His ways are not our ways. JOE GUARINO

HOLIDAY IDEAS

The Christmas after Johnny Thiem died, I found a Snowbabies ornament of a little angel playing a drum and gave it to his parents in his memory. He played drums in our high school band with my sons.

Every year I hang my daughter's stocking with the rest of ours. On the stocking is a poem, inviting anyone to share memories and put them into the stocking. There is always paper and a pen handy. My sister always remembers to write a note. Two of my nieces mailed us notes for the stocking. JULIE CHRISTENSEN

I decorated a little artificial Christmas tree, about two feet tall. The ornaments and beads are permanently attached to the tree so the wind wouldn't blow them off. I placed it in a gold basket and put fake presents under the tree. I take that Christmas tree out to our daughter's grave each year. JULIE CHRISTENSEN

Purchase something for an underprivileged child who is the same age your friend's child would have been and let the family know what you've done. JULIE CHRISTENSEN

December twenty-fifth will be two months to the day since Dad died. Marilyn Heavilin dropped by to give me a Christmas ornament in Dad's honor. It comes from Precious Moments. It is in the shape of a locket, and when it is opened up, there is a picture of Dad on the left and the words, "You have a special place in my heart," on the right-hand side.

The Memorial Tear® also makes an ornament in pewter and sterling silver with the same message, "This is a teardrop, to be worn in memory of someone loved." There is a rose inside as a symbol of the love that never dies. It may be purchased through:
http://www.memorialtear.net/

Give angel ornaments in memory of people who have died. Knowing that I have special memory ornaments representing family members who have died, Uncle Jim sent me three of Aunt Katie's angels for our tree with a note that read, "Enclosed are three of Katie's angels for your three angels to hang—remembering her. I am delighted to send them to you, and I know they will be honored well in your home."

RECIPES

Taking food to families in a difficult situation has been a long-standing tradition. However, as our lives get busier and more moms are working, preparing a home-cooked meal becomes a bigger chore. I have gathered a selection of my own recipes and recipes from friends that are interesting and unusual, but most importantly, they are quick and easy to prepare.

When my close friend Jan Frank heard about Dad's death, she prepared homemade lasagna. It is my favorite meal that she cooks. She drove for an hour from her house to mine and slipped it in my outside refrigerator along with some French bread and salad fixings. I was still out in Palm Springs with Mom, but she came anyway, wanting me to have some of her "comfort food." The next day, we all left Palm Springs and drove to Redlands, where I live. We had to go to the mortuary and finalize the arrangements. As we were finishing, I called home to my son Bryan and asked him to put the lasagna in the oven. When all ten of us gathered, there was a wonderful, home-cooked meal waiting for us. What a blessing it was not to have to think about what we would eat or find time to prepare it. Betty Southard and her friend Jan Stoop prepared a huge roasting pan filled with roasted potatoes, carrots, and roast beef for our meal following the visitation. We had over thirty people at our home for dinner that evening.

My sister Marita has participated in a "casserole shower" where each person prepared a casserole that could be frozen and brought it as a gift. The idea was, the recipient didn't have to worry about cooking meals during a particularly difficult time in his or her life.

As a gift to my sister-in-law when she had her baby, Marita purchased all the food ingredients, went to Kristy's house, and spent the day preparing uncooked meals that could be frozen and then pulled out and put in the oven for a freshly cooked meal. The recipes came from the cookbook *Don't Panic...It's in the Freezer.*[1] It was a blessing to Kristy to have a freezer full of meals that required no preparation time.

I suggest that you double most of these recipes and keep a meal for your own family. If you are going to the effort to prepare the meal, be sure to feed your family as well.

Here is a practical suggestion when taking food. Put everything into containers or plastic bags, etc., that do not have to be returned. It is overwhelming to face empty dishes and need to find their rightful owners. For example, tossed salad can easily go into a clear plastic bag. Paper, plastic, or foil dishes/pans will do the rest. The recipients will love you for this favor. LYNNE REITZ

In my home church, when a family is in need, one person takes charge of the meals. For instance, I would step in and say, "I will manage the meals." Then, I would call everyone who I think might want to take a meal, and I schedule them so the recipient doesn't have to worry about it. I tell the recipient if anyone calls about meals to have him or her call me. Then I give the recipient a list of who is bringing meals and their addresses, so the recipient will have all the information he or she needs to write thank-you notes. Sometimes I even address the thank-you notes and include them with the list if I know that the individual will want to send notes and that I could save them some worries by doing so. RHONDA WEBB

To be ready to meet the needs for food

❖ I buy the large package of ground beef, and I cook the whole amount on the stovetop in my big roaster pan, crumbling it up. Then I bag it into Ziploc bags, lay it nice and flat in the freezer, and shake it after awhile so it does not freeze in a solid block. Now I'm ready to make soups or casseroles; I can just pour out as much as I need.

❖ I do the same with roasts. I fit two nice boneless roasts in the crock pot and cook them all day. Then I remove them and slice them into generous 1 ½-inch thick slices. I freeze these slices in Ziploc bags so they do not touch and freeze together. These slices can be used in stews, topped with gravy, put into pot pies, or cooked in tomato sauce and then pulled apart with a fork as it cooks for wonderful sloppy joes.

❖ I buy a big bag of frozen boneless chicken pieces and cook them in a roaster pan, either on the stovetop or in the oven. When they are cooked, I cut each piece up into small cubes and freeze them in bags. This chicken can then be used to make salads, soups, pot pies, or to add to gravy, etc.

ELAINE HARDT

JAN FRANK'S FAMILY LASAGNA

10 oz. lasagna wide noodles (uncooked)

3 c. ricotta cheese

16 oz. cottage cheese

½ c. parmesan cheese

2 tbsp. parsley flakes

3 eggs, beaten

1 ½ tsp. salt

½ tsp. ground black pepper

1 lb. mozzarella cheese, grated (save a handful for the top.)

6 c. of your favorite spaghetti sauce, meat or meatless

Spray 9" x 13" pan with nonstick spray and spoon in a thin layer of sauce. Combine all ingredients except mozzarella, sauce, and noodles. Place half of the noodles in the bottom of pan. Spread half of cheese-filling mixture over noodles. Sprinkle half of mozzarella on top and half of spaghetti sauce. Repeat layers. Sprinkle remaining mozzarella on the top. Bake at 375° F for one hour, covering with foil for 45 minutes and removing foil for remaining 15 minutes. Let sit 5–10 minutes before serving.

The following is a recipe from a dear friend who brought this dish to our home after my dad died. I thought it was so good, I asked her to share her recipe.

CHICKEN ENCHILADAS
CONNIE SHEPSON

3 c. white sauce*

8 oz. sour cream

4 oz. chopped green chilies

2-4 tsp. jalapeño peppers, chopped (according to taste)

2 ½ c. cheddar cheese, grated (½ cup reserved for top)

2 c. green onion, chopped

10-12 flour tortillas

3 c. chicken, chopped

Add jalapeños to the white sauce and simmer on low heat, being careful to stir so sauce does not scorch. Add sour cream to sauce mixture. Spread a thin layer of the sauce mixture on bottom of 9" x 13" casserole dish. On each tortilla, spread about a tbsp. of the sauce, then chicken, chilies, onion, and cheese. Roll tortilla up tightly and place in casserole dish. When dish is full, pour remaining sauce on top to moisten all tortillas. (Any unused chilies can be added to the sauce.) Sprinkle remaining cheese on top. Bake at 350° F for approximately 30–40 minutes, or until bubbly.

*WHITE SAUCE:

3 tbsp. butter	3 tsp. chicken bouillon
6 tbsp. flour	pepper to taste
3 c. milk	

Melt butter in heavy saucepan. Add flour, and mix until smooth. Slowly add chicken bouillon and milk, stirring constantly over low to medium heat until slightly thickened.

Note: 3 cans of cream of chicken soup can be substituted for the 3 c. of white sauce.

This is the meal I take to folks: Chicken Spaghetti, Spinach, and Mandarin Orange Salad and Bread. RHONDA WEBB

CHICKEN SPAGHETTI

1–2 oz. spaghetti, cooked

1 lb. boneless skinless chicken breast, cooked and cubed

2 tbsp. butter or margarine

1 onion, chopped

4 stalks celery, chopped

8 oz. fresh sliced mushrooms

14 oz. light Velveeta, cubed

10-¾ oz. can condensed mushroom soup (I use Healthy Request.)

10-¾ oz. can chicken broth (I use low sodium, low fat.)

In saucepan, melt butter. Add onion, celery, and mushrooms. Cook about 10 minutes, or until mushrooms are dark. Stir in chicken broth and mushroom soup. Cook until smooth (less than 5 minutes). Stir in Velveeta and cook until smooth. In two 9" square pans (I use disposable foil pans), halve ingredients equally and layer: spaghetti on the bottom, then chicken cubes, and finally, pour vegetables/sauce over the top.

Cook uncovered at 350° F for 30 minutes.

This dish can be frozen for quite some time. I usually fix half for my family for dinner and keep the other half in the freezer so I will have it available at a moment's notice. I deliver it ready to bake so my friends can prepare it at their convenience.

SPINACH AND MANDARIN ORANGE SALAD

Fresh spinach leaves, torn

1 small can mandarin oranges, drained

3 green onions, chopped

French fried onions

Salad dressing*

Put spinach and green onions in large Ziploc bag. Put mandarin oranges and salad dressing together in small Ziploc bag.

Put fried onions in another small Ziploc bag.

Recipient can combine all ingredients in the large bag right before dinner for a fresh salad.

*SALAD DRESSING

In a pint-size jar, add:
> ½ c. sugar
> ¼ c. apple cider vinegar
> ½ c. extra virgin olive oil
> 2 tbsp. minced onion
> ½ tsp. or so celery seed

BREAD

One-half loaf of fresh French bread wrapped in foil, ready to heat. Partially slice so bottom is still connected. Then brush melted butter with thyme and rosemary between slices.

LITTAUER FAMILY SPAGHETTI SAUCE

> 1 lb. ground beef
> ½ lb. Italian sausage links
> 1 c. chopped onion
> 1 tsp. chopped garlic (fresh or from the jar)
> 3 tbsp. olive oil
> 2 (1-lb.) cans Italian plum tomatoes
> 12 oz. can tomato paste
> 1 c. red wine or ½ cup of balsamic vinegar
> 1 tbsp. sugar
> 1½ tsp. salt
> ½ tsp. pepper
> 1 ½ tbsp. oregano (I usually use Italian seasoning)
> 1 bay leaf

Sauté onion and garlic in the oil in a large pot. Add remaining ingredients and heat to just under a boil. Simmer for at least an hour. (I usually keep it simmering most of the day.) Before serving, brown meat and add to mixture. Serve over your choice of pasta.

HOT CHICKEN SALAD
MARILYN HEAVILIN

4 c. cubed chicken, cooked
1 c. salted cashews
1 c. green pepper, chopped
2 c. mayonnaise
½ c. pimento
1⅓ cans fried onions (save ⅔ can onions for top)
2 c. celery, diced
⅓ c. lemon juice
½ tsp. salt
1 c. milk or chicken broth

Mix all ingredients and bake, covered, for 40 minutes at 350° F. Top with paprika and ⅔ can of onions. Bake 5 minutes longer.

BRIGGS' SIMPLIFIED TEXAS BARBECUE

Cut one onion in eighths and place in the bottom of the crock pot. Place 2–3 lb. beef brisket on top of onions, fat side up. Pour a bottle of your favorite BBQ sauce over the meat, and turn the crock pot on high. Once the items are warm, turn down to low and allow to cook all day. To serve, remove beef carefully; it will be very tender. Place on cutting board and slice. Top with additional BBQ sauce. You may separate the fat from the drippings and puree the onions and BBQ sauce in a blender and use as a sauce. (I rarely do. I just use new BBQ sauce.) I usually prepare boxed creamy noodles and frozen baby peas with this. You may prefer the traditional baked beans and cole slaw.

MARITA'S CROCK POT GREEN CHILE STEW

2 lbs. country style pork ribs, pork shoulder steaks, or stew beef
2 c. onions, chopped
3 c. green chilies, chopped (I use fresh/frozen rather than canned)
2 large tomatoes, chopped
1½ c. chicken broth (use beef broth if using beef rather than pork)
½ tsp. garlic powder
2 tsp. salt
¼ c. pasta sauce (optional) (I use Classico Spicy Roasted Red Pepper)

Cut the meat into 1" cubes. Brown meat in a skillet over medium high heat. Place meat and all other ingredients in a crock pot. Stir lightly to mix ingredients. Cover and cook on low all day. Serve in bowls. Make 4–6 servings.

CHUCK WAGON CASSEROLE
JANET SATERLIE

1 lb. ground beef
1 onion, chopped
6 oz. can tomato paste
1 can whole kernel corn
1 pkg. of macaroni and cheese

Brown ground beef and onion. Drain. Add tomato paste and corn. Let simmer 5 minutes. Then add prepared package of macaroni and cheese. Stir together to let the flavors blend, and serve.

CANNED MEAT CASSEROLE
JODIE HEINRICH

1 bag wide egg noodles
1 family-size can cream soup (mushroom for tuna casserole, chicken for chicken casserole, or celery for salmon casserole)
Canned meat (2 large cans of tuna, 2 large cans of white meat chicken, or 1 large can of salmon)
1 can baby peas
1 bag shredded mozzarella cheese

Boil noodles until softened to desired texture. Drain noodles and pour into a large mixing bowl. Empty soup, drained meat, and drained peas into the mixing bowl. Using a large rubber spatula, mix all ingredients together. Place mixture in 13" x 9" casserole dish. Cover with cheese. Bake at 350° F until cheese is melted and turning slightly brown. Serve warm. Can be frozen and reheated.

CHICKEN AND STUFFING CASSEROLE
ELAINE HARDT

Steam 1 chopped onion and 2 zucchini, sliced and unpeeled, with a little water for 5 minutes. In a big bowl, mix ½ c. melted butter, 1 can undiluted cream of chicken soup, 1 c. sour cream, and 1 c. chicken broth. Add to this mixture 3 c. of cubed cooked chicken. Stir in contents of one 8-oz. round box of chicken Stove Top stuffing. Add the warm onion and zucchini. Mix and pour into 9" x 13" inch baking dish. Bake at 350° F approximately 45 minutes or until hot and bubbly. Serves 8.

CHICKEN ROTINI COMFORT CASSEROLE
SHERRY TAYLOR CUMMINS

4 boneless chicken breasts
4 slices bacon
10 ¾ oz. can cream of mushroom soup
16 oz. carton sour cream
16 oz. box rotini pasta

Wrap each chicken breast with a bacon slice and place in 13" x 9" baking dish. Bake at 350° F for 30 minutes or until tender with clear juices. Cook rotini in salted water as directed on package. Drain. Add sour cream and mushroom soup to rotini. Mix well. Add drippings from chicken pan. Mix well. Remove breasts from pan. Pour noodles into baking dish. Top with chicken breasts and bake 15 additional minutes or until noodles are hot.

QUICK ENCHILADAS
LISA COPEN

1 lb. hamburger
1 small onion, finely chopped
1 pkg. dry enchilada sauce mix
    prepared according to directions on packet
1 small can tomato sauce
1 (8-oz.) or 1 dozen pkg. tortillas (corn or flour)
2 c. grated Mexican cheese combo

Brown hamburger and onion and make enchilada sauce according to directions on packet. Mix half the sauce in with hamburger. Fry tortillas in a bit of olive oil and let them dry on a paper towel. Drop a couple of spoonsful of meat mixture and a bit of tomato sauce into each tortilla and fold in half, stacking on each other a bit. When done, pour remaining enchilada sauce and grated cheese over the top. Can be taken somewhere like this and baked later at 375° F for 30 minutes. Freezes well. This recipe can be made the night before, refrigerated, and then reheated.

INDIAN POT ROAST
LANITA BRADLEY BOYD

3–4 lb. boneless chuck roast
½ tsp. salt
1 tbsp. flour
2 cloves garlic, crushed (fresh or from jar)
5 tbsp. olive oil
1 large onion, sliced
12 whole peppercorns
12 whole allspice berries
1 bay leaf
1 tbsp. grated horseradish (from jar)
½ cup water
½ c. burgundy or ¼ c. balsamic vinegar
6 carrots, scraped and quartered
4 potatoes, peeled and halved

Sauté garlic in hot oil in a Dutch oven. Sprinkle roast with salt and dredge in flour. Add to garlic oil and brown on all sides. Remove the roast from the pan, laying it in the lid. Place onion slices in the pan and place the roast on top. Add peppercorns, allspice, bay leaf, horseradish, water, and wine. Bring to a boil. Cover, reduce heat, and simmer for 2 hours. Add carrots and potatoes and probably more water. Simmer 30 minutes or until tender. To serve, remove carrots and potatoes. Blend remaining sauce on high to make an easy gravy. Serves 6–8.

(This is a good one to do when you are home to keep an eye on it, and the family you take it to can easily reheat it in oven or microwave when they are ready for it.)

SAUSAGE BISCUITS
LANITA BRADLEY BOYD

I just fry sausage and use the biscuit recipe on the Bisquick box. Nestling them in attractive paper napkins in a box furnishes a container that doesn't have to be returned. I used to do an inexpensive basket and cheap cloth napkin but found that, no matter what I said or that it was not labeled, it always came back.

AUNTIE'S SIMPLIFIED CHICKEN ENCHILADAS
ELAINE HARDT

Pour a 10-oz. pkg. of white corn tortilla chips into 9" x 13" baking dish. Mash them slightly with potato masher. Take out half of the chips, leaving half in bottom of the baking dish. Mix together in large bowl: 1 c. sour cream, 2 undiluted cans of cream of chicken soup, ½ c. minced onion, 1 small can green chilies, ½ c. milk, and 3 c. of cubed cooked chicken. Pour over the chips in baking dish. Sprinkle over this 1 c. of shredded jack cheese. Now top with the rest of the slightly crushed tortilla chips you reserved. Top this with 1 more c. of shredded jack cheese. Bake at 350° F for about 30 minutes.

Serves 6 to 8.

NON-MEAT ITEMS

THREE CHEESE SPINACH TORTE
MARITA LITTAUER

2 c. bread crumbs from French bread
8 tbsp. melted butter (one stick)
10-oz. pkg. frozen chopped spinach, cooked according to package directions and drained
2 (8-oz.) pkgs. cream cheese
¼ c. whipping cream
½ tsp. salt
1 tsp. Dijon mustard
4 eggs
1¼ c. (4 oz.)grated gruyere cheese
¼ c. grated parmesan cheese
¼ tsp. paprika
⅛ tsp. cayenne pepper
¼ c. chopped green onions

Preheat oven to 350° F. Combine bread crumbs and melted butter and press into the bottom of a spring form (cheesecake) pan. Bake 8–12 minutes until lightly browned.

In a large bowl, beat together cream cheese, whipping cream, and mustard until smooth. Add eggs, one at a time, and beat well after each addition. Add the cooked spinach, grated cheeses, paprika, cayenne, and green onions. Beat on low speed until well mixed. Pour mixture into baked crust or directly into spring form pan lightly sprayed with cooking oil.

Bake 1 hour and 15 minutes or until filling is set and lightly browned. Cool for 15 minutes. Remove the outside of the spring form pan. Cut into wedges. Serves 10–16 as appetizer or side dish, 6–8 as main course.

GREEN CHILIES AND CHEESE CASSEROLE

KIM JOHNSON

1 lb. cheddar/jack cheese (more if you like cheese)
3 (7-oz.) cans of whole green chilies (split open and rinsed)
1 can evaporated milk
3 tbsp. flour
4 eggs
1 small can enchilada sauce

Grease or spray a 9" x 13" baking dish with nonstick spray. Layer green chilies and cheese, starting with green chilies, retaining approx. 1 c. of cheese. (1½ cans of chilies per layer.) Mix canned milk, flour, and eggs and pour over the top of the layers. Then carefully pour the can of enchilada sauce over the entire casserole, but do not stir or mix it in. Bake at 375° F for 25–30 minutes. Remove from the oven and sprinkle with the remaining cheese. This recipe can be made the night before, refrigerated, and then reheated.

BROCCOLI CASSEROLE

KATHY BOYLE

3 boxes frozen chopped broccoli
1 cup mayonnaise (do not use light mayo or Miracle Whip)
2 cans cream of mushroom soup
3 eggs
1 tbsp. fresh onion, diced
Cheddar cheese (shredded)
Ritz crackers (small box)

Preheat oven to 400° F. Cook broccoli according to package direction. Drain well with cold water. In a 9" x 13" glass baking dish, mix the mayo and soup until well blended. Add the eggs. Using a whisk, blend well. Add the diced onion and mix in well. Fold in the well-drained broccoli. Shred the cheddar cheese over the top. Lightly fold in. Then shred another layer of cheese and lightly fold in. Crumble the Ritz crackers on top, covering the entire casserole. Bake for a total of 40 minutes. After 30 minutes, cover the casserole with foil so that the crackers do not burn. Turn off oven at 40 minutes, and let the casserole remain in oven an additional 10 minutes. Remove and allow to stand about 15 minutes before serving.

EGGPLANT PARMESAN
SUSAN GAINES

1 large eggplant, sliced (with peel) into ½" slices
2 c. dry Italian bread crumbs
¾ c. parmesan cheese
½ tsp. crushed basil leaves
1 jar spaghetti sauce
1 c. flour in plastic bag
3 eggs beaten in tin pie plate
½ tsp. garlic salt
1½ c. mozzarella cheese, grated
Olive and corn oil to ½" depth in pan

Heat oils in large non-stick fry pan. Slice eggplant into ½" slices. Shake in bag with flour. Beat eggs in tin pie plate. Mix seasonings and ½ c. parmesan cheese with bread crumbs in separate pie plate. Dredge flour-coated eggplant in egg mixture, then in bread crumbs. Fry 3–4 pieces of eggplant at a time till golden brown on both sides. Drain on paper towels. Repeat till all eggplant is cooked.

Place single layer of eggplant in bottom of glass baking dish (may need to divide slices of eggplant to cover bare spots in dish). Generously sprinkle mozzarella cheese over eggplant and pour sauce over cheese. Repeat, ending in sauce. Sprinkle additional mozzarella lightly over top and any remaining seasoned bread crumbs and parmesan cheese. Bake covered in 350° F oven till bubbly, about 45 minutes. Serve with lightly buttered wagon wheel pasta and tossed green salad. Cold leftovers make a great snack. Notes: This is one of our favorite vegetarian dishes and one of my finest originals because it is so easy and consistently good. In my opinion, salting and draining eggplant on paper towels like most cookbooks recommend is a waste of time and nutrients.

GAINES' SCALLOPED POTATOES
SUSAN GAINES

4–5 large russet potatoes, peeled and sliced
½ onion, finely chopped
1 can cream of mushroom soup
2 c. cheddar cheese, grated
1 soup can whole milk + additional
Salt and pepper to taste

Layer potatoes, onion, salt, pepper, and grated cheese in a large baking dish. Repeat. Mix soup and milk together and pour over potatoes. Add additional milk if needed to within ½" from top of potatoes. Cover with foil and bake at 350° F for 1 hour. Remove foil and continue baking until knife inserted in casserole comes out easily and potatoes are golden brown. Reheat leftovers in hot non-stick fry pan. No oil needed. Cover pan and fry on medium high heat till bottom becomes crusty. Turn and brown other side.

SPINACH CHEESE MANICOTTI
MAXINE MARSOLINI

1 pint ricotta cheese
1 egg, beaten
½ pkg. frozen chopped spinach, thawed and water squeezed out
1 c. grated mozzarella cheese
½ c. grated parmesan cheese
½ tsp. nutmeg
1 tsp. minced garlic

1 jar spaghetti sauce
1 pkg. manicotti shells, uncooked
2 c. water

Mix ricotta, egg, spinach, mozzarella, Parmesan, nutmeg, and garlic together in a mixing bowl. Combine ¼ cup of spaghetti sauce with ½ c. of water. Divide this between two 8" square baking dishes. Spread evenly over the bottom of the dishes. Fill the manicotti shells with the cheese mixture and place half of the shells in each dish. Mix 2 c. of spaghetti sauce with 1½ c. of water and pour ½ of this thinned sauce over each pan of manicotti. Sprinkle manicotti with Parmesan cheese. Cover and bake at 375° F for 45 minutes. Heat the remaining spaghetti sauce; ladle over the manicotti when ready to serve. Sprinkle with additional Parmesan cheese. Serving size: 2 manicotti per person.

SOUPS

LITTAUER FAMILY CORN CHOWDER

½ gallon milk
Salt and pepper to taste
1–2 tbsp. parsley, finely chopped
¼ lb. bacon, chopped
1 onion, chopped
Add 2 c. of potatoes, cubed and cooked
Add 2 cans of creamed corn
Add 1 can of niblet corn

Fry bacon and set aside. Sauté onions in bacon drippings. Add potatoes an corn. Over medium heat, slowly add ½ gal. milk. Add salt and pepper to taste. Add bacon and parsley. Add rest of ingredients.

Heat thoroughly, but don't boil. This is wonderful reheated the next day and will probably need more milk added.

CHICKEN TORTILLA SOUP
PENELOPE CARLEVATO

Combine:

5 (14-oz.) cans of chicken broth
4 c. chicken breasts, cooked and cut into bite-sized pieces
28 oz. Mexican stewed tomatoes
1 bunch green onions, chopped
1 can Mexican corn
2 cans black beans, drained
1 bunch fresh cilantro, chopped

Bring to boil in Dutch oven. Turn off heat and add cilantro. Cool and refrigerate until ready to transport. Serves 6.

Include a bag of tortilla chips and 2 c. of shredded Jack or cheddar cheese with soup.

Add chips and cheese to each bowl of soup. (Soup can be heated up one bowl at a time.)

CREAM OF BROCCOLI SOUP
SHERRY TAYLOR CUMMINS

1 small carrot, peeled and grated
1 small onion, diced
13 ½ oz. can chicken broth
10 oz. pkg. chopped broccoli, thawed and drained
1 c. shredded cheddar cheese
6 tbsp. melted butter
8 tbsp. flour
1 quart half-n-half
Salt and pepper to taste

In 4-qt. saucepan, combine carrot, onion, salt, pepper, chicken broth, and broccoli. Let simmer until carrot is tender. Add shredded cheese and half-n-half. Simmer (don't boil) for 10 minutes. Mix melted butter with flour. Stir slowly into soup mixture, blending well. Bring to simmer without boiling, slowly, until thickened. Serves 5. I often double the recipe because one serving just isn't enough. I add extra broccoli. The base for this soup may be used for cauliflower soup, potato soup, etc.

Serve with a home-baked loaf of sourdough bread. I visit the local bakery for fresh baked rounds of herbed breads. Often, when people are not feeling well or grieving, they are not hungry for a big meal and are quite happy to have a warm and cozy soup for dinner. Soup warms the soul as well.

KID'S LOVE IT HAMBURGER SOUP
DEAN CROWE

1 lb. ground chuck, browned
2 cans Veg-All, drained
1 envelope onion soup mix

1 can diced tomatoes
2–3 c. water

Throw everything in the pot. Bring to a boil. Simmer and cook 25 minutes. (Also add anything you might have in the refrigerator that goes with vegetable soup, like leftover pasta, rice, or veggies—it's excellent with squash!)

Bake up a couple of packages of corn bread, and you have a great meal!

EASY BROCCOLI SOUP
JUDY WALLACE

1 medium onion, chopped and sautéed in 1 stick butter
2 boxes chopped broccoli, cooked and drained
2 cans each:
cream of mushroom soup
cream of chicken soup
cream of potato soup
6 soup-cans milk (I use less to make it thicker and richer.)

Combine all in Dutch oven and warm through, or you may put it into a crock pot. Serve with grated cheddar cheese on top. It is wonderful, and we all know soup soothes the soul!

SUSAN GAINES' BEST WHITE BEAN SOUP

Place ingredients in a 5-qt. crock pot in the order given:

4–5 chunks of frozen ham (chunks off the bone, fat removed, stored in a quart-size sealed freezer bag)
1 lb. small white beans, sorted carefully for clay pieces
1 carrot, ends removed, cut into thirds (or several peeled petite carrots)
½ onion, peeled
4 large cloves garlic, peeled
2 dried bay leaves
1 rib of celery, cut into thirds (optional)
1 mounded capful of loose chicken bouillon or 2 large cubes chicken bouillon
Black or white pepper to taste
Water to within ½" of top of 5-qt. crock pot

Cover and cook on high till beans are creamy and tender. I normally cook from 7:00 AM to 5:30 PM while at work. With slotted spoon, discard bay leaves. Place onion, garlic, and celery in blender and puree with 1½ c. juice from beans and scant ½ tsp. dried basil. Pour back into beans. Break up ham into smaller pieces as desired. Occasionally, I add a small can of undrained diced tomatoes. Serve steaming soup with hearty pieces of buttered bread or corn bread made with buttermilk.

COOK'S NOTE: The basic recipe above is essentially how I cook any bean, adjusting some ingredients and the end process depending on the choice of bean and desired result. I always keep chunks of ham or ground beef in the freezer in qt.-size plastic freezer bags, and rice and beans in the pantry. I never bother to soak beans. Never "dump" beans into a pot without sorting for clay. If you ever get a mouthful of cooked clay, you'll never be too lazy to sort them again! With lentils I focus on diced garlic, carrots, and jalapeño chili peppers.

CREAMY CHILI BEANS: Use 4 c. of pinto beans. Eliminate bay leaves, celery, and black pepper. Use either large chunks of frozen ham or ground beef. When you get home from work, ladle carrot, garlic, onion and a few scoops of beans and bean juice into blender. Add 2 tbsp. each of corn meal and mild red chili powder and puree in blender. Return to bean pot and simmer while cooking either rice or corn bread. If serving with rice, sprinkle grated cheddar cheese over steaming rice and ladle beans over rice.

PLAIN PINTO BEANS: Use 4 c. of pinto beans, ham, onion, garlic, carrots, and chicken bouillon. Eliminate bay leaves and black pepper. When beans are fully cooked, remove and discard all vegetables except carrots. Spoon beans, ham, carrots, and the clear bean broth into bowls and serve with buttered sourdough bread, corn bread, or any substantial type roll or bread.

BLACK BEAN SOUP: Use 1 small bag black beans (eliminate bay leaves, celery, and black pepper). At end of cooking process, ladle carrot, onion, garlic, and a couple of scoops of beans and juice into blender. Add 1 or 2 canned smoked Chipotle chilies (remove seeds and stem). (They're very hot.) Puree and return to bean pot to simmer an additional ½ hour while cooking corn bread to accompany soup. Ladle soup into bowls and top with dollop of sour cream, chopped red onion, and chopped, seeded, fresh tomato.

SALAD

LAUREN'S SPECIAL MANDARIN ALMOND SALAD

6 c. salad greens (I use romaine lettuce.)
1 c. finely sliced green onions
1/3 c. slivered almonds, toasted
> (I toast in a toaster oven. Watch carefully, they burn quickly.)

2 large cans mandarin oranges, drained

Toss all items with desired quantity of dressing.

DRESSING

3 tbsp. sugar
3 tbsp. malt vinegar
1½ tsp. salt
¼ tsp. almond extract or amaretto
1½ c. vegetable oil

Dissolve sugar and salt in vinegar and extract. Whisk in vegetable oil.

CHINESE CHICKEN SALAD

1 head iceberg lettuce, shredded or torn
2 c. chicken, cubed and cooked
4 green onions
¼ c. slivered almonds
2 tbsp. sesame seeds
Rice sticks or noodles

Toss all items with desired quantity of dressing.

DRESSING (I usually double this.)

2 tbsp. sugar
1 tsp. salt
3 tbsp. rice vinegar
½ tsp. ground pepper

¼ c. salad oil
1 tbsp. sesame seed oil

Mix dry ingredients in vinegar until sugar disolves. Whisk in oils.

FRESH CITRUS SALAD

1 bunch romaine lettuce, torn into pieces
2 grapefruit, peeled and cut into sections
1 medium red onion, peeled and thinly sliced
1 c. nuts of your choice (may use candied nuts)

(I often add crumbled blue cheese or substitute oranges for grapefruit.)

Toss all items with desired quantity of dressing.

DRESSING

⅓ c. red wine vinegar
1 tsp. salt
¼ tsp. ground pepper
¼ tsp. dry mustard
⅔ c. olive oil (I prefer vegetable oil)
1 tbsp. lemon juice
3 drops Tabasco sauce

Mix first 4 ingredients, then add oil, lemon juice, and Tabasco. Shake or whisk well.

YUMMY CHILLED DILL TUNA SALAD
DEAN CROWE

8 oz. small pasta shells, cooked and drained
2–3 cans (6.5 oz) albacore solid white tuna in spring water
   (Don't substitute; I use 2)
1 c. celery, thinly sliced
⅓ c. minced onion or green onions
6 tbsp. mayonnaise
6 tbsp. lemon juice
3 tbsp. white wine vinegar
3 tbsp. dried parsley flakes
1½ tsp. dill weed
1½ tsp. salt
1 tsp. black pepper

In a large bowl, combine tuna, pasta, celery, and onion. In a small bowl, combine mayo, lemon juice, vinegar, parsley, dill, salt, and pepper. Mix well until smooth. Pour over tuna mixture and toss well. Refrigerate at least 8 hours or overnight to blend flavors. Serve with fresh tomatoes and crackers. I add more salt, pepper, and dill. Also, I use fresh parsley when I have it. It is so good.

TUNA LEMON MOLD
BARBARA ANSON

This one sounds strange but is delicious and works for a light summer dinner.

3-oz pkg. lemon gelatin
1 tbsp. vinegar
½ c. mayonnaise
6 oz. can tuna, drained
½ c. celery, diced
2 hard-boiled eggs, chopped

Dissolve gelatin in 1 c. hot water. Add ½ c. cold water, vinegar, and mayonnaise. Mix with rotary beater. Refrigerate till firm. When firm, whip till fluffy. Add tuna, celery, and eggs. Refrigerate till firm in an 8" square or 9" x 5" Pyrex dish. Serves 6–8.

BROCCOLI SALAD
BARBARA ANSON

This one is surprisingly tasty, and I don't even like broccoli!

Large head broccoli cut into small florets
½ c. raisins
½ c. red onion, chopped
½ lb. bacon, cooked and crumbled
Dressing: ½ c. mayonnaise
                             2 tbsp. sugar
                             1½ tbsp. rice vinegar

Marinate broccoli, raisins, and onion in dressing at least 1 hour. Add bacon just before serving. Serves 8.

24-HOUR GREEN SALAD

BARBARA ANSON

ARRANGE IN LAYERS IN 9" X 13" PYREX DISH:

1 head lettuce, broken or shredded
1 c. frozen peas, cooked and drained
1 bunch green onions with tops, choopped
1 small bell pepper, chopped
1 c. celery, chopped
1 small can chopped black olives, optional
1 c. cucumber, chopped (optional)
½ lb. bacon, cooked and crumbled

Spread mayonnaise lightly over the top, and top that with grated cheddar cheese. Refrigerate several hours or overnight for best flavor (can be eaten immediately).

DESSERTS

LAUREN'S SUMMER COBBLER

1 c. sugar
1 stick (4 oz.) butter
1 c. milk
1 c. Bisquick
Fresh fruit of your choice, or 1–1½ bags of frozen fruit.
(My favorite fruit is peaches.)

Melt butter and put in 9" x 13" pan. Add fruit. Sprinkle both sugar and Bisquick over fruit evenly. Pour milk over all and toss lightly. Bake at 350° F for 45–55 minutes.

MARITA'S APRICOT CRUMB CAKE

2 c. flour
1 c. brown sugar
1½ sticks butter (¾ c.)
1 egg
1 c. buttermilk
1 tsp. vanilla
1 tsp. baking soda
1 c. dried apricots, diced into about ¼" pieces
1 c. chopped pecans

In a medium bowl, using your fingers, blend the first three ingredients until well blended and a crumbly consistency. Remove 1 c. of this mixture and set aside.

In a larger bowl, beat egg with a fork or whisk until well blended. Add buttermilk, vanilla, and baking soda and beat until well blended. Add remaining dry ingredients (not the one c. that has been set aside) and stir until blended. Batter will be slightly lumpy.

Lightly spray a 13" x 9" pan with nonstick spray. Pour batter into pan and spread evenly.

In the bowl that formerly contained the dry ingredients, combine the 1 c. of crumb mixture and the apricots and pecans. Sprinkle this mixture evenly over the batter and press it lightly into the surface of the batter to set.

Bake at 350° F for 30–35 minutes until nicely browned and evenly risen and a toothpick inserted near the center comes out clean. Allow to cool for 5–10 minutes. Slice and serve warm. Will keep for 2–3 days in an airtight container.

DUMP CAKE
SHARON GRESHAM

1 c. flour
1 c. sugar
1 stick butter or margarine, melted
1 can fruit filling

Mix together and bake about 1 hour at 350° F.

SUGAR-FREE CHOCOLATE PIE
CANDY ARRINGTON

This pie is so simple, but folks always like it. Since my husband is diabetic, I try to think about others on sugar-free diets. People on sugar-restricted diets will feel special because someone made an effort to prepare a dessert they can eat.

> graham cracker crust or cooked pie shell
> 1 large box sugar-free instant chocolate pudding
> 3-oz. pkg. reduced-fat cream cheese
> chopped pecans (optional)
> lite whipped topping

Soften and beat cream cheese. Add pudding prepared according to directions on the box. Blend together. Sprinkle chopped pecans on the bottom of the crust. Spoon pudding and cream cheese mixture into crust. Refrigerate until firm. Top with whipped topping just before serving.

CHESS PIE, AN OLD SOUTHERN CLASSIC
LANITA BRADLEY BOYD

Preheat oven to 400° F. Get frozen pie shell out of the freezer. Melt 1 stick of margarine or butter in a mixing bowl in the microwave. Add 1½ c. sugar to melted butter and stir. Put pie shell in the oven and set timer for 1 minute. As soon as the minute is up, take it out and crimp edges all around. (You may use refrigerator piecrust and not need to put it in the oven for 1 minute.) To butter and sugar mixture, add 3 eggs, 1½ tsp. corn meal, 1½ tsp. vinegar, and 1 tsp. vanilla. Beat well with wire whisk. Pour into pastry shell and bake at 400° F for 15 minutes. Then reduce oven heat (without opening oven) to 325° F and bake 25–30 minutes until crusty on top and only slightly quivery in the middle. Cool, cover with aluminum foil, and easily transport anywhere without having to retrieve a pie plate.

YUMMY YELLOW CAKE
ELAINE HARDT

Mix up 1 pkg. of yellow cake mix, adding the eggs, water, and oil as directed. Unwrap and place on large plate 2 8-oz. pkgs. of cream cheese. Microwave the cream cheese for 1 minute on high, then add to the cake batter along with ½ c. of sugar. Beat. It will still have small lumps in it. Prepare 2 round cake pans with parchment paper cut out to fit the bottoms. Divide batter into the 2 pans. Bake a few minutes longer than recommended on the cake mix directions. This cake needs no frosting and tastes almost like cheesecake. Serve it with fresh berries or open a can of any flavor fruit pie filling. Then serve topped with a dollop of whipped topping on top. Refrigerate the cake. Makes 2 cakes. Serves 16.

CHOCOLATE CHIP CHEESECAKE
LANITA BRADLEY BOYD

2 8-oz. pkgs. cream cheese
1 roll chocolate chip cookies (5-dozen size)
2 eggs
1 c. sugar
1 tsp. vanilla

Slice off 15 cookies and save for top. Spray 9" x 13" pan with nonstick spray and spread out remaining cookie dough in the pan. Mix cream cheese, eggs, sugar, and vanilla. (This is simplest in a food processor.) Spread over cookies in pan. Top with 15 cookies. Bake at 350° F for 30 minutes.

VERY SIMPLE MUFFINS
JENNIE BISHOP

Take a box of generic cake mix (the simplest, cheapest kind—not the kind with pudding or extras) and mix it with a 15-oz. can of pumpkin. That's it! Spoon into a muffin pan and bake just as it says on the cake box—350° F for 30 minutes. You can add some chocolate chips or raisins. My family likes them hot and with butter. They don't last around here!

NEIGHBORHOOD FAVORITE PEAR DESSERT
ELAINE HARDT

In 9" x 13" baking dish, pour 1 large can of sliced pears with its liquid. Take another can of sliced pears and drain off the liquid, then add the pears to the baking dish. Sprinkle 1 pkg. of white or yellow dry cake mix over top of the pears. Melt 1½ sticks of butter in the microwave. Drizzle the butter over the dry cake. Bake at 350° F for about 45 minutes, till golden brown and bubbly around the edges. Serves 10.

APPETIZERS

ZESTY CHEESE SPREAD
AUNT VIRGINIA LITTAUER

8 oz. cheddar cheese	1 tsp. curry
8 oz. cream cheese	1 jar mango chutney
2 tbsp. sherry	1 bunch green onions

Mix first 4 ingredients. Mold into a mound or block. Refrigerate for ½ hour or chill until firm. Chop chutney (take off syrup if too liquidy) and push into the block of cheese so it won't slide off. Chop green onions and sprinkle on top. Add chopped nuts if desired. Serve with crackers.

TACO CHEESE BALL
BRENDA NIXON

1 can bean with bacon soup
4 c. sharp cheddar cheese, finely shredded
¼ c. onion, finely chopped
¼ c. green chili peppers, chopped
¼ c. taco sauce (Add more if needed for consistency)

Mix ingredients together until smooth. Chill on waxed paper. Shape into a ball and roll in chopped walnuts or pecans. Serve with tortilla chips or cheese crackers.

HOT ARTICHOKE DIP
JOE GUARINO

PREP TIME: 10 MINUTES; COOKING TIME: 25 MINUTES

14-oz. can artichoke hearts, drained, chopped
10-oz. pkg. frozen chopped spinach, thawed and well drained
1 c. Kraft real mayonnaise
1 c. (4 oz.) grated Romano cheese
1 garlic clove, large, minced (more if you're a real garlic lover)

Heat oven to 350° F. Mix all ingredients. Spoon into 9" pie plate or shallow ovenproof dish. Bake 20–25 minutes or until lightly browned. Serve with tortilla chips, crackers, or assorted cocktail bread slices. Makes 2 c.

AN ESTRANGED OR REBELLIOUS CHILD

1. Brendan O'Rourke Ph.D. and DeEtte Sauer, *Hope of a Homecoming* ©2003. Used by permission of NavPress-www.navpress.com. All rights reserved.
2. Ibid.
3. Ibid.
4. Ibid.

INFERTILITY—FAILED ADOPTION

1. Jan Coleman, *After the Locusts* (Broadman and Holman Publishers, 2002), 56

WHAT IS LOSS?

1. Bertha G. Simos, *A Time to Grieve* (Family Service Association of America, 1979), 1.

LOSS BY SUICIDE

1. Comments from Dr. David W. Cox and Candy Arrington, authors of *AFTERSHOCK: Help, Hope, and Healing following Suicide.* Broadman & Holman Publishers, release date, October 2003.
2. Ibid.
3. Ibid.
4. Ibid.
5. "Helping Survivors Survive" by Victor M. Parachin, *Bereavement Magazine*, January, 1991.
6. Comments from Dr. David W. Cox and Candy Arrington, authors of *AFTERSHOCK: Help, Hope, and Healing following Suicide.* Broadman & Holman Publishers, 2003.
7. Ibid.
8. Ibid.
9. Ibid.
10. Comments from Dr. David W. Cox and Candy Arrington, authors of *AFTERSHOCK: Help, Hope, and Healing following Suicide.* Broadman & Holman Publishers, 2003.
11. Ibid.

PRAYER

1. Marita Littauer, *Come As You Are* (Bethany House, 1999), 200.

GIFTS

1. Marilyn Heavilin, *Roses in December* (Harvest House, 1987), 32.

RECIPES

1. Susie Martinez, Bonnie Garcia, Vanda Howell, *Don't Panic ... It's in the Freezer.*

ABOUT THE AUTHOR

Lauren Briggs has been referred to as a true "Renaissance Woman"; multi-talented, accomplished, and credentialed in her professional, spiritual, and everyday life. She is multi-faceted with interests in music, theater, literature, and history . Blended with her spiritual depth, her most important ability is to see heartache and concern in people's lives and minister to them compassionately. She has been helping hurting hearts for over twenty years through her writing, speaking, seminars, and various support groups.

For more information go to www.laurenbriggs.com.